internet cool guide

2001

internet
cool guide
.COM

INTERNETMEDIAHOUSE.COM
THE @NETWORK

internet cool guide is an InternetMediaHouse portfolio company.

contents

4	Introduction
5	Ratings
6	Net by the Numbers
8	Is Your Search Engine Right for You?
14	Cheaper, Better, Faster: Tools for Expert Shoppers
18	On Your Terms: A Privacy Bill of Rights
20	Beyond Basic Browsing
22	Art & Culture
27	Beauty
29	Books
32	Business
37	Careers
40	Cars
44	Chat
46	Communities
49	Computers & Internet
59	Directories & People Finders
60	Education
64	Entertainment
70	E-Services
72	E-Zines
75	Fashion

77	Film
81	Finance & Investing
87	Food & Drink
91	Games & Gambling
95	Health
101	Home & Living
108	Kids
112	Law
114	Love & Sex
119	Men
121	Music
126	News
129	Parenting
132	Politics & Issues
134	Reference
139	Religion
141	Science & Nature
143	Seniors
145	Shopping
162	Sports
169	Streaming Media
173	Teens
174	Travel
181	TV
184	Women
186	Glossary
190	Index
199	Credits

introduction

Dotcom commercials during the Super Bowl, Web site mascots in the Macy's Thanksgiving Day parade ... this Internet thing is here to stay. But you don't have to be a techie to take advantage of all the Web has to offer. With a little guidance from the experts, you'll know where to take a tennis lesson, find a stir-fry recipe, watch a film festival, or chat with a celebrity, all online.

In the following pages, we've selected the best sites on the Web in 40 categories, hand-picked for quality, coolness, and overall appeal. You'll also find information on Internet innovations—everything from quirky surfing tools to image search engines—along with need-to-know information on privacy rights, shopping online, and making the most of your wired life.

Don't Log on Without it (But if You Do ...)

That thing in your hand? It's online, too. Check out our site, internetcoolguide.com, for even more of the best sites out there, plus features, tips, and cool interactive tools. Each week covers a different theme, with an in-depth article, related surfing shortcuts, and our homegrown Top Ten lists. Think of us as an electronic roadmap with the most direct route to your online destination—and a few fun roadside attractions along the way.

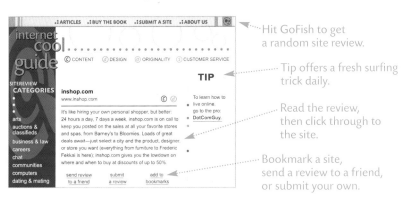

How the Sites are Chosen

internet cool guide editors constantly scour the Web to find the best sites and services around, researching thousands of sites to bring you the small collection here. What do we look for in a Web site? First and foremost, we seek compelling content. Is the information interesting and relevant? Is the design elegant and user-friendly? Do the help pages explain tricky concepts? Is the site fun?

ratings

Rating symbols are assigned to sites that are particularly outstanding in any of four areas: content, design, originality, or customer service.

© content

The content rating indicates that the site offers an awesome amount of top-quality content and tools, such as well-written articles, a stellar list of MP3s, or a big database of movie reviews. Highly interactive sites with loads of personalization and services also get the content rating.

ⓓ design

The design rating is awarded to sites that combine cutting-edge graphics with a user-friendly, well-organized layout. These sites often take advantage of Web technology like streaming audio and video and Flash animation.

ⓞ originality

Sites that receive the originality symbol offer a unique, creative, and sometimes offbeat concept or service. It may be a new concept that is only possible online, or a fresh spin on an old idea.

ⓢ customer service

Sites that receive the customer service icon excel at making the shopping experience smooth and hassle-free. They have detailed help pages and generous return policies, are super responsive to phone calls and questions, and offer a toll-free phone number, a privacy policy, order confirmation, and in some cases, free shipping.

Net by the Numbers . . .. .

Number of Internet users worldwide: **330** *million*

Number of U.S. households joining the Internet per hour: **760**

Number of Americans who access the Internet on a typical day: **55** *million*

Percentage of users who
would watch less TV to spend more time online: **62**

Number of email messages sent per day in the U.S.: **9.4** *billion*

Number of Americans who say they have
learned more about their families since they began using email: **16** *million*

Fraction of those who email family members
who like e-communication because
it makes it easier to say frank or unpleasant things: *one-***third**

Percentage of Internet users who "like spam or have some use for it": **3**

Number of completed auctions
at eBay in the first quarter of 2000: **53** *million*

Chance that an eBay auction is a fraud: **1** *in* **25,000**

Percentage of Web-surfing
teens who shopped online in 1999: **67**

Teen online spending projected for 2003: $**1.2** *billion*

Percentage of nine to 17-year-olds
who say the Internet has improved
their attitudes to attending school: *more than* **40**

Number one female name in online searches for 1999: *Britney Spear*

Number one male name: *Ricky Martin*

Percentage of the world's top 500 companies
that recruit new staff on their corporate Web sites: *80*

Percentage of major U.S. companies that engage in
electronic monitoring of employee communications and performance: *45*

In 1999, average percent increase
in stock price for pure Internet companies at IPO: *233*

Percentage of Internet users
who have bought stocks online: *12*

Number of Internet startups
with Queen Elizabeth II as an investor: *1*

Reported number of stock options received by
William Shatner for advertising for Priceline.com: *125,000*

Sale price of the
domain name business.com: $*7.5 million*

Ratio of parents who worry about their kids
giving out personal family information online: *3 in 4*

Ratio of children who said they'd be
willing to give out family information in exchange for a free gift: *2 in 3*

Number of people the band Metallica
accused of illegally trading its music on Napster: *317,377*

Age of Shawn Fanning when he
invented the software program for Napster: *19*

Number of viewers who logged onto the
live webcast of Victoria's Secret's 2000 fashion show: *2 million*

Number of daily visitors to
sexhelp.com, a site for sexual addicts: *17,000*

Number of surgeons who bid
to perform a lower lid lift for
a user logged onto "Bid for Surgery"
at medicineonline.com within 72 hours: *5*

Net by the Numbers

Is Your Search Engine Right For You?

One mouse. One billion Web pages. Here, 14 top search tools to help you tame the Net.

Portals

AltaVista www.altavista.com

AltaVista has long been ahead of the pack with its sophisticated search options, large index (350 million sites and growing), and stellar multimedia and foreign language searches. But AltaVista may be trying to do too much. The main page is advertising-heavy and overloaded with features, news, and a hodgepodge of services. The site performs well on keyword searches but falls short when the search comes in the form of a question. When asked "What is the population of New Mexico?" in plain language, AltaVista was way south of the border: Mexico was the subject of nine of its top 10 hits.

What to love: The dizzying array of Boolean query options; search URLs, titles, and images, for starters.

When to leave: Don't know a Boolean query from a barmaid? Try Google instead.

Snap www.snap.com

Like AltaVista, NBCi's Snap is a search engine-cum-portal with tons of tools and features. While the search results are impressively diverse and accurate, the lists lack order: returns are rarely ranked according to relevance, and often several pages from the same site are repeated. In a search for "baseball," Snap yielded three subsites of the official Major League Baseball site but not the site itself. As a portal, though, Snap's interface is light years ahead of its competitors, allowing you to follow anything and everything from upcoming IPOs to the weather in Uzbekistan.

What to love: Click on High Speed Features (for broadband connections) for a slick, Flash-enhanced page equipped with heat-seeking features like a power search and free Web storage.

When to leave: Want to know which sites are most surf-worthy? Hotbot's engine, which ranks sites by popularity, is a better bet.

Yahoo! www.yahoo.com

That's right—one of the most popular search engines around is also one of the best. According to the *San Jose Mercury News*, "Yahoo! is closest in spirit to the work of Linnaeus, the 18th century botanist whose classification system organized the natural world." Yahoo! does a great job organizing its seven-figure archive of sites into thousands of categories for its directory. Under a search for "bag-pipe sheet music," Yahoo! successfully delivered what appears to be one of the most substantial (yeah, you guessed it) bagpipe sheet music sites on the Web, Viper Piper (viperpiper.hypermart.net). Watch Yahoo!'s competitors play follow the leader.

What to love: The well-organized directory format can't be beat: you'll find what you're looking for eight times out of 10 and have a blast while you're at it.

When to leave: Because Yahoo! searches are based on categories of sites, a query for specific text on a Web page is better accomplished at AltaVista or Google.

All-Purpose Search

HotBot www.hotbot.com

HotBot is a strong overall performer boasting accurate results for both keyword and more specific searches. It also gives surprisingly smart results to searches posed in question form. The intuitive inter-face, streamlined design, and responsiveness to plain English terminology are great for beginners. Surfers with time-tested skills will appreciate HotBot's vast selection of advanced search options (e.g., it will return sites containing specific types of media like RealAudio). Results are ranked according to their place in Direct Hit's popularity rankings, a real plus that's sorely missing on other major engines. The top 10 results for a "music" keyword search pro-duced general music sites that get the most traffic on the Web like IUMA, MP3.com, and CDNOW.

What to love: The popularity rankings, and pull-down menus that make basic Boolean searching easy.

When to leave: For news headlines, stock tickers, and other portal paraphernalia, click elsewhere.

Metasearchers

MetaCrawler www.metacrawler.com

Metasearch engines take your search request and run it on a num-ber of search engines simultaneously, saving you the hassle of figuring out which engine works best. An inspired idea, but with a few flaws. For one thing, metasearchers don't return every result from each engine—only a small selection from each—and their rank-ings are sometimes unhelpful, jumbling the best sites with lesser sources. Go2Net's Metacrawler, however, prides itself on being the most popular and most powerful metasearch on the Web: it searches Yahoo!, Lycos, Infoseek, WebCrawler, Excite, AltaVista, Thunderstone, About.com, and Looksmart simultaneously.

What to love: Quirky tools like MiniCrawler (a tiny window that gives you desktop access to the MetaCrawler engine) and MetaSpy (to see what others are searching for).

When to leave: When MetaSpy queries like "super chicken" and "erect nipples" shake your faith in humanity.

Pure Search

Google www.google.com

This sleek, simple alternative to the portals has become the hands-down favorite for fast, no-nonsense searches. Since launching, Google has grown to include a university database, a foreign language search, and a mature content filter. It's also gone wireless—and to rave reviews. Boasting 500 million indexed sites and access to 500 million more, this engine finds thousands of sites in a fraction of a second—all organized by relevance to your search query. Found a site and want more like it? Type the URL into the query field and have GoogleScout look for similar sites. A note: simple, one- or two-word queries work best since Google will drop all the words it thinks are irrelevant in a question or long phrase.

What to love: Amazingly accurate results.

When to leave: Google doesn't support Boolean search commands; if you seek complex search capabilities, AltaVista might be more your speed.

Raging Search www.raging.com

A competitive half-brother to Google, Raging is a straightforward, ad-free, and swift search engine for hardcore search enthusiasts. With great customizable options that let you filter mature content or set the number of listed results per page, Raging also has all the benefits of being AltaVista's stepchild—like access to their index of more than 350 million sites and innovative BabelFish translator. Searches are fast but work best for single-word queries. For multiple word searches, Raging tends to search each word separately and not list sites by relevance. Works great for obscure topics, but for more popular queries, you may get more hits than you can handle.

What to love: No ads!

When to leave: For simple searches, you just can't beat Google.

Research Engines

Northern Light www.northernlight.com
For surfers with a serious research agenda, Northern Light is the hi-tech mining tool of choice. It's a search engine and full-text database service all in one. That means that the results for any given search will consist of "premium" for-pay material from its Special Collection of sources, along with ordinary pages. The Special Collection is an online library of 6,200 full-text journals, books, magazines, newswires, and reference sources (like *American Banker* and *ABC News Transcripts*). Most of the 20 million articles are available for under $5. Northern Light's innovative sorting system also presents results in folders according to source, subject, language, and document type.
What to love: The Special Collection, which is excellent and unique on the Web.
When to leave: Northern Light can be annoying for ordinary searches; you'll have to wade through premium content which you may not want to pay for.

Directory

About.com www.about.com
For a site directory with personality, head to About.com, where (human!) guides maintain pages on thousands of categories with hand-selected links. There you'll find site recommendations, news, chat, and the community you need to keep your most vital interests alive online. Love soap operas? Bet you didn't know that there are more than 10 sites where you can trade *Days of Our Lives* videotapes. The guide sites are vast, sophisticated, frequently updated, and addictive to explore.
What to love: It's comprehensive, covering everything from Computer-Aided Design to Saltwater Fishing.
When to leave: Simply looking for sites? Seek elsewhere—About.com is more about finding information.

Question-based Search

Ask Jeeves www.ask.com
Jeeves isn't your typical butler—no food, no drinks, just facts. Ask Jeeves any question in plain English or take a peek at the live questions posted from other readers, such as "How much should I weigh?" or "Where can I find a study guide for *A Clockwork Orange*?" Jeeves has links to more than seven million prepared answers as well as lists of similar questions. While the value in these trivia bits

depends entirely on your research needs, Jeeves provides a refreshingly human-friendly way of "asking" a search engine for information. But remember, it's Ask Jeeves, not Ask Einstein. Be sure to keep your questions simple.

What to love: Ask Jeeves will answer questions you didn't even know you had.

When to leave: When Ask Jeeves can't answer the question you do have.

Kids

Yahooligans! www.yahooligans.com

Fans of Yahoo! can feel safe entrusting their young ones to Yahooligans!, the popular Web giant's search engine for kids. Almost as soon as boys and girls can click a mouse, Yahooligans! is there as a basic guide to the Web. More sophisticated young adults may find it a bit generic, but some of its better virtues are a bright, simple design (although it does squeeze in about one banner ad per page) and helpful guides for parents and teachers. Little ones with questions can click on the Yahooligans! Ask Earl feature.

What to love: A safe jumping-off point for the youngest Web surfers.

When to leave: When Barbies and Pokémon begin to fade. Older kids will need a more sophisticated engine.

MP3

Palavista www.palavista.com
Our favorite one-stop MP3 search engine. Palavista's digital music metacrawler searches MP3 engines like Kermit, MP3 Lycos, FastMP3, and 2Look4, among others. The site also offers advice and answers in a helpful FAQ (and you will have questions if you are new to MP3s and FTP sites). A search for "the Beatles" on Palavista was highly productive: more than 600 hits were scored on three differ-ent engines, very few of which were dead links.
What to love: Best chance of finding the artist and song you want.
When to leave: There's no guarantee that every MP3 hit will pan out. Move on to a song database like Audiofind if you keep getting broken links.

Multimedia

Streamsearch www.streamsearch.com
Why not take advantage of your high-speed broadband connection or give your snail-paced modem a run for its money? Streamsearch provides an excellent directory and search function for the Web's ever-expanding selection of multimedia programming. A search for "international news" across all types of media turned up a wide-ranging selection of more than 20 different audio and video news files, though none of them were live and few were very recent. A search for the same topic in the News category elicited no results.
What to love: The site lets you know whether or not you have the necessary players and plug-ins.
When to leave: If you're looking for live or upcoming events, you're out of luck here. Go to an event directory like ChannelSeek instead.

Message Boards

Remarq www.remarq.com
Search here for Usenet groups and email lists. A search for "radical politics" garnered a list of approximately 100 relevant, active discus-sions (including six non-English) that ranged all over the spectrum—from Rush Limbaugh to the politics of marijuana. You can find postings by specific message board authors or zero in on specific topics in the directory.
What to love: Well-organized, comprehensive, and where else can you find a round-the-clock discussion on Buddhism?
When to leave: When the chia pet discussions get old, or when extremist postings turn you off.

Is Your Search Engine Right For You?

Cheaper, Better, Faster: Tools for Expert Shoppers

It's no news that the Internet is revolutionizing the way we shop. From Pokémon to Peruvian cold remedies, everything and anything is just a click-and-drop away from your virtual shopping cart. Luckily new sites are popping up every day to make shopping faster, easier, and much more user-friendly than before. With your own shopping assistants and "sale finders" hunting down the bargains, choosing the  perfect gift, and even fetching dinner and a movie, all you need to do is relax, kick back, and enjoy the ride.

Better Technology & Service

Let's face it, shopping online doesn't compare to the real thing—no clothes to try on, no friends to laugh with in the dressing room. But some sleek new sites are putting the sizzle in online shopping with fancy tools and technologies. Landsend.com lets you shop and chat online with a friend simply by logging on to its Web site simultaneously. You can both browse the selection of summer dresses, gift baskets, furniture, and accessories, even put all your items in the same shopping cart. The site also offers a virtual model for specific body types to try on the swimsuits you'd never dare to in real life. At Girlshop.com, shopping assistants will suggest the proper dress for a cocktail party, and the Tell A Friend button lets you email pals for a second opinion. Purpleskirt.com even hosts virtual makeovers for lucky surfers who send in their photos. Home decorating sites like Living.com, HomePortfolio.com, and GoodHome.com are spicing things up with virtual "room designers" that allow you to select and arrange furniture, even down to selecting the colors for your new virtual chair—without ever having to leave yours.

If The Pickings Are Slim, Design It Yourself

If you finally found the perfect lamé shirt for your '70s retro party—but gold really isn't your color—some online shops let you customize clothing to suit your tastes. Even big names like

Nike.com are now letting shoppers choose the design and color of their athletic shoes as well as stitch their nicknames into the body of the shoes. New sites like getCustom.com offer a variety of products from golf clubs and DVD players to clothing that can be made to order. But Starbelly.com is the site leading the way in customized clothing by designing and building Web stores for corporate sites that let you pick from hundreds of logoed designs. Or blend your own lipstick and foundation color at Reflect.com; customize your new bike to fit your shape and size at Airborne.com; or mix a personal CD for that special someone at CDNOW.

Take the Legwork Out of Giving and Getting

Remember making your Christmas list and sending it to Santa? Now kids and adults alike can fashion virtual wishlists at gift registry sites like Wishlist.com and Della.com. A smarter way to give (and receive) better gifts, you create your own wishlists directly on the sites and let friends and family log on to buy your choices. Wishlist.com links to more than 400 Internet retailers searchable by price, brand name, or product type. Della.com features products from stores like Amazon.com, Banana Republic, and Williams-Sonoma—enough variety for any picky relative.

Another snazzy gift for the lazy shopper is to send Flooz.com's online gift currency via email. Recipients spend Flooz just like money, purchasing exactly what they want without the hassle of returns. Or send online gift certificates from GiftCertificates.com, redeemable at stores like iBeauty.com and Benihana.

Some Sushi, Some Bubbly, a Midnight Flick, and Make It Quick

The phenomenon of the go-for-it man may seem a little archaic in this day and age, but it's the idea that spurred two of the hottest e-commerce sites around—Urbanfetch.com and Kozmo.com. Kozmo.com (located in 10 major cities, including Chicago and New York) promises to deliver movies, videogames, music, books, magazines, food, and gifts straight from the Internet directly to your door—in under an hour. Urbanfetch.com, on the other hand, can suggest something to suit any peculiar fancy, although that lobster bisque and bottle of vintage red might take a little longer to deliver. But unless you reside in New York City and select parts of Brooklyn, you'll have you wait a while longer before Urbanfetch.com comes knocking at your door. New Yorkers also have a friend in Homedelivery.com, a site that lets them order from local merchants who deliver in their neighborhood. Just enter a zip code and shop for groceries, pet supplies, flowers or takeout. Stay tuned; all three of these sites have plans to expand.

Cheaper, Better, Faster: Tools for Expert Shoppers

Searching for a good deal on the Internet can be as frustrating as battling overwrought crowds at the after-Thanksgiving sales. A shopping bot (robot) is a good way to save time and money. Tell a bot exactly what you want and it will search online stores for the best deals. Bots like DealTime.com, Bottomdollar.com, and mySimon.com search thousands of products, and are excellent tools for those who want to peruse a wide selection of items. Those looking for specific bargains are best served by specialized bots like CNET Shopper, which deals strictly with computers and electronics, or BestBookBuys.com for a huge selection of reading material. For shoppers determined to pay no more than a certain price, sites like Dealtime.com will page or email you if your desired price comes along.

But while bots are a quick and efficient way to comparison shop, they aren't perfect. For instance, not all categories (sports equipment or clothing) are well represented in the main bots because smaller, cheaper retailers often don't list their products online. This gives you a smaller selection and higher prices. Another limitation is that Internet merchants sometimes block bots from

Safe-Shopping Checklist

Keep in mind the following criteria to help ensure that any online shopping experience is a safe one.

 The site is secure. The checkout page should use encryption such as Secure Sockets Layer (SSL) or SET Secure Electronic Transaction to scramble the purchase information you enter. Look for the padlock icon at the bottom of your screen and "https" in the URL field to be sure a site is secure.

 You know the company. Anyone can set up a shop online, so if you're not familiar with a merchant, seek out the 800 number and return policies before you order.

 The privacy policy is posted. If there is no policy, there's no telling how a company may use your personal information.

 The store or auction takes plastic. Credit card transactions are protected by the Fair Credit Billing Act, which gives you the right to dispute charges under certain circumstances (e.g. defective or damaged items).

 You've kept a record. Print a copy of your purchase order and confirmation number for your records.

their sites, limiting a search's scope. One last tricky issue: on many bots, online stores pay to receive "preferred" placement in search results, even though their prices may not be the lowest. A new generation of bots from Frictionless Commerce (compare.friction-less.com), whose software technology also powers Lycos Shop and Brodia, are heating up the race for the best shoppers on the market. By offering more features to choose from, these bots let you search not only for the best price, but also for the best quality and service. They also have the added bonus of being freestanding, which means merchants can't pay for preferential listings.

Super Sale-Finders

If you subscribe to the "Don't go to the sale, let the sale come to you" mantra, sites like StyleShop.com and inshop.com are putting their motto where your money is. StyleShop.com lists sample sales or clearances by city and category, and gives store locations, directions, and bargains. inshop.com gives you the lowdown on where and when to buy at discounts of up to 50%. A huge discount clearinghouse, Shoppinglist.com is updated hourly and keeps you informed via email of what's on sale at stores like Pier 1, Ralph Lauren, and Crate & Barrel. Another great site to save at is Freeshipping.com—with more than one million products and 125 retailers to choose from, items are shipped at no cost to the consumer. It's a smart way to purchase hefty items like furniture or electronics, whose shipping and handling fees can really pile on the extra charges.

Coupon Crazy

At CoolSavings.com, do away with clipping coupons for good. The site has thousands of printable money savers on its site that are recognized at national chains like Kmart and eToys.

Anywhere You Go, The Digital Wallet Is There For You

Like most shoppers, you probably don't want to deal with the hassle of filling out order forms. Digital wallet to the rescue. Feed all of your data into it—name, address, credit card numbers, passwords, shipping information—and when you're ready to buy on any site anywhere, just click on the wallet and the order fills itself out. Some wallets like NextCard are stored on your computer, while others remain on the computer of a host. Netscape and Microsoft now support wallet technology on their browsers; other free wallet services include eWallet.com and Gator.com.

Cheaper, Better, Faster: Tools for Expert Shoppers

On Your Terms: A Privacy Bill of Rights

It's 10 PM. Do you know where your profile is?

The fact is, when you surf the Web and collect information from a site, the site also collects information from you. A recent study found that around 93% of sites gather data on your IP address, browser, and operating system. It is as if you're leaving a trail of electronic footprints. And if you've ever given information voluntarily (by registering or filling out a survey), you can bet it was filed away somewhere. The result is an electronic profile of your personal information.

On the whole, sites use this information to your advantage. Every personalized homepage, saved wishlist, and e-commerce shopping cart relies on the fact that the site can keep track of you. But if you've ever had your inbox buried under a flood of spam, you already know that some companies share, and even outright sell, information about you and your preferences.

So far, the United States government has taken a hands-off approach to regulating what sites can do with users' personal information. The Federal Trade Commission (www.ftc.gov) has outlined a federal privacy policy similar to the one recently adopted in Europe that would make unfair use of information a legal issue with clear penalties. But until this policy is actually passed, the burden of watching out for invasive practices falls to the consumer. To that end, we've put together the following Online Privacy Bill of Rights:

The Right to Consistent and Clear Privacy Policies

A privacy policy explains how a site will use or distribute any personal information it gathers. Very few laws govern privacy policies, and a recent survey found that less than 20% of the sites surveyed had a policy that met even the general standards. Policies aren't required to be brief, understandable, or even in the consumers' favor—if a site's small print states that it will indiscriminately share personal info, it legally can.

Be especially careful when dealing with sites that link you to a partner site—the policy on the new site may differ from that of the referring page. Also note that policies can change if a company is bought by another company, a gray area for consumer rights.

The Right to Opt-in or Opt-out

One popular band-aid solution to the problem is the opt-in, opt-out method of personal control. You've probably seen a checkbox when you registered or made a purchase that gave you the option to receive further information. If you click the box to receive further information (known as opt-in) the site may disperse your personal information; if you click to opt-out you forbid the site to share information that it otherwise might. While it isn't ultimate control, it's still steps ahead of having no choice at all.

The Right to Review Personal Data

Being able to correct erroneous information in your profile is a basic part of the standards proposed by the FTC, but for now there isn't an easy way to do it. If you remember registering on a site, you'll know to check your profile there, but you may not want or even be able to chase down all the other profiles. It's easy to see why losing control of personal information remains the top fear of two thirds of Internet users.

The Right to Anonymity

Companies like to track users' surfing habits because it makes it easy to target advertising to them. But you don't necessarily have to give information away while you surf. Anonymizers are down-loadable programs that function like a screen between the user and the Web; when a site looks for personal information about you, all it sees is the anonymizer.

Likewise, programs called remailers can erase the traceable trail that comes from sending email from a personal account. They strip away identifying information like address and user name before passing the message along—useful when posting to bulletin boards and other public forums.

The Right to Retribution

The FTC has already begun to step in when companies demonstrate extremely deceptive practices—Geocities and YoungInvestor have both received citations for misleading consumers about their privacy. But in general the lack of regulation has left no real way to make sure that a site is punished for a breach of privacy. What we do have are third-party groups like TRUSTe (www.truste.com) and the Personalization Consortium (www.personalization.org), that set privacy standards for their members. Check these sites for steps you can take to ensure your privacy online.

On Your Terms: A Privacy Bill of Rights

Beyond Basic Browsing

You've set your home page, stowed a couple of bookmarks, and gotten to know Google. Congratulations, you've passed Web Surfing 101. Ready to go for an advanced degree? These browser shortcuts and online utilities will get you started.

First, get a browser upgrade.
The newest versions of both Internet Explorer and Netscape are free, and the improved features are worth the 20-minute download time. Get them at www.microsoft.com/windows/ie or home.netscape.com/download.

Know thy browser. Just about every tool bar and menu is customizable; you may want to replace seldom-used buttons or add a fun browser skin. Internet Explorer users should take advantage of add-on tool bars like a stock ticker or news headlines bar, available at www.microsoft.com/windows/ie/webaccess.

Ax the images and ads. Images and banner ads can be major speed bumps on the info highway, making pages load 18 times slower than they would without them. If you're using a slow Internet connection, you may want to try turning off images and viewing Web sites in text-only mode. Also check out software designed to block banner ads. We recommend ADfilter (www.adfilter.com), though like most ad-blocking software, it detects ads only about 75% of the time.

Cache in. Every second counts when you're browsing the Web; savvy surfers will want to get to know the ins and outs of their cache to save precious download time. How does caching work? While you browse, information about each Web page you visit is stored in the cache on your hard drive so that your computer doesn't need to download the page again the next time you visit. For anyone who regularly visits the same sites, it pays to increase the size of your cache in order to browse more quickly.

Experiment with accelerators. Accelerators take the idea of caching pages one step further by pre-caching pages you might link to from the site you're on. So, if you're visiting Salon.com, an accelerator will not only cache the main page, but all the pages linked up to it as well—before you even visit them. Click on a link and you'll find it loads superfast, thanks to the accelerator. Want to try it? Download InterQuick for Windows (www.interquick.com).

Meet metabrowsers. Metabrowsers let you view several Web sites at the same time, on the same page. Pages are stacked right on top of one another and are accessible through tabs at the bottom of your screen, letting you look at one page while waiting for other pages to load. Sound cool? NetCaptor (www. simulbrowse.com) is a browser that can keep track of 30 different pages at once and uses indicator lights on the tabs to show whether a page is stuck (red), loading (yellow), or ready (green). If you'd rather not download a whole new browser, tools like Quickbrowse (www.quickbrowse.com) simulate the convenience of metabrowsers for Netscape and IE users.

Try search shortcuts. Several Web utilities can deliver searches right to you so you don't need to visit a search engine to look for links. ThirdVoice (www.thirdvoice.com) is a unique tool that scans the text in the Web page you're looking at and creates links based on words on the page. So, if you're reading about Puerto Vallarta and want to learn more, ThirdVoice turns the words "Puerto Vallarta" into a link for more Puerto Vallarta pages on the Web. Alexa is another great bet for getting site recommendations as you surf. Download the Alexa toolbar (www.alexa.com) for lists of links to sites that are similar to the one you're viewing.

Boost your bookmarks. Have all your personal must-surfs resulted in a motley list of bookmarked URLs? Online bookmark services like Backflip (www.backflip.com) are a better way to store favorites. Each time you hit Backflip's bookmark button, Backflip sorts the site into the proper category in your online collection of bookmarked sites; it's like creating your very own Web directory.

You can also bypass the browser altogether and use DoDots (www.dodots.com), little windows that sit on your desktop and give you instant access to online content. One dot might contain a dictionary search engine, another a calendar or news ticker that updates automatically from the Internet.

Ditch the major browsers. Maybe you've mastered the big two (Netscape and IE), or perhaps you're just ready for a change. Few people realize that these aren't the only browsers available. Venture over to Internet.com's Browser Watch (browserwatch.internet.com) to view a massive list of alternative browsers to fit your operating system. NeoPlanet (www.neoplanet.com) is a fun one to experiment with, offering features similar to the major browsers in a package that looks like a rocket cockpit.

art & culture

ArtandCulture.com www.artandculture.com © ⓓ

The best new art site on the block this year, ArtandCulture.com takes a refreshing approach to its coverage of cultural movements by plowing right through the typical pop art/high art pigeonholes. Search using keywords like Lush and Cool for intelligent coverage of the movements and personalities that are carving out our cultural landscape: Pablo Neruda, Patsy Cline, John Woo, and trip-hop, for starters.

Playbill Online www.playbill.com ©

The ubiquitous theater magazine and program boosts its informative content to a new degree online, providing news, features, and interviews for Broadway, off-Broadway, London, and regional performances. Browse or search current show times and venues, buy tickets, even book hotel rooms and restaurant reservations. Playbill Online's memorabilia boutique and links to Amazon.com's theater bookshop come to the rescue for anything you may have forgotten to pick up at the show.

foto8 www.foto8.com ©

Put simply, foto8 is sleek Web technology and international photojournalism at its most sophisticated. Enter a slide show on Brazilian rainforest fires or experience a political uprising in pictures. While the content here is selective, the library of back issues more than compensates. After you board this tightly run ship, other sites may start to look a little unkempt.

Whitney Museum of American Art www.whitney.org

Exploring the Whitney Museum's Web site is like getting one tasty bite of a very big meal. The site offers two virtual slide shows, a peek at recent acquisitions, and an overview of the museum's 12,000 classic American artworks. Though there are plenty of thumbnail images from the permanent collection peppered throughout the site, anyone seeking in-depth content will quickly exhaust the offerings here.

Photography In New York www.photography-guide.com ©

A slick and comprehensive guide to photography galleries and exhibitions in New York, across the United States, and worldwide. The extensive contact information and cross-referenced photographer listings here are the best available online. Find Brassaï or Ansel Adams in your city or across the globe, or search for the latest photo exhibits in a specific area.

art & culture

World Wide Arts Resources www.wwar.com

The perfect portal for quality art sites. Each site submitted to WWAR is categorized and reviewed for relevance—subject areas range from movements and artists to antiques and film. For planning offline art experiences, peruse the Local Arts section, which provides a handy list of galleries, museums, and theaters in your area.

Dance Online www.danceonline.com

A dance destination without a tutu in sight, Dance Online captures contemporary dance culture with a definite slant toward the New York scene. Aside from news updates and reviews of current shows, the site serves up sizable articles and QuickTime video clips of dance performances. Aspiring dancers will appreciate the site's strong community focus: chat forums, job postings, and the soap opera-esque *Chronicles of Dancer X* column encourage community and commiseration.

ZoneZero www.zonezero.com

ZoneZero chronicles photography as it moves from analog (film) to digital, with online exhibitions that marry still images, audio, and animation. Some of the exhibits extend work that has already appeared in books, like Lauren Greenfield's *Fast Forward.* Start out with the site tour, which maps out the site's contents and helps you optimize your browser settings.

The Museum of Modern Art www.moma.org

©

Elegant and tech-savvy, just as you'd expect, the MoMA site links to more than a dozen Web art pieces commissioned by the museum. You can also view selected works from its permanent collection—complete with audio commentary—and shop for beautiful, funky tchotchkes in the MoMA's online store.

The National Portrait Gallery www.npg.si.edu

The online home of the National Portrait Gallery is the only place to view the museum's 42 presidential portraits until the museum reopens in 2003. Log on here to check out Bill Clinton's bronze bust or Chester A. Arthur's bewhiskered visage. Other wings of the gallery house famous Native Americans, members of the Seneca Falls Convention, and ("Happy birthday, Mr. President") Marilyn Monroe.

DoubleTake Magazine www.doubletakemagazine.org

Fascinating photography down to the last pixel: *DoubleTake* Magazine puts the best of its quarterly print publication into its online companion. Each Web issue has three or four photo features excerpted from the magazine, intriguingly presented in contrasting pairs (punk rockers and swing dancers to name one) for heightened visual effect. If the current issue leaves you wanting more, visit the archives (which date back to 1995), or take advantage of the special Web subscription rate.

Walker Art Center www.walkerart.org

The Walker Art Center Web site is an exhibition unto itself, a combo of light and contrast that reflects the style and feel of its art. Jasper Johns, Marcel Duchamp, and Edward Hopper anchor the permanent collection, while Gallery 9 features digital works that affirm the Center's long-held position at the vanguard of modern art. Some screens are near unreadable (dark writing on dark background), but the site map is clear and panoramic tours lend a sense of "being there."

Disinformation www.disinfo.com

There's information ... and then there's information from the front. Disinformation is the counterculture center of the Web, with info on Bolivia's cartel-like government, Japanese garbage wrestling, the new e-poor, and other antiestablishment rants. The site features RealVideo interviews, cartoon clips, and a continuously updated talk show, as well as chats, forums, and a shop stocked with Timothy Leary-esque books, videos, and gear.

State Hermitage Museum www.hermitagemuseum.org ©

The five buildings of this veritable Russian Louvre house some three million artifacts, weapons, paintings, and sculptures from "The Stone Age to the 20th Century," B.C. to Y2K. Though the site has just a selection, it's huge. And how often do you get to see St. Petersburg? The design, formal from font to photography, might induce whispers of awe during the virtual tour, but go ahead and gaze.

Musee d'Orsay www.smartweb.fr/orsay

All the light and airiness of the tangible, actual museum for 19th-century art. Hi-fi navigation makes the touring stellar—use the panoramic viewer to walk through the museum simply by clicking on a rotating photo. The accompanying floor plan will let you know exactly where in the museum you are and provide running commentary. Approximately half of the collection—Degas, Renoir, Rodin—is online.

Voice of Dance www.voiceofdance.com

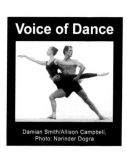

If you live and breathe dance—ballet, modern, or classical—Voice of Dance might be talking to you. Articles, interviews, and the latest news and criticism are all here. But the extra steps that stretch this site's performance are the thoughtful content (e.g., a section on eating disorders), a comprehensive worldwide schedule with an option to buy tickets, and a listing of auditions for North America and Europe.

Damian Smith/Allison Campbell,
Photo: Narinder Dogra

CEPA Gallery Online cepa.buffnet.net

Although Buffalo isn't exactly known for its trend setting culture, the city's CEPA Gallery Online is decidedly flashy. Experimental modes of navigation lead you through the online shows of "post-photographic art," event listings, local links, and a very small store. We only wish they would beef up the content; though witty and thoughtful, the limited offerings leave us wanting more.

PBS.org: Arts www.pbs.org/neighborhoods/arts ©

If PBS did a show on the topic—architecture, drama and dance, film, fine art, literature, music, pop, or folk art—you'll find it here. The making of *Citizen Kane*, "The Irish in America," and Ralph Ellison's *The King of the Bingo Hall* are a few examples, and all shows come with transcripts, clips, fantastic links, and teachers' guides.

The Metropolitan Museum of Art www.metmuseum.org

Take a virtual tour of the 200,000-square-foot, 125-year-old art museum without leaving your chair. Floor plans of the Met's dozens of galleries allow visitors to view selections from the three million works in the permanent collection spanning 5,000 years of cultural history. Medieval armor, marble reliefs from ancient Greece, and Kandinsky paintings—it's all here. Visit the museum shop for gift ideas and online shopping.

Artstar.com www.artstar.com ©

1001 ways to slice and dice the art world: Artstar.com has made a science of sorting artists and images into user-friendly, cross-referenced categories. Say you've fallen in love with Van Gogh's *Cornfield with Cypress*; click into the Explore interface to easily uncover works by the same artist, in the same medium (oil on paper), or on the same subject (fields). Artstar.com is really a poster shopping site, but the extensive content sets it apart from other poster peddlers.

Sothebys.com www.sothebys.com © ⓢ

While $150,000 may not buy as much as it used to, it will get you a rather nice two-thousand-year-old Egyptian bust. For antiquities, jewelry, sculpture, and paintings, Sotheby's reigns supreme—drop in here for a peek at all the gorgeous stuff and the opportunity to place a bid. An expanding section of collecting guides details the ins and outs of buying and caring for silver, paintings, watches, books, and the like.

NextMonet.com www.nextmonet.com © ⓢ

Want to find out what's up in the art world? NextMonet.com will bring you up to speed with weekly feature articles and an amazing custom search tool that breaks down new art by medium, style, characteristic (like color and balance), and subject. After five minutes of absorbing the artworks and their descriptions, you'll be ready to find and buy the perfect asymmetrical still life for your dining room.

CultureFinder.com www.culturefinder.com ©

Tickets for Cher? Don't be gauche. Load up this URL to find out about ballet, theater, and opera performances in your area. CultureFinder.com has special ticket offers on events all over the country, plus loads of articles on the art forms. There are even crash courses in every discipline for the culturally curious. Finally, a coherent plot summary of *I Pagliacci*!

eyestorm www.eyestorm.com

Purists may be turned off by the price tags, but this commercially driven site also happens to be one of the best places on the Web to view contemporary art and photography. A polished, Flash-driven interface steers the viewer through works by big art-world names like Damien Hirst and Andres Serrano, adding artist profiles and additional information where appropriate. If you like a particular piece, click My Space to add it to your personal slide show of favorites. If you hate it, head to the Discussion Space for lively debate.

eArtGroup www.eartgroup.com

Enough with the browsing. If you're looking to buy, consult eArtGroup to research, appraise, and even purchase esteemed works of 20th-century art and photography from reputable dealers worldwide. Prices run the gamut, from a few hundred thousand dollars for an Andy Warhol painting to a few hundred for a lithograph by Merce Cunningham. It's designed for experienced collectors, but registration is free and there's a ready-to-assist staff to help beginners. Or, spend nothing and start your own virtual collection, gratis.

Butterfields www.butterfields.com

Founded in 1865 and recently linked to eBay, this San Francisco-based art and antiques consignment shop offers real-time bidding capabilities for their online auctions. Check the sundry research materials, registered appraisal services, and catalogues the site provides before you lift your virtual paddle for that Navajo blanket or post-modern vase.

Antique Networking www.antiqnet.com

Antique Networking looks like an antique shop—stuffed to the gills, with something in every corner and then something behind that. Gird up, though, because there's a wealth of antique information here (fair listings, appraisals, opportunities to buy), designed for enthusiasts but clear enough for neophytes. You'll find the antiques equally easy to search and buy, whether you know exactly what you want or only have a vague idea.

beauty

beautyscene
www.beautyscene.com

Beauty may be only skin deep, but a lot rides on that fraction of an inch. Use beautyscene.com's My Kit feature to look calm, collected, and exceptionally cool. My Kit keeps track of the makeup and beauty supplies you frequently buy and sends you a reminder when it's time to reorder. You'll have to become a member to use it, but registering (for free) also gets you free samples and beauty advice from a dermatologist, a fitness expert, a plastic surgeon, and *Cosmopolitan* founder Helen Gurley Brown.

iVillage Beauty www.ivillage.com/beauty ©

Though it's tempting to spend a half an hour on this site's Makeover-O-Matic section alone, you'd miss all the other features that make this site so overabundant in beauty content. There's also the Looking Glass, which quizzes you to determine your personal style, the Fragrance Finder, and a separate expert for practically every facial feature. Registered members can save a personal My Beauty page that tailors beauty advice to fit their hair type, skin color, and style.

Beauty.com www.beauty.com

Their motto is "The world of beauty online," but it's more like, "An online beauty store." The cosmetic e-tailer has a vault of glitzy, glittery, glammy potions and powders from the trendiest lines (think Anna Sui and The Face), and a strong collection of men's products. Advisors staff the live chat forum, if you have a pressing question. But the feature non-pareil is makeup magician Kevyn Aucoin's column, with before and after pics that are see-to-believe extraordinary.

Changeslive.com www.changeslive.com

For you rough diamonds in need of a little polish: the British beauty specialists at Changeslive.com are well-equipped to help you unearth your inner supermodel. The site offers a stellar array of quality products and guidance to steer you to the good stuff. Articles on the psychology of lipstick, sleep disorders, and fitness exemplify their commitment to first-rate beauty and living and super-clean Flash graphics complete the package.

Sephora.com www.sephora.com

With a sleek black design and beauty advice from the likes of François Nars and Vincent Longo, Sephora's site attempts to recreate the luxe and sparkle of its real-life stores, with mixed results. The makeup and fragrances, tools, and accessories live up to the hype, but why the ingredient lists? Who really cares that Hard Candy Disco 2000 contains epoxy resin-coated polyethylene? For makeup purists, though, the site's superior selection redeems.

indulge.com www.indulge.com

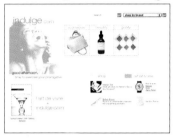

A patent on self-pampering with a price tag that is nothing if not indulgent. indulge.com's three sections cover accessories, beauty products, and pretty home trinkets—see the first for Modo sunglasses, the second for Bloom lip gloss, and the third for Naturopathica bath candles. The design is elegantly spare, and the super attentive customer service includes live chat, a toll-free number, and personal shoppers. If you're looking for more information, link through to the site's monthly mind and body magazine.

Spafinder.com www.spafinder.com

Rich, indulgent, or seriously stressed? The resorts listed at Spafinder.com run the gamut from simple day spas to week-long retreats where pampering is an extreme sport. Spa searches are locale-based but can take other criteria into account (non-smoking, vegetarian, pet-friendly, etc.). If you don't know what type is right for you, send them an email to get a personalized recommendation. Frazzled New Yorkers take note: search results for some areas (like the Northeast) are surprisingly lacking.

reflect.com www.reflect.com

You mean you don't have your own personal line of beauty products? Dahling, you really must get with (or rather, download) the program. Shockwave, that is. You'll need it to make your way through the intuitive personalization process at this gorgeous site. Members (registration is free) can enhance their experience with a preferred reading list, horoscopes, chat, tips from the experts, and wishlists.

hair-news.com www.hair-news.com

It's easy to find hair how-to sites that are slicker than pomade; the hard part is getting information that's not undermined by heavy product promotion. hair-news.com has unbiased tricks, from getting what you want at the salon to fixing hair snafus once they've happened. We especially liked the Lab, a cookbook of recipes for beauty products like detangler and conditioner.

ingredients.com www.ingredients.com

ingredients.com wraps its beauty products in the standard mix of impressive Flash animation and cute, strategically bubbled naked models frolicking onscreen. Some little touches try too hard, like the word-search puzzle required to access the site's magazine, but the navigation is one of a kind. Users can search by ingredient (green tea, St. John's wart, etc.), product, and even "benefit" (antiseptic, balancing, energizing).

books

Barnes & Noble.com www.bn.com

Could 2.9 million people in more than 215 countries be wrong? At Barnes & Noble.com, the numbers speak for themselves: 750,000 titles in stock, 50% discounts on *New York Times* best-sellers, and 2,500 books under five dollars. The Out of Print section may be one of the best features: there are millions of used, rare, and out-of-print books in the searchable database here. Listen to B & N's online radio station while you peruse the selections.

Borders.com www.borders.com

What's cool about Borders.com? The community. While you may not be able to sip a mochaccino while you're there, the online NetCafe offers staff recommendations, author interviews, and a forum for your opinions. You'll also find a huge selection of music and videos here (for a total of 10 million books, CDs, and videos), and discounts of up to 50% on forthcoming books and *New York Times* best-sellers.

BookBrowse www.bookbrowse.com

Loitering in bookstores may get you a dirty look from the clerk, but logging on to Book-Browse will get you sample chapters from fiction, nonfiction, and children's books. Find John Grisham's latest (or the two before that), the new one from Isabel Allende, Tom Wolfe, Salman Rushdie, and, of course, *I Ain't Got Time to Bleed* by Gov. Jesse "The Body" Ventura. Each excerpt also comes with a plot summary, review tidbits from the popular press, and a bit about the author.

MP3Lit.com www.mp3lit.com

If you're itching to hear Kerouac read from *On The Road* in his beatific Franco-American voice, surf this way. MP3Lit.com provides free spoken word recordings of hundreds of famous authors. The selection ranges from the edgy spoken word of contemporary poet Wanda Coleman to the more obscure, drunken slurrings of 60s luminary Charles Bukowski. Don't expect full-length works, however; you'll have to click through to purchase them from Barnes & Noble.

Bookreporter.com www.bookreporter.com

Refreshingly free of the requisite book reviewer pretension, the employees of this site seem to actually enjoy reading—even mainstream novels. The discerning academic may be put off by the emphasis on best-seller favorites and novels adapted for movies, but the average reading enthusiast will appreciate Bookreporter.com's aim to provide intelligent commentary for a broad audience.

January Magazine www.januarymagazine.com

January Magazine's simple presentation makes it a standout in the online literary jungle. The focus here is on well-written book reviews, frequently updated and divided into basic food groups like fiction, nonfiction, fantasy, and art. Close examination reveals a perceptible emphasis on the crime fiction category. You'll also find an extensive list of author interviews complete with links to their personal Web sites.

The New York Review of Books www.nybooks.com/nyrev Ⓒ

An intellectual nirvana with reviews from Joan Didion, John Updike, and other heavy-hitting thinkers, book lovers will find the site hard to pass up. Although design lacks, a searchable database of reviews from the last 35 years lets readers in on a virtual conversation with some of the most notable writers and thinkers of modern literature.

Fatbrain.com www.fatbrain.com Ⓒ Ⓢ

Stuff your head to bursting with science, math, computer, and business books from Fatbrain.com. Their books and manuals, interactive training software, and same day shipping are great for those times when you need to learn SQL, DBS, or C++, fast. Quick-response customer service and extras like the customized corporate bookstore are tops.

Alibris www.alibris.com

For out-of-fashion favorites, turn to Alibris; the site's Book Hound will search out any title that isn't in their impressive collection of out-of-print, rare, or first-edition books. After you've tracked down your grandmother's cookbook or your favorite childhood story, head to the Interact section, where sci-fi fans, book experts, and other bibliophiles opine online.

VarsityBooks.com www.varsitybooks.com

To a college kid being sucked dry by the high cost of tuition and Dominos delivery, a 40% discount off textbook prices is nothing to sneeze at. VarsityBooks.com has 350,000 different book titles, including graduate level material and fiction as well as nonfiction and undergrad. When you start a search here, go armed with specific titles or the ISBN numbers of the books you need—searching by course list is hit or miss. Delivery takes one to two days.

Project Gutenberg www.promo.net/pg © ©

"Anything that can be entered into a computer can be reproduced indefinitely." Sure, we know that now—dancing hamsters—but in 1971, those words from Project Gutenberg's founder were pretty radical. Applied to books, that means that 2,700 texts "in the public domain" are available in full. Download quickly and freely major works of literature: either "light" (*Through the Looking Glass, Alice in Wonderland*), "heavy" (the Bible, *Moby Dick*), or reference. The site looks a little, well, bookish; that's entirely the point.

Online Originals www.onlineoriginals.com

London-based Online Originals stocks its cybershelves with novels, nonfiction, and children's books—all exclusives. Pay $7, of which the author gets a cut, and you get a full-length book emailed to you. E-books in Braille are also available. It's a great service, but not all the selections are page-turners. Read sample chapters before you buy.

iUniverse.com www.iuniverse.com ⓞ

Aspiring writers may want to spend their next $100 on actually getting published. For $99 and up, iUniverse.com takes your manuscript, designs a cover, and prints the finished product—a real live book!—in fewer than 60 days. The book will be available to thousands of book-sellers and on the Barnes & Noble.com and Amazon.com book pages. If you're stuck writing the title page, you may want to check out their numerous writer resources: reviews, classes, and marketing advice.

BookSwap www.bookswap.com

The theory: if a student pays for a book, uses it, then resells it, the net expense is virtually nothing. That's why we have BookSwap, a textbook classifieds for students in the U.S., Canada, and U.K. If a book you're looking for isn't yet posted, register a Want Ad and receive an email if it turns up. The only flaw is the conspicuous lack of customer service—it's up to the buyer and seller to work out shipping and returns themselves.

Best Book Buys www.bestbookbuys.com

You want the book, but at the prices they charge these days … Best Book Buys searches high and low, online and off, major publishers and minor ones, for the cheapest price. The number of results depends on the search, but the savings are significant (e.g., a best-selling hardcover at $13 to $26). You search, you get the price (cost of shipping included), you link to the store/site, you buy, and soon, you read.

Fortune www.fortune.com

The who's who in business won't miss a beat: *Fortune* magazine's full print content is online—and then some. Browse categories on careers, technology, business life, and the key to *Fortune*: lists of the top 500 companies across the globe. Additional resources include a career advice column, a peer job counseling forum, and strategies for job hunting online.

Fast Company www.fastcompany.com

A *Wired* for the business world, Fast Company dives into technology with grace and style. The site is filled with all the wit and wisdom you've come to expect, including business advice and tips on sanity maintenance in the workplace. The only difference between the Web site and the print version seems to be that there's more of it on the Web—searchable archives, expanded resources, community polls and events, and the delectably efficient convenience of the Internet.

SmartOnline.com www.smartonline.com ⓞ

Unless you like the challenge of learning 27 different software applica-

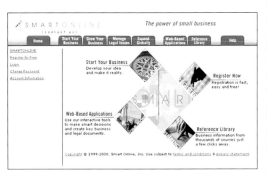

tions to manage your small business, you'll appreciate SmartOnline.com's more compact approach. The site offers Web-hosted software applications for daily functions (finances, legal forms, sales) that all have the same basic look and structure. Most applications are free, though a few require a per-use fee ranging from $10 to $25. While you're there, don't miss the extensive How-To section, with articles that range from "Start Your Business" to "Expand Globally."

BusinessWeek Online www.businessweek.com ⓒ

More resources than would ever fit in one print magazine, BW Online offers multiple tiers of access (from free to full subscription) and a broad array of services. The weekly email newsletter, the comprehensive Daily Briefing section, plus resources for small business, entrepreneurs, technology, and investing are open to the general public. The real meat of the magazine costs, but those seriously interested in business will likely find it well worth it.

Forbes.com www.forbes.com

Cher made the cut but Madonna didn't. We're talking about Forbes' Celebrity 100 list, one of the publication's many lists of famous and wealthy people available online. Forbes.com also provides everything the print magazine offers plus pages of unique information and tools, including calculators for college savings, retirement, and life insurance; 12,000 company profiles; and a financial glossary.

U.S. Department of Labor www.dol.gov

Often people have a general understanding of what should and should not happen in the workplace—but better to be certain. The U.S. Department of Labor provides guides that explain the rules regarding small businesses, retirement, health benefits, safety standards, and wage requirements. The Statistics & Data section offers a particularly engaging window into the state of employment in the country today.

FT.com www.ft.com

Before you attain world domination, you'll need to know what's going on outside the immediate five-mile radius. FT.com (progeny of the *Financial Times*) aims to be the reference of choice for business people seeking global savvy. Is it successful? Partly—its financial information is solid, with market indices, news from 3,000 different sources, and a directory of business links. But the excess of other content, such as the city guides and travel features, can leave a surfer confused.

Office.com www.office.com

While you probably won't be looking for information on managing sewage sludge and distributing digital music at the same time, you can bet that you'll find both at Office.com. Divided into six manageable sections, this content-rich site aims to help small-business managers run their offices' daily operations. The Market-

place provides convenient access to everything from hardware to postage through streamlined links, and, while small, the Community section allows users to network through informative bulletin boards.

Dow Jones Business Directory
www.businessdirectory.dowjones.com

The business Yellow Pages straight from the source. Search by site name, category, or keyword for the best business sites, complete with ratings and reviews based on content, design, speed, and navigation. A great jumping-off point for business and financial resources on the Web.

U.S. Patent & Trademark Office www.uspto.gov

The USPTO does its best to make it easy for anyone to learn about patent and trademark application procedures, with archives and detailed FAQs on the process from submission to acceptance. Its Electronic Business Center offers a bevy of tools for filers to submit or check the status of a pending application.

addAshop.com www.addashop.com   Ⓓ Ⓞ

Wanna-be small business owners can get their feet in the virtual door by starting a store at addAshop.com. You sup- ply the Web address, pick a color scheme, and decide which of the two million product options you want to sell; five minutes later, the site will have your online storefront up and operational. addAshop.com also helps manage inventory, customer service, ship- ping, and billing. The cost of such easy, turnkey e-commerce? Nothing.

The Web of Culture www.webofculture.com

"Thumbs up" in the States may be a good thing, but in Iran, it might put your life in jeopardy. Since etiquette can make or break a business deal, The Web of Culture has listings of proper gestures, current global headlines, and even some geography that frequent business travelers will want to commit to memory. The site also offers help on finding embassies and consulates, and online dictionaries to prevent embar- rassing language *faux pas*.

Demandline.com www.demandline.com   Ⓞ

Whatever happened to the little guy in today's world of dotcoms and big business? Demandline.com allows small businesses to pool their resources and get low corporate rates on core services from providers like GTE. A reverse auction process (explained within) offers some of the lowest available prices for services like 401(k), credit-card processing, and Web hosting, without difficult negotiation.

Inc.com www.inc.com   Ⓒ

By providing access to in-depth advice from colleagues, mentors, and industry experts, Inc.com takes the legwork out of learning how to be a successful entrepreneur. Extensive advice and discussion sections let users seek out answers to their specific quandaries, while the database contains local service providers for specific business needs. Register to be listed in the site's directory and to use the My Inc.com, a personalized page for storing articles, research, and contacts.

inc·com
YOU INCORPORATED

AllBusiness.com www.allbusiness.com   Ⓒ

When sales manager, accountant, and secretary are all the same person, you know you're working for a small business. This site was created to help small business owners perform the tasks that eat up their time, like checking employee backgrounds, collecting on bad debts, or run- ning a trademark search. But while AllBusiness.com arranges its vast resources into easily accessible categories, be prepared to wade through layers of information before getting to your target topic.

NewWork News www.newwork.com
Adding a little edgy interpretation to its information, NewWork News has articles that question traditional perspectives on work, the economy, and politics. Some material is original, while other features are culled from sources such as the *Christian Science Monitor* and the *Nando Times*. But don't expect flashy graphics or even well-formatted text—at this bare bones, non-commercial site, only content counts.

Bizzed.com www.bizzed.com
Bizzed.com is a network of partners who provide online services for the

budding business. The site can link you to a company to get your Web site up and running, another company to analyze the competition, and another to craft a business plan. Bizzed.com pools your request for the service with other members' requests to get a group discount rate. Free resources on the site include informational articles and message boards for networking.

Onvia.com www.onvia.com
Onvia.com's Emarketplace provides a profusion of information for small-business people looking to take advantage of the new economy. Cook up a marketable plan and head straight to their News and Tools section for hundreds of worksheets, forms, checklists, how-to guides, and business articles spe-

cific to your industry and location. Once you have (fingers crossed) employees and an office, return to the site to buy and sell products and services by auction.

EDGAR www.sec.gov/edgarhp.htm
The SEC's searchable database, called EDGAR, will bring you the latest information on annual reports, prospectuses, and mutual fund filings straight from the mouth of the Securities and Exchange Commission. While most people won't exactly flock to this dry, no-nonsense site, corporations and investors will find its wealth of information invaluable.

EntreNetwork.com www.entrenetwork.com
When they said not to put all your eggs in one basket, they said nothing about incubators. EntreNetwork.com is a networking tool for local entrepreneurs, leading them to resources and funding that will help get their idea off the ground. The site's strength is its listings of seminars and offline support organizations; feature articles are well written but infrequent and the online resources it lists belong to its partner sites.

Garage.com www.garage.com

Since the tiny startup operation at 367 Addison Avenue in Palo Alto spawned Hewlett Packard, the very word garage has come to symbolize the aspirations of every fledgling Internet company. Appropriately, Garage.com's *raison d'etre* is linking startup companies that need money to venture capitalist "angels" who have it. The only catch? Entrepreneurs have to attend the site's Startup Boot Camp before they can get to Heaven (the virtual boardroom).

Hoover's Online www.hoovers.com   ©

Dubbed "the reigning king of corporate profiles" by *Fortune*, Hoover's provides its paid subscribers with detailed information on more than 15,000 public and private companies around the world—perfect for investors, executives, and job seekers. The pithy and well-researched profiles sketch out the company's history, ownership, and position within the industry, and include 10 years of fiscal data. Pay $109.95 for the full deal—or access mini versions for free.

office supplies

OfficeDepot.com www.officedepot.com   © Ⓢ

Office Depot's awesome online store offers way more than just staplers and file folders. The site is loaded with extras like their office toolkit (complete with downloadable contracts, forms, and business letters) and tips on how to get organized, set up a home office, and even start a company Web site. To get the most out of the site, set up an account and take advantage of customized shopping lists.

Staples.com www.staples.com   ©

Buying office products can be quite a chore—marching up and down warehouse aisles, choosing fine-tip or extra fine-tip pens. For simpler shopping, head to Staples.com, the comprehensive source for pins, pens, file folders, furniture, and everything else. Become a registered shopper and the site adapts to you by keeping track of your purchase history and favorite "aisles," or product genres. The more you shop, the better the site knows you and the faster you can get back to work.

OrderZone.com www.orderzone.com

Ranked one of the top business–to–business Web sites, OrderZone.com is a one-stop online service for hundreds of products. Uniforms and apparel, electronics and office supplies—all from brand merchants, all in one place. The easy ordering feature is a real time-saver for those who want to avoid the hassle of multiple order forms and invoices.

careers

Vault.com www.vault.com

Taking insider journalism to the job market, Vault.com profiles hundreds of companies and industries (such as consulting and high tech) with alarming insight. Get the skinny on top firms and internships, or read about the players in the Silicon Valley scene. The job search form lets job seekers select criteria, then sit back and relax while the site emails reports on positions that match their skills and experience.

CareerPath.com www.careerpath.com ©

With job postings culled from 90 newspapers and additional listings submitted directly to the site, CareerPath.com is the place to start your nationwide job hunt. Search for openings at specific employers, see who's offering your minimum salary, or locate recruiting events and job fairs in your area. The only drawback to having 350,000 openings at your cursor tip is that search returns can be overwhelming; be specific for best results.

Monster.com www.monster.com © d

The undisputed champion of online job hunting. The job listings alone make Monster.com a must see—not to mention the "My Monster" start page, which lets you store your resume, cover letter, and job prospects online. Special features include company profiles, advice guides, personalized job search agents, and a global search function.

Jobtrak.com www.jobtrak.com

If you're nowhere near the college or university you attended, Jobtrak.com can put you back in touch with the job-hunting resources of your alma mater. Having contracted with over 900 college career centers across the country, Jobtrak.com manages and posts job opportunities for alumni and students. You'll also find car-buying advice, a tutor finder, and real-time tutoring sessions online.

ArtHire www.arthire.com

Great art doesn't come cheap, but with the help of ArtHire, it can come easy. This site creates a place where artists and employers come together for mutual benefit—potential employees can post resumes and portfolios online (including Flash and QuickTime files), and potential employers can get a sneak peek at work done by the person they're considering. If you're just shopping for art, you can do so, or visit the Extras section for quirky games.

mediabistro.com www.mediabistro.com

New name, same outstanding source for media professionals. Formerly HireMinds.com, mediabistro.com is a respected place to go for news and job opportunities in both new and old media. The Resources section sports links for journalists (like news wires and writer's guides), and helpful pages on finding grants and other means of self-employment. The focus, however, is the cache of jobs listed for a variety of editorial and design positions.

HotJobs.com www.hotjobs.com

The site whose single-fingered icon has become a signpost to a more satisfying career, HotJobs.com's simple design and quality content one-up the run of career sites. Job listings include entry-level and startup, with the hottest prospects noted by site staffers. Even non-members can contact the employers—a job site rarity. See the HotJobs 411 e-zine for everything you need to know during your hunt and post-hire.

JobReviews.com www.jobreviews.com

Find out what a company's employees really do all day (and how much they enjoy it) before the final round. JobReviews.com asks current and past employees of major companies like Price Waterhouse and Microsoft to post the real scoop on their duties, corporate culture, and salary. It's a quid pro quo approach, so you'll have to dish before you can see their goods. The site is still growing–smaller companies and obscure positions aren't well covered yet.

careerjournal.com www.careers.wsj.com

Career advice from the people who know business. The *Wall Street Journal*'s career magazine continues to uphold the quality of the print publication, but for free. It also offers a hefty tool kit of e-services, such as relocation guidance, salary data by industry, job postings, and career Q & As. Useful information, engaging features, updated daily.

Headhunter.net www.headhunter.net

A recruiting site that takes its statistics seriously: resumes, job postings, and users here total more than 150,000. Employers can control the priority of their job postings by "upgrading" their listing or invest in the VIP Résumé Reserve to check out the newest and most attractive resumes before they're put in the batch with the rest. A great site for more passive job seekers and recruiters.

6FigureJobs.com www.sixfigurejobs.com

Unsatisfied senior executives can't exactly leaf through the classifieds. At 6Figurejobs.com, professionals can apply for top-tier positions and employers can post premium opportunities to a pre-screened pool of candidates. The Job Search Assistant lets you keep up to three search profiles with varying criteria (location, salary, etc.). Should you find an interesting ad, the one-click-apply tool sends an employer a full rundown of your current credentials.

Guru.com www.guru.com

Executive freelancers, moonlighters, and hired guns wear the additional label of guru at the site that considers them the top tier of workforce quality. Like most career sites, Guru.com lists openings, which include creative and media positions as well as Web and technology ones. But it also dishes out financial, legal, and professional resources essential to the solo businessperson. Register to save a list of attractive job prospects and to have new postings emailed to you.

WetFeet.com www.wetfeet.com

Here we have one of the few career sites without a job database. But anything else you might want to know about finding and keeping a job is here. We're talking company profiles, search tips, helpful books to purchase, and tools to use. Get specific by exploring career descriptions by category, or go for more general help in resume-building and self-marketing. The lack of external links is a good thing—all of the active text points to original content.

FreetimeJobs.com www.freetimejobs.com

Find a way to trade idle minutes for spending money; this unique job posting service catalogs limited, minimum-commitment positions like handyman, temp bookkeeper, and holiday retail help. Seekers can browse listings and sign up for the weekly newsletter without paying, but Premium Membership (read: $10 a year) is required to be able to put in a bid on a project.

JobMonkey.com www.jobmonkey.com

You won't find opportunities in Alaskan fisheries at your run-of-the-mill job Web site, but such alternative types of employment are JobMonkey.com's forte—cruise ships, casinos, park service, and the aforementioned fisheries are just some of the options. The site can even help employees secure lodging and insurance, and offer suggestions on what to take. The only place we were disappointed was the discussion boards, where activity was surprisingly sparse.

govWorks.com's Jobs in Government
www.jobsingovernment.com

Your country, state, or city wants you. Heed the call at govWorks.com's career site, Jobs in Government, the definitive site for job openings in the public sector. Sanitation and road construction, you think? Recent listings included lifeguard, nutritionist, librarian, and tree surgeon. Head to the Resources section for information that goes beyond the individual job descriptions, such as resume tips and what (they say) it's like to work for the government.

FreeAgent.com www.freeagent.com

Love the freedom of freelancing but hate the hassle of chasing down projects, invoicing, and the rest? Become a member of FreeAgent.com and you can have a personal assistant take care of all that nasty paperwork for you. Need health insurance? No problem. Help with tax payments? A breeze. You do your work, and FreeAgent.com takes care of the rest—for a fee, of course.

Net-Temps www.net-temps.com

Nothing lasts forever, even great employment. Net-Temps specializes in contract and temporary jobs in traditional fields (clerical, IT, and sales to name three). You can sift through the 100,000-plus jobs yourself or set up a personal Job Seekers Desktop, and let the site go to work. Additional help comes in the form of discussion forums, job seekers' news, and advice on career development. Sign up for the email newsletter if you want to skip to the juicy parts.

myjobsearch.com www.myjobsearch.com ©

If you uploaded an experienced career counselor to the Internet, you'd have myjobsearch.com. The mass of helpful information on this site is staggering, with tips on finding, winning, and keeping the job of your dreams. Unique among career sites is the Salary section, where you can use real pay scales to determine your asking price. If you take advantage of the services here, that price may be more than you think.

cars

Motor Trend Online www.motortrend.com ©

The folks at Motor Trend Online understand that there is more to buying a car than simply haggling with the salesman. There's also a world of information that includes automotive recalls, safety concerns, new models, auto shows, and accessories. You'll find all that here, as well as video clips, screen savers, and the indispensable Buyer's Guide, with extensive ratings and reviews of all the latest autos.

The Tire Rack www.tirerack.com ©

Do you have a spare in your trunk? If not, get thee to The Tire Rack, where you can quickly search for a new set of wheels by tire size, car model, year, or brand. Need help choosing? There are plenty of articles here to assist, plus an interactive guide that lets you see how particular wheels look on your car.

Car And Driver Online www.caranddriver.com

Joie de piloter, or joy of driving, is what differentiates *Car and Driver* readers from mere commuters. The magazine's Web site encompasses the print's feature articles, as well as some more frequently updated online exclusives. We loved the 100 Best Roads section, a list of top places to drive and recommended pit stops along the route. But because the site relies on the magazine's archives to beef up its offerings, you may encounter features written in 1997.

cars

AAA Online www.aaa.com

The official Web site of the American Automobile
Association can set you up with a membership,
which does, indeed, have its privileges: discounts
on hotels and rental cars, traffic reports, tour
books online, road maps, and driving directions.
But if you decide to veto paid membership, you
can still get to the automotive tips, tows, and savings section.

BreezeNet's Guide to Airport Rental Cars
www.bnm.com

Featuring more than 110 major auto rental companies at more than 140 airports in the United
States and abroad, BreezeNet is a great way to
reserve a set of wheels at a reasonable price—
before you reach your destination. The site
links you directly to agencies in your destination
city, and explains potential gas charges and the
limits of "unlimited mileage." There are even listings for limos and luxury cars—why take a taxi when
you could take a Jaguar XJS?

PickupTruck.com www.pickuptruck.com

The top spot for vehicle sales
doesn't go to family sedans
or sport coupes, but rather
pickups, year after year.
Truck owners can connect
with other members of their
dedicated demographic in
the chat rooms and bulletin
boards of this community
hub—brand war was the hot
topic when we checked.
Other features include truck
news, a Truck of the Week
pictorial, and details on emerging luxury trucks.

Edmunds.com www.edmunds.com ©

The car-buying scenarios on this site read like Stephen King (no one
said getting inside the head of an auto dealer would be pretty), but if
you're in the market for a new or used car, you'll find them very
informative reading. Here also are price lists, pros and cons, and war-
ranty information for the makes and models you like. Before buying,
see how a vehicle holds up in the Long Term Road Tests, or find out
how similar models match up using the Comparison Tests section.

CarsDirect.com www.carsdirect.com © ⑤

This is a perfect example of how the Internet can empower consumers
and make their lives a whole lot easier. CarsDirect.com's clever service
takes you step by step through the process of choosing a car, getting
financing or a lease, and ordering your vehicle. If you finance your purchase through the site, they'll also give you roadside assistance for six
years. We'll withhold our praise until the site can cook us dinner,
though.

The IntelliChoice Car Center
www.intellichoice.com

The components of a car's price can be more mysterious than the ingredients in a Christmas fruitcake, but this site will help unravel the mystery—it goes beyond the sticker price and shows the luxury tax, gas-guzzler tax, dealer incentives, and rebates that result in the final cost. Still unsure if you're getting your money's worth? Stop by the Competitor Reports to see how four competing models measure up.

SoundDomain.com www.sounddomain.com

Who cares if your car stalls, skids, or slides? The real question is, does it rock? The stereos, speakers, and electronic doodads at SoundDomain.com can make your car's sound system the envy (or terror) of the neighborhood. Browse for a Blaupunkt, Alpine, or JVC CD player, pick up some crunchy Boss subwoofers (essential for rattling pedestrian teeth), or talk shop with aficionados in the chat rooms.

Trader Online www.traderonline.com

A high-tech alternative to putting a For Sale sign in your rear window, TraderOnline.com is a vehicle classifieds clearinghouse that hosts separate areas for cars, trucks, RVs, planes, boats, and SUVs. Each section includes a sidebar of helpful references such as price checkers, parts finders, and links to pertinent publications. Placing an ad online is free, as is browsing the 100,000 ads already listed.

Autoweb.com www.autoweb.com

With something for every stage in the lifecycle of auto ownership, Autoweb.com offers information that is (almost) unsullied by commercial influence. The site's research section walks buyers through exploration and purchasing, while the Maintain portion gives current owners help with care and repair. A whole caddy of online tools includes recall notices, rebates, and a lease vs. loan calculator.

Cars & Culture www.pathfinder.com/carculture

With more than 17 million cars manufactured each year, cars have become an undeniable influence on our contemporary culture. Cars & Culture focuses on the parts of life spent getting from A to B and the traditions that have evolved out of them, from road-trip stories to driving games to popular songs about cars. The Odd Car Facts section makes interesting reading, as do the first-person accounts of classic car tours and events.

The Jalopy Journal
www.jalopyjournal.com

The cars here are closer to hot rods than anything the Beverly Hillbillies might drive, but the site definitely has a down-home feel. Self-labeled an "electro-zine thing," it offers a community-oriented look into the world of rodding, complete with slide shows, greaser diversions, and classifieds. See the Bench Rodding section to read members' nostalgic accounts of past cars and races.

ClassicCar.com www.classicar.com
A community dedicated to the celebration of cars and the people who love them. Whether you're a passionate collector and restorer or simply curious, the super search engine here is a gateway to features and forums, auctions, car parts and services, and appraisals. The community features and listings of clubs, museums, and events are stellar; the design, on the other hand, could stand to be revamped .

iMotors.com www.imotors.com

Your old clunker has bitten the dust but you don't have time to test drive a dozen new ones. Head over to iMotors.com and let the pros search on your behalf. You tell them what kind of car you want; they find it, buy it, try it, and make it like new. A seven-day, 700-mile return policy keeps it risk-free in case you don't agree with their assessment. Available in limited areas at the moment, but we're hoping they expand.

MotorcycleWorld.com www.motorcycleworld.com
A motorcycle hub that's two parts Honda and one part Harley. Choose a model and get all the latest specs; pick a photo of a bike for your computer's wallpaper; or enter the make of a bike and your zip code to find a dealer near you. There are also thousands of pictures of bikes, both old and new, along with facts and figures.

ExpressAutoParts.com www.expressautoparts.com
Here are a few perks you won't find at the local dealer: 24-hour shopping for five million auto parts, clear descriptions of every one of them, and mechanics available for live consultation online. But even if you're not shopping, the site's resource center offers helpful information on repair and restoration, and general news. Register for membership to keep all your vital vehicle stats on the site.

chat

Talk City www.talkcity.com ©
Talk City boasts more than five million visitors a month to 20 topical
neighborhoods that are easy for beginners to navigate. More experienced users should check out the eFriends feature, which lets you start
your own online club by simply entering a title and inviting friends to
join. You'll earn reward points for each person who visits; points are
redeemable for movie tickets, gift certificates, and dinners.

The Palace www.thepalace.com
In The Palace chat rooms, members interact in richly textured, graphic
environments (read: cartoon rooms), where each participant is
represented by an avatar (cartoon character). When you type, a speech
balloon pops up next to your avatar. Click and drag your character
around the room to virtually cozy up to—or run from—the person
you're chatting with.

Yahoo! Chat chat.yahoo.com
Yahoo knows its signature style can be a little overwhelming. That's
why it makes chatting here super simple, requiring no downloads and
giving members a personal home page to save their favorite rooms and
buddies. Otherwise, returning to a chat would be like finding a needle
in a haystack—there are almost 20 rooms on specific TV shows alone,
not to mention scores of group- and interest-specific rooms (in four
languages!).

Delphi.com www.delphi.com
Got an ax to grind or just want to jaw? Delphi lets you create your own
 chat room and bulletin board for
whatever's on your mind. Just want
to browse? You can get guitar
guidance, troubleshoot a computer
problem, exchange stock tips, or play
poker at the hundreds of existing
forums. Be sure to register for the
My Forum feature, which keeps
track of the chats you're a part of
and sends an email when someone responds to your post.

chatalyst chat.novia.net
A lurker's paradise and a chat room rarity: chatalyst lets you join a
room without registering. Just choose a handle (or remain anonymous)
and go. Each room has a maximum occupancy; large gathering spots
like the Forum can take up to 21 people, while the more intimate Back
Seat only holds two (which tells you something about the nature of the
chat in both). Know a friend is logged on but don't know which room?
The Locate Someone feature will tell you if they're around.

ICQ.com www.icq.com

A unique instant messenger that lets you know when friends are at their computers, ICQ (I Seek You) is by far the most popular way to personalize the Internet. Download ICQ software (free for a temporary trial) and create a network of friends to chat with in real time, no matter what ISP they have. It's cheaper than long distance, and way more addictive.

CU-SeeMe World www.cuseemeworld.com

The natural next step in the rapidly evolving world of chat technology, CU-SeeMe World is a live chat network with video and audio as well as text. A $50 webcam, a microphone, and a quick software download let you see and be seen, but you can still participate in the discussion if you're lacking one or all of the components. Don't expect *Star Trek* yet—this technology is developing, and it's not as fluid as it might be.

AOL Instant Messenger www.aol.com/aim

"You've got mail!" is quite the catch phrase, but it's so . . . 90s. Today's netizens keep connected with AOL Instant Messenger, the most popular instant messenger available. Like most, it uses the "buddy system" of compiling contacts for chat and messaging, but also features an easy file transfer for sending images and sound. Best of all, it's independent of America Online's ISP services, so you don't have to subscribe to download it for free.

Activeworlds.com www.activeworlds.com

Active is right—in this 3D chat environment, the avatars jump, fly, laugh, and even dance the Macarena. One thousand unique worlds are at your disposal once you download the software (Windows directly, or Mac with a Windows emulator), ranging from grassy parks to high-tech cafes. You can try much of it without paying, but $20 will get you access to the best parts for a year.

Topica www.topica.com

Pick the brains of people who share your passion for slack-key guitar, Cajun cooking, or tech stocks. No live chat here, but rather a system of email lists in which anyone can participate and newsletters (written by one person and received by subscribers) which cover a cornucopia of themes. Things can get heated—check Macintosh vs. Wintel, for example—but most of the discussion is amiable and instructive.

VZones www.vzones.com

The 3D Disneyland of chat environments, VZones pack a huge variety of background graphics and avatar options into its site. Choose the cartoon character that represents you and then dive right into the online activities, which include games, music, and shopping as well as basic conversation. You can even rent and decorate your own virtual living space, enjoying the comfort of home from the comfort of home!

Tribal Voice www.tribal.com

Forget that adage about computers reducing social interaction; Tribal Voice plugs you into a vibrant worldwide community. The buzz centers around PowWow, the site's super-popular and versatile instant messaging software. In addition to plain text, PowWow sports sound messaging, voice chat, and text-to-voice capabilities. It even plays common abbreviations as sounds—type LOL for Laugh Out Loud and hear it laugh. Download it free from the site, if you have Windows.

The Avatar Factory www.theavatarfactory.com

Put your best face forward, even if it isn't exactly your face. The artists at The Avatar Factory have been manufacturing high-quality visual chat icons since 1996. Inventory includes cartoon characters, celebrities, and sexy pin-ups, some with multiple versions that show different emotions. Check the instructions for compatibility first, then outfit yourself in the best virtual threads the Net has to offer.

communities . . ..

theglobe.com www.theglobe.com ©

Get yourself connected. theglobe.com houses member-created email clubs for people to talk about health, hobbies, humanitarian ventures or anything else—with more than 120 million emails sent between club members each month. Join an established club or register (free) and create your own. Registering also gets you 25 MB of memory and access to the uPublish Web design program so you can create a home page with your resume, a fan site, or a personal profile.

The Park www.the-park.com

Welcome to the new world clique in this globally oriented community. The Park emphasizes public service, with special rooms for crisis support and environmental organizations. There are also rooms set up for a whole host of different age groups and interests (though the teen and no-holds-barred topics get the most action, as you might guess). Many of the rooms are hosted during certain hours (the schedule will show you when) and some support the FireTalk voice chat software.

CollegeClub.com www.collegeclub.com ©

Looking for a job? An apartment? A chance to study abroad? Then stop posting those misspelled fliers in the laundromat and head for CollegeClub.com, which can set you up with everything from a gay roommate to a new religion. The wonderfully comprehensive site deals with the educational, social, and financial sides of college life—a truly impressive amount of content. The Road Trips from Hell page may make you reconsider that bus trip home, though.

AsianAvenue.com www.asianavenue.com

With more than 600,000 members,
AsianAvenue.com is a fully equipped virtual city

designed specifically for people of Asian descent. You'll find a handful
of chat rooms in the lounge, topic-specific informational pages in
Venues, and a list of Asian-focused events posted by members. One
catch: though membership is free, the registration form here asks more
personal questions than the Census Bureau.

PlanetOut www.planetout.com

PlanetOut offers an online forum for lesbian, gay, and bisexual people, and anyone
else who wants to be informed of gay-relat-
ed issues. It does everything a good
people-site should, keeping readers updated on news in the community and helping
like-minded folk connect with one another.
Become a member and the site lets you
register a profile—complete with your vital
stats, interests, and preferences—that other
members can view while you chat.

BET.com www.bet.com

The BET (Black Entertainment Television) network has expanded into

an online community
with all its appeal intact.
Features on Money,
Lifestyles, Home, Health,
Careers, and Love sit
alongside the latest
interviews and news on
everyone from Mary J.
Blige to Mumia Abu-
Jamal. The content is
original, searchable, and
includes plenty of
streaming audio, down-
loads, and chat
opportunities.

FortuneCity www.fortunecity.com

FortuneCity is a general community site hosting chats, message boards,
and Web pages on hundreds of topics. To aid in navigation, some categories organize homepages by "most popular sites" (although one
wonders how the "Greenway High Alumni Page" could be first on anyone's list). The best things about this site are the variety of chat
topics—from Celtic history to Anime (hosted by someone named Toi-
letpaper Goddess)—and the creativity of the homepages.

MyFamily.com www.myfamily.com

Strengthening those family bonds can be as easy as (downloading the
recipe for Grandma's) apple pie. MyFamily.com lets you set up Web
sites for you and your kin where you can exchange photos, recipes, and
stories, or set up a family tree online to archive who begat whom. If
you're wired but feeling out of touch, use the site to send emails or
schedule family chats.

BlackVoices.com www.blackvoices.com

What this site lacks in design, it makes up for in resources like a comprehensive job search, shopping, chat, even a feature that lets you search the Web for streaming video by typing in a keyword. The Chocolate Cities feature is especially cool—it allows members to chat, post messages with people from specific geographical areas, or just find out what's going on around them. Extensive bios and photos are encouraged, so the members' voices, and faces, really show through.

We Media www.wemedia.com

Part magazine, part online community, We Media is a comprehensive resource for people with disabilities. Unlike other sites whose articles seem tacked on, We Media provides excellent, daily content that is well written and tuned-in. Read about the latest documentary about a boy with cerebral palsy, locate new workshops in your area, join a forum about discrimination, even research jobs. Register for membership to be notified when new sections of the growing site go live.

sixdegrees www.sixdegrees.com

Cashing in on the theory that everyone is connected through a chain of six people or fewer, sixdegrees has devised a way for you to access an ever-growing pool of contacts. When you meet people you like in one of the site's topic-driven chats, you add them to your list and you get their lists. You can then see exactly how you're related to the people you chat with, instant message, and email. If the theory proves correct, you could end up connected to everyone who's registered.

Gay.com www.gay.com

A solid hub that covers the gay angle on lifestyle topics like health, finance, relationships, and travel. Some sections are better than others—news offers excellent coverage of important gay and lesbian issues, while food and entertainment are a little scant. Registered members get to post a personal profile, store preferences like horoscope and favorite chat, and get an @gay.com email account, useful when giving out info in the chat rooms and on the bulletin boards.

VirtualJerusalem.com www.virtualjerusalem.com

Acquaint yourself with the Jewish community outside your local synagogue by logging on here. This extensive resource for all things Jewish hosts discussions about the Torah, a live 360-degree picture of the Wailing Wall, and the latest news about the West Bank. There's also a weekly Ask the Rabbi feature that would be something like Dear Abby, if Abby offered choice bits of Talmudic wisdom.

myprimetime.com www.myprimetime.com

Unashamed to call itself a "baby boomers portal," MyPrimeTime provides clearheaded lifestyle content for the forty- and fifty-something sets. Despite an Oprah-esque self-improvement slant, the articles are savvy and original (a guide to trip-hop for music-ignorant parents, for instance). Think of it as what would have happened if the cast of *The Big Chill* had stopped arguing long enough to come up with aWeb site.

eGroups www.egroups.com

Stay connected with family and co-workers, or find a group that shares your hobby. The eGroups site supports many independent email communities where members share messages, plan events, and generally keep the dialogue flowing. Any member can create his own group, or join one of the thousand extant lists on topics like the arts, the stock market, and the Internet. A fierce anti-spam policy filters out bulk mail and kicks off the members who send it.

computers & internet

CNET.com www.cnet.com ©

If you haven't visited CNET.com, please step calmly away from any technological devices. Its comprehensive content makes it one of the first destinations for both consumers and insiders. Plentiful buyer's guides and investigative articles offer information vital to a successful foray into computer shopping. Getting wired, however, is only one slice of the pie—there's browsing to be done, and the site will lead you to free downloads, online games, and surfing tools.

Dell.com www.dell.com

Dell's site may not give you a warm, fuzzy feeling, but it can help you install, manage, and upgrade your computer in two shakes of a lamb's tail. Sure, you can probably find better prices at the bigger discount stores, but they won't be able to customize your system the way these folks can. Best of all, Dell.com is prepared to serve customers in more than 67 countries. Ah, the joys of doing business with the big guys!

Outpost.com www.outpost.com Ⓢ

Whether you want a monitor the size of a movie screen or a dinky handheld, Outpost.com will ship it to you overnight for free. With that in mind, go ahead and pile your shopping cart high with desktop computers, digital cameras, and stereo speakers—there are 160,000 to choose from. The site doesn't have product comparisons or reviews; come here when you know what you want and you want it quick.

Slashdot www.slashdot.org

"News for nerds" summarizes the content on Slashdot, but "news by nerds" would better define the site. The majority of the writing posted here is submitted by readers, not high-falutin' journalists. As such, the focus remains honed in on what netizens consider significant, whether it's tech talk or the world's largest game of Tetris. If features like "MIDI Support for Linux" don't butter your toast, you're better off in a different kitchen.

ZDNet www.zdnet.com

The godfather of pixel-to-paper publishing, ZDNet (a.k.a. Ziff Davis) is home to *PC Magazine, MacWorld,* and *Yahoo! Internet Life,* to name a few. But you don't have to link through to them to get information—the portal itself is chock full of tech news, products, and wireless developments. In fact, the amount of content borders on unmanageable, so take advantage of MyZDNet to narrow down the selection or download the Alerts software to get news without even logging on.

NECX www.necx.com

Sporting a refreshingly simple design, NECX is a business-to-business dealer whose site is geared toward consumers. Product comparisons and the incredibly useful list of manufacturer rebates and coupons help customers uncover sizable bargains on semiconductors, electronic components, computer products, and networking equipment. The one thing that NECX doesn't offer is free telephone ordering; if you don't want to buy online, you'll have to pay $25 for the phone call.

Price Watch www.pricewatch.com

Practical information for comparison shopping. Price Watch's spartan design makes it easy to browse products ranging from handhelds to memory, software, and consumer electronics. Type in a product to get a chart comparing brand, product description, price, and shipping information in surprisingly little time. Technology costs, but having gotten the best deal out there, at least you'll have the peace of mind.

Jumbo! www.jumbo.com

Step right up, folks, to the greatest site for shareware and freeware on the Net. Featuring more than 300,000 programs, Jumbo's got tons of fun stuff like games, skins, and cool wallpaper. The software demos can be frustrating, cutting you off just when a program gets useful or interesting, but that's probably the point. An endlessly fascinating place to surf, it's practically impossible to walk away empty-handed.

Chumbo.com www.chumbo.com

A computer without software is like peanut butter without jelly: totally useless. Complete your machine with software from Chumbo.com; they've got Mac and PC programs that do everything from designing greeting cards to transcribing your lecture notes. Chumbo.com's super-navigable and cool-looking design has garnered accolades from *PC Magazine* and *U.S. News & World Report*. Check it out to see why.

Gateway www.gateway.com
There's a reason why Gateway's black-and-white spotted boxes have become such a familiar sight: its computers are powerful and user friendly. Shop at Gateway for desktops, portables, and networking devices. Its tech-support pages are some of the best around, giving easy-to-follow instructions on how to construct the perfect machine for your needs. Easy, no-hassle shopping.

Tucows www.tucows.com
The software marketplace of the future takes the form of Tucows. This site provides both freeware and commercial programs for a variety of operating systems and uses, from from the simple (desktop themes) to the complex (server tools). Frequent news updates keep you posted on the "whys" behind the "whats" that you're downloading, while a comprehensive user ratings system can guide you to what you need.

MacMall www.macmall.com
Mac devotees rejoice: MacMall offers great deals on software, hardware, and iMacs in all their many flavors. The site also has a Memory Configurator service
that will tell you exactly what you need to upgrade your system, a list of current hot discounts, and a guarantee that covers your purchases for five years. How ya like them apples?

Compaq www.compaq.com
What good is the info superhighway when you're still driving an Edsel? Compaq has computing solutions for home, office, and small business that will get you zooming along in no time. Can't afford one off the showroom floor? Access the Factory Outlet, which features refurbished machines for less. An extensive menu of services is also available online (like free training for small businesses).

Egghead.com www.egghead.com
Forget the day after Thanksgiving; the sale is going on all year at Egghead.com. The e-tailer sells computers, software, and electronics for a song, or lets you name your own price in its Onsale auctions. You just might walk away with Norton Antivirus at a sickeningly cheap price. Comparison shopping within the site isn't easy, but with prices often cheaper than other online megastores, you may not need to.

SoftSeek www.softseek.com
ZDNet throws its hat into the shareware ring with SoftSeek, a den of downloads nearly unrivaled on the Net. The breadth of Windows applications, tools, and games available should be enough for any PC user. And though the interface isn't the most aesthetically outstanding, it does get the job done quickly and efficiently. Use the hot lists to help you pick a peck of software solutions.

Shareware.com www.shareware.com

Mom always said sharing was a great thing; Shareware.com proves it beyond a shadow of a doubt. If you have a software problem, it's a near certainty that CNET's freeware site has a downloadable software solution. 250,000 items are available for five different platforms, including everything from gaming to memory management utilities. A handy rating system lets you know how reliable the files are.

MyHelpdesk.com www.myhelpdesk.com ©

MyHelpdesk.com is a wallet-friendly alternative to calling the manufacturer hotline ($16 a minute?!) when you need support references, troubleshooting, and tips on hardware and software. Topics include simple issues like driver updates as well as complex ones like desktop reconfiguration. And the whole site is personalizable, so you can set it to display information specific to the hardware and software you use.

MacAddict.com www.macaddict.com

Sometimes it's hard to be a Mac lover in an increasingly Windows world, but Apple aficionados have a safe haven in MacAddict.com, a site where serious news and technical how-tos

share space with community activities and entertainment. A user-friendly layout makes finding anything from product reviews to step-by-step software tutorials fairly painless, and the feel-good atmosphere is almost palpable.

PC World.com www.pcworld.com

PC World.com addresses the gamut of topics critical to informed computing; the mysterious inner-workings of Microsoft Excel, the case against downloading music, and the e-commerce landscape, to name three. The FileWorld section is particularly useful, with shareware gathered from sources around the Web, as are the interactive ISP and product finding bots. If you're in the market for a new machine, sign up for its daily review e-newsletter.

McAfee.com www.mcafee.com

There's a world of software-related hurt out there—viruses, memory leaks, junk file buildup, etc.—and McAfee.com has the cures. Down-loadable software solutions are available for purchase here, meaning you can fix your glitch without ever unwrapping a box or plugging in a disc. The company also offers a firewall service to keep your PC safe from hackers and free virus software updates and information on hoaxes, available upon registration.

Service911.com www.service911.com ©

Dailing 911 works for computer emergencies, too—Service911.com, that is. A rich, user-friendly portal for online tech support, it covers hardware, software, Internet use, and even consumer electronics. If the text tutorials or video guides can't help you, certified experts are available for one-on-one chat. The personal touch makes frustrating bugs that much more bearable, and the fact that it's free just sweetens the deal.

Sharky Extreme www.sharkyextreme.com

Just when you thought it was safe to tinker, Sharky Extreme attacks!
This site offers gamers and technology enthusiasts a full range of coverage on the hottest in hardware and software. Get guidance from the
multitude of buyer's guides, reviews, and statistics, including constantly
updated price lists. Or, if you'd rather have the dirt on developments in
the tech sector, sneak a peek at the Private Eye column.

Expertcity.com www.expertcity.com

Tech problems don't conform to the
nine to five schedule of most customer
service hotlines. When your PC sticks at
3 a.m., you can turn to the staff at
Expertcity.com. The site's desktop
streaming technology makes it possible
for them to see your screen and (with a
quick plug-in download) actually
manipulate your computer remotely.
The cost of having a human trouble-
shooter looking over your shoulder? Free the first time, determined by
the expert each time thereafter.

GirlGeeks www.girlgeeks.com

Anyone who's seen the men's room line at a computer convention
knows how much of a boy's club the wired world can be. GirlGeeks is
the definitive online gathering place for women in technology, offering
mentoring, training, job opportunities, and amusements. The Geek-O-
Meter will tell you if you "qualify" for membership, but whatever your
score, you're welcome to chat, study up, and plug in to the *femme*
perspective.

The Iconfactory www.iconfactory.com

The self-labeled Mac evangelists at The Iconfactory have
rounded up a virtual warehouse full of fab miniature
icon art that's free to download. The showroom holds
the newest cool sets (how about dragons or candy
hearts?), while the Icon Cold Storage section has hundreds of archived ones. While you're there, download
the Icon Dropper, the site's exclusive freeware that lets you switch an
icon by dragging and dropping (instead of tedious cutting and pasting).

Freeskills.com www.freeskills.com

Expertise doesn't come cheap in the IT world, but this site can actually
teach you 200 different technology skills usually found in private, for-
pay courses. You don't even have to register to get at the classes, which
cover computer programs (Windows, Access, Photoshop) and soft
skills like organization. Lessons come in Adobe Acrobat Reader format,
which makes them easy to flip through but, sadly, not downloadable.

ZDNet FamilyPC www.familypc.com

This branch of the ZDNet publishing dynasty aims to enlighten parents on the issues that come with buying a family computer. Safety concerns for younger surfers, how to find a school online, and birth announcement Web pages were three recent topics in a list that spanned several screens. Visit the Activities section for on- and offline projects that families can do together, or Fun & Games for pithy reviews of recently released computer games.

Skinz.org www.skinz.org

Skins are pictures and patterns that decorate the frames of your office applications, instant messengers, and MP3 players—like wallpaper for application windows. Skinz.org is the place to get them, a virtual warehouse with thousands of user-submitted variations (there are 1,200 choices for WinAmp alone). To see the skins, choose an application or download its special skins browser to flip through the images quickly. Due to the titillating nature of some skins, kids under 13 aren't allowed.

internet

Yahoo! Internet Life www.zdnet.com/yil

Apparently, this quote-unquote Internet thing is here to stay. Yahoo! Internet Life's jingoistic attitude toward all things online may not be responsible for this, but it does make excellent reading for anyone longing to be among the plugged-in cognoscenti. Topical feature articles, incredibly useful sites, and strange only-on-the-Web curiosities are among the easily digested contents. What lurks in the hearts of the wired? Only the ever-helpful Surf Guru knows for sure.

internet.com www.internet.com

Just because tech professionals have their fingers on the pulse of the networked nation doesn't mean they can go without news and views. For that, they have internet.com, a massive network of sites, newsletters, and discussion lists dedicated to the mother of all networks. An insider's view, to be sure, but well worth perusal for those looking to go from interested to educated.

TheStandard.com www.thestandard.com

Did you hear that some people are making money on the Internet? And where can the enterprising executive go for an insider's perspective on the new face of business? TheStandard.com, that's where. Statistics, references, and features on such topics as the effects of technology on immigration (and vice versa) address the current economy with a depth rarely seen outside of subscription services. Sign up for a topical newsletter to get the news delivered to your virtual doorstep.

i-drive www.idrive.com

Infinite memory for files from the Web and 50 Megs more to save desktop stuff is the offer that i-drive is making you. And at the low, low price of free, there's no reason not to accept. Once a user has registered and downloaded the software, he can put away as many MP3s, photos, games, and whole Web pages as his packrat heart desires. Saved folders are accessible from any browser, and can be made public, accessible only by friends, or completely private.

Learn the Net www.learnthenet.com

So you had to know a little bit to get to this site, but for the worldwide curious, education awaits at Learn the Net. Though light on content and limited in scope, the site does offer easy tutorials in English, Spanish, French, Italian, and German, on topics ranging from Web navigation to email, newsgroups, conferencing, research, and making the most of multimedia.

Webmonkey www.webmonkey.com

The Webmonkey's been wired since 1994, and has bequeathed all he's learned to the Lycos Network. His site offers light-hearted guidance to aspiring webmasters, graphic artists, and network engineers in the form of in-depth informational articles and an extensive glossary. The Quick Reference section is particularly useful, with one-click access to a number of code guides. The Monkey relies heavily on his archive for content, so expect to see something from 1999 on the homepage.

Homestead www.homestead.com

Stake out your spot on the Web with Homestead. While not the only free Web page hosting service online, the absence of pop-up advertisements is a welcome relief. Plus, Homestead's simple Web publishing tools lets you click and drag your page to perfection—without knowing one letter of HTML. A great beginner-friendly tool.

Webopedia www.webopedia.com ©

If you confuse SCSI with SSI or PCI (or have no idea what any of them stand for), Webopedia is the place for you. But the information provided here goes much deeper than simple definitions. Links associated with many entries provide gateways to information on the inner workings of the Internet and the people and organizations that make it go. Even better, Webopedia can go with you wherever you surf through a slick browser plug-in.

whatis www.whatis.com ©

The only thing that develops as fast as technology is the lingo that describes it. Keep on top of both common and obscure words at whatis.com, an eminently useful interactive tech glossary. The Top Twenty section ranks the most frequently requested words of the week and compares last week's rankings. An invaluable reference guide—bookmark immediately!

Yahoo! GeoCities www.geocities.com
No need to get caught up in HTML when Yahoo! GeoCities will walk you through every step of creating your own Web page. Set up a free account and they'll give you clip art, Java applets, and interactive add-ons (like guest books and hit counters) to go along with your own pictures, sounds, and text. They've even done away with the pop-up windows we hated so much.

Bigfoot.com www.bigfoot.com
As rare as a genuine photo of Nessie is an email address you can keep for life. Members of Bigfoot.com receive a free, permanent address they can use to forward mail to any number of other accounts. The idea is that you won't miss a message even if you change jobs or ISPs. Bigfoot.com can also filter incoming mail into different inboxes—perfect for keeping business mail separate from personal messages.

The Webby Awards www.webbies.com ◎
There are no celebrities and (thankfully) no Joan Rivers, but that doesn't make The Webby Awards any less prestigious than its higher-profile brethren. Presented by the International Academy of Digital Arts and Sciences, The Webbies spotlight the best and brightest Web sites in a large range of categories. Here, you can find records of past winners, info on the selection process, and (one night a year) the live broadcast of the Oscars of the Internet.

Namedroppers.com www.namedroppers.com ◎
Wait to buy a URL for your business and you may end up stuck between arock.com and ahardplace.net.

n@medroppers.com
Domain Name Searching Services

Namedroppers.com is a URL search engine that locates variations on prospective addresses that have already been snapped up. If you actually find an available (and viable) choice, the site will link you to its partner, register.com, to secure it. Take a second to try your name while you're there and revel in the ego-surfing possibilities.

100hot www.100hot.com
Cutting out the low-grade clutter that confounds most search results, the 100hot directory delivers the 100 most popular sites in general categories like arts, music, lifestyles, and technology. Selections are based purely on traffic, yielding a collection of fairly mainstream and commercial picks. Take note that the Jokes and Celebrities categories bring you lists of actual jokes and celebrity names rather than sites.

Backflip www.backflip.com

Like bookmarks, but better: Backflip is a browser-based book-mark service that files pages you want to remember in a directory it creates just for you. To get started, download the browser plug-in and use the new Backflip it! button on your toolbar to mark a page you like. Because the service keeps your records online rather than in your computer, saved pages are accessible anywhere and are easy to swap with friends.

ditto.com www.ditto.com

Sure, you can find pictures of Britney Spears using any search engine, but what about Pat Benatar? Our search on ditto.com, an image search engine, produced 221 hits for pictures of the leather-clad '80s diva. Use the keyword option to browse popular categories like sports and animals; those who seek more obscure images can submit the request to the Ditto Detective, which will email results within 24 hours.

Hotmail www.hotmail.com

There was a time when email accounts could only be accessed from specific terminals. But that all changed when Hotmail debuted, bringing much-needed flexibility to the concept of electronic messaging. Since then, the site has continued to evolve and now offers spam filtering, cell phone alerts for new mail, and the ability to check up to four other email accounts from the inbox. You can be signed up and sending email in minutes, with nary a registration fee or download.

Mail.com www.mail.com

The word that follows that @ in your email can mean a lot, so it only makes sense that you should choose it. Mail.com is a free email provider that offers suffixes like @usa.com, @doctor.com, @engineer.com, and literally hundreds of others. The site's other services include firewalls and e-faxes, making it a must-browse for the Internet job seeker and work-at-home entrepreneur.

Anonymizer.com www.anonymizer.com

The ability to browse without baring all (email, IP address, and other personal info) is an invaluable boon to anyone concerned about online privacy. Anonymizer.com works like a virtual screen to keep sites from seeing the details they might otherwise be able to glean from your hard drive. Though using the service will slow page loading, such is the price for a little confidentiality. Anonymous email and online privacy news are also available here.

handheld computing

PDAStreet.com www.pdastreet.com

The intersection where personal digital assistants meet their reviewers, buyers, and competition. At PDAStreet.com, product reviews, news, discussion, hardware specs, software downloads, and everything you need to know about Windows CE is collected. Look here for "before you buy" info, articles, classified ads, and links to selected retailers both in the online neighborhood and off.

PalmGear H.Q. www.palmgear.com

The fastest-selling invention since the slinky, the Palm Pilot will change your life, guaranteed. Now, with accessories and programs cropping up like bunnies, it's easier than ever to expand your PDA's power. Search products by type (hardware, software, etc.), phrase, or popularity, or just browse the "essentials" to ensure maximum organization.

MemoWare www.memoware.com

Looks don't matter, it's what's inside that counts. MemoWare offers thousands of freeware documents (databases, literature, maps, technical references, lists) formatted to be easily added to your PalmOS device, Psion PDA, TI Avigo, or WinCE PDA. News, books, how-tos, and even downloadable literature will take your hand's favorite device to the next level.

HandheldNews.com www.handheldnews.com

Whether your handheld is just an organizational tool or as necessary as food and water, you'll need an online source for info and extras. Get a load of freeware, news, discussions, and the general lowdown on Palm devices at this site. The reviews of software and peripherals are must-have material for new users. You'll find all sorts of neat stuff like health care-related utilities available for download right here.

Vindigo www.vindigo.com

You're on the corner of 25th Street and 3rd Avenue—quick, where's the nearest hot spot for neo-French cuisine? You'd know if you had Vindigo, the super-cool software for handheld computers that specializes in pinpointing restaurants, stores, and movie theaters near your exact location. Almost reason enough to invest in a Palm Pilot (and move to one of the few cities Vindigo covers).

directories & people finders

Switchboard.com www.switchboard.com ©

Switchboard®

Let your mouse do the walking: Switchboard is as useful as the Yellow Pages, and a whole lot smarter. Its excellent business finder offers search options by name, type, and location. For the latter, simply type in your address to get business listings displayed with addresses, phone numbers, and distances in miles, as well as optional maps, directions, and information on nearby shops.

SMARTpages.com www.smartpages.com ©
What you're looking for isn't on this site, but the tool to help you find it is. SMARTpages.com holds a dozen different kinds of search engines for locating business listings, people, restaurants, driving directions, and more. Links on the home page give one-click access to the most popular search terms, and a traditional form is available for more unusual requests. A useful tool for finding both specific companies and general types of services in your zip code.

Yahoo! People Search www.people.yahoo.com
In the old days, the only way you could find someone's email address was to call her. Things are changing slowly but surely, and typing a first and last name into Yahoo! People Search is a fine place to start. The site can also be used to find the phone number of that guy who owes you 20 bucks from the Holyfield/Tyson fight of '97.

uspublicinfo.com www.uspublicinfo.com
Sometimes a telephone number just isn't enough. This site specializes in people location and background checks. While many of the services it offers cost money (between $5 and $20), the No Find-No Fee policy makes the bill easy to justify. Response time is immediate for nearly all services, though a couple of them take up to a week.

Ancestry.com www.ancestry.com
A database of records nearing the one-billion mark makes it easy to understand why Ancestry.com should be your first stop in tracing family roots. With both free and premium areas, helpful guides on how to begin your genealogical search are here, as well as extensive lists of databases, magazines, books, and message boards. Discover your roots and watch the tree grow.

*Ancestry.com*ᔆᴹ
Part of MyFamily.com, Inc.

ClassMates.com
www.classmates.com   ©
See who's paired off, who's washed out, and who's got a bun in the oven. ClassMates.com has 5.9 million registered alumni in its database already and adds about 20,000 new registrants each day. Enter your contact information to gain access to message boards and a list of your classmates who have also registered; to get any of their contact information in return, you'll have to join and pay $30.

SuperPages.com www.superpages.com   ©
Find a doctor, dentist, mechanic, florist, or (gulp) funeral home in a time of need. GTE SuperPages.com is a complete online version of the Yellow Pages, with search features that make it easy to find specific products, driving directions, or business phone numbers and addresses. Check out the city guides for shopping information that's customized to your locale. If you're hosting a party, buying a car, or starting a business, the Idea pages will point you in the right direction.

teldir.com www.teldir.com
The only reason to tolerate design this basic is the extreme utility of the site that sports it. teldir.com gives you access to 350 different yellow pages, white pages, business directories, and email listings in 150 countries. When a country has multiple directories available, the list is ranked for quality with three stars as the highest.

Planet Alumni www.planetalumni.com
Whether you wanted to lose touch with your senior prom date or not, thanks to Planet Alumni you can at least keep informed. This site has evolved into an online community where students and alumni of high schools, universities, and Greek organizations can reconnect. You'll be able to see which class members have entered contact info once you register, but you'll have to pay to actually get it.

education

Hungry Minds.com www.hungryminds.com
An autodidact's paradise, Hungry Minds.com is an online directory of how-to information. Every niche in the galaxy of hobbies, pedestrian interests, and highbrow entertainment is represented, either by the site's own experts or links to authoritative pages. A random search found reams of info on nuclear physics, tax filing, and crochet. User reviews on the various sources are currently sparse, but could in time provide a good guide to this mass of material.

education

Embark.com www.embark.com ©

Applying to college can be one of the most nerve-wracking experiences ever, but the Internet is helping to ease the strain. Offering easy ways to find, apply, and get into the right program, Embark.com can cut down on those agonizing meetings with school counselors eager to turn budding painters into business majors. There's also advice on financing your education and forging the career you want.

Lightspan StudyWeb www.studyweb.com

Like an *Internet Cool Guide* for homework, StudyWeb organizes its 121,000 URLs into categories like animals, computer science, and criminal justice, and rates each one of them. Click on Study Buddy to get a take-along window with instant access to time-worn study aids like the encyclopedia, thesaurus, CIA World Fact Book, language dictionaries, and a host of converters and calculators.

familyeducation.com www.familyeducation.com ©

This all-in-one family resource site has done its homework. The network offers articles on what to do when the kids sneak into R-rated films, suggests games, and provides comprehensive Expert Advice that has pediatricians, family therapists, teachers, and learning disabilities specialists on call. The site is navigable by age group and user location, and you can browse the weekly updated articles, polls, and quizzes.

Kaplan www.kaplan.com

While Kaplan's site aims to get you to register for its courses, the amount of information it offers in the process makes this site a must-see for college, grad, law, or medical school preparation. If articles on current issues in test prep don't pique your interest, click through the categories for detailed information on planning, tests, financial aid, school selection, getting in, and getting through the first year.

U.S.News .edu www.usnews.com/usnews/edu

If you simply must go to a school that offers extracurriculars in both rodeo and radio, U.S. News will find the school for you. The leader in school rankings puts its research to even better use online, making it easy to search for schools based on 15 criteria, including distance from home, cost, and diversity. It also provides a college personality quiz and message boards with an abundance of advice for frazzled seniors dead-set on higher learning.

FinAid www.finaid.org

It's good to know that while college costs are soaring, quality scholarship information can still be had for free. FinAid is the first stop for figuring out how to pay for your education. Sections focus on the different kinds of aid and scholarships available, how to qualify, where to look, and how to get them. The site also offers guides and FAQs specially tailored to the needs of parents, students, and educators.

Council on International Education Exchange www.ciee.org

An umbrella site for study, work, volunteer, and travel abroad opportunities, CIEE is the heart of international educational exchange. The Travel section is bursting with tools for the would-be student traveler, including information on airfare, rail passes, hostels, and cool tours to take. But though the site is geared toward students, fares are often open to anyone or available at a slightly higher rate.

Learn2.com www.learn2.com

Sometimes it's hard to ask for help–at Learn2.com, often there's no asking required! With hundreds of "2torials" featured and in searchable archives, learning how to tie a tie, fix a running toilet, or repair a scratched CD (is this possible?) is cost and embarrassment free. They now even have online courses–some free, some paid–on computer applications, the Internet, and finance.

ePALS www.epals.com

How can kids in notoriously insular America learn about cultures outside the U.S.? ePALS is an online service that connects entire classrooms full of Bart Simpsons with their counterparts all over the globe. The site actually translates kids' letters into foreign languages (currently there are six European languages to choose from) and vice versa. The site also includes teachers' guides, maps, and information on culture and geography abroad.

The world's largest online classroom community

American School Directory www.asd.com

An Internet gateway connecting 108,000 K-12 schools in the United

States, the American School Directory provides links to school information, alumni directories, and even online yearbooks for participating schools. At the online payment center, parents can pay for everything from school meals to tickets to the prom; but the site would be much-improved if it offered objective information on private and public schools for relocating families.

StudentU www.studentu.com

If StudentU takes off, the dreaded 8 a.m. class might just lose its sting. Servicing students at America's largest universities, the site provides clean, legible (yes, it's possible) notes to a range of liberal arts and techie courses. While currently the site doesn't have that many notes—it needs campus correspondents—it does have study guides for specific books and test-taking difficulties. Take advantage while it lasts; if the universities have their say, sites like this may be short-lived.

Homeworkhelp.com www.homeworkhelp.com

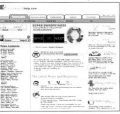

A massive, Alexandria-like online library filled with the type of information middle and high school students need while cramming or just trying to figure out what the heck happened in class that day. Basic (free) service provides lots of info, but premium (not free) service yields video clips, interactive games and tutorials, and other bells and whistles.

DIAL www.dialnsa.edu

When Plato founded the Academy, he didn't know how far it would go. DIAL, a division of New School University in New York, is a degree-granting program where students register, participate in discussions and lectures, and hand in homework all online. Over 150 graduate and undergraduate courses are offered in the full range of university departments, and price per credit averages about $600 (lower if you're not working toward a degree).

Lightspan www.lightspan.com

In most classrooms, the students probably know more about computers than the teachers. Lightspan.com attempts to redress this imbalance by providing kids with educational games and teachers and parents with lesson plans and guides on how to stay one step ahead of Johnny and Jane. Classrooms can also share results of Lightspan.com science projects with each other or take site-guided virtual tours.

SmartPlanet www.smartplanet.com

It seems odd to go to the same place to learn how to make *and* fly a kite *and* get yourself out of credit card debt *and* study DNA, but the same thing happens at continuing ed programs all over the country. Why not do it on the Net? SmartPlanet offers just such a panoply of courses for a variety of fees (few more than $20). Their instructors are first rate, and the syllabi are truly impressive.

Student Advantage www.studentadvantage.com

Student Advantage aspires to be the confused undergrad's first stop on the Net. With topics ranging from getting into business school to the health hazards of marijuana (supposedly a lot of college kids smoke the stuff), this huge hub has the lowdown on everything the college crowd needs. Stick to the original feature content—most of the useful tools you'll find were provided by the site's sponsors.

Englishtown www.englishtown.com ⓓ

They say watching American TV is the best way to learn English, but for people who would like to move their literacy past "stay tuned" and "now, this," Englishtown offers another option. Students can sign up for a free English-as-second-language course on the site and chat online with teachers and students—a great way to build writing and conversation skills simultaneously. Other services include searches for local schools, learning resources such as CD-ROMs, and dictionaries.

CliffsNotes www.cliffsnotes.com

No, this isn't every teacher's nightmare (free book summaries online!), but it is a better place to buy the handy summaries than perpetually understocked bookstores. The full range of titles is available in both the regular paper form and a downloadable version you can immediately access. It's nice to know that even the oldest of our (ahem) educational aids has kept up with the times.

The College Board www.collegeboard.org ⓒ

Those horrible, drab people who run the SAT test aren't as horrible or drab as we thought. Their remarkably informative and easy-to-use site provides information on all College Board programs, including prep course-quality tips for taking the test. Financial aid info is also available, as is a version of the site in Spanish. The tests themselves may still be riddled with trick questions, but at least their site gives you a fighting chance.

PowerStudents.com www.powerstudents.com

PowerStudents.com seeks to, er, empower high school and college students by providing glossy magazine-style stories on everything from sex to college admissions and possible career paths. While the content can be a bit preachy, the site is cleanly designed and links to a pack of student-related sites, like College Cams and FunkandWagnalls.com.

entertainment . . .. .

EW.com www.ew.com ⓒ

Read up on all the doings in Tinseltown and add your own two cents about the latest stinker you had the displeasure of seeing at the local cineplex. You'll find enough news, reviews, polls, links, and features to warrant enrollment in a 12-step program. (Repeat after me: "My name is Joe, and I am a Buffy-holic.") Nothing earth-shattering here, but definitely smart, organized, and enjoyable reading.

The Onion www.theonion.com

Tongue-in-cheek doesn't even begin to describe The Onion, the weekly e-newspaper of legend. Brandishing headlines such as "Charlize Theron Has Opinion," and "Alex Trebek Deftly Prolongs Agonizing Small Talk," the site's stories are odd and hilarious—think *South Park* meets the *New York Times*. Syndicated humor columns such as Dan Savage's "Savage Love" and several riotous comics are sprinkled throughout.

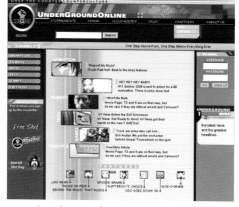

UnderGround Online
www.ugo.com

An entertainment hub
worthy of the moniker
UnderGround Online,
UGO Network is a fun,
if diverse, collection of
online amusements,
from games to TV and
music picks. Chat about
all things *The Simpsons*,
declare your undying
adoration for Gary Coleman, or shop for your favorite games online. If
that doesn't suit your fancy, check out the sites on UGO's alliance of
unconventional links.

Media Nugget www.medianugget.com

People with infinite pop culture knowledge are modern-day gurus.
Become one of them with Media Nugget, a site that packages pop trivia
into one 100-word blurb each day. The primary focus here is on print,
film, television, and computers, but pretty much anything is game.
Don't think only in terms of what's new—the staff is more than willing
to post an item on *Young Frankenstein* over twenty years after the film's
initial release.

E! Online www.eonline.com

From Tom Cruise's summer blockbuster to Robert Downey Jr.'s minimalist new home, E! Online lays out who's hot and who's not in
Hollywood. It's got down-and-dirty showbiz news in addition to
celebrity-hosted chat and Q & A with the it boys and girls of the
moment. For a laugh, don't miss games like Boy Band-o-rama and Live
and Let Dice.

Shockwave.com www.shockwave.com

Yes, that's right. Directing your own *South Park*
cartoon is no longer an impossible dream. Not if
you stop by and see what the experts at Shock-

wave.com can do with their fun, cutting-edge technology.
Traditionalists can play classic arcade favorites or try animated games,
while music lovers can watch a music video or tune in to Sonicnet
Flashradio, the first visual radio station that combines non-stop
animation with the latest hits.

EnSpot.com www.enspot.com

While some people may enjoy a rousing game of "I don't know. What
do you want to do tonight?" others will prefer to go the EnSpot.com
route. Register your email and zip code, slog through a forest of check
boxes to tell the site your interests, and the site delivers event listings
for your area—sporting events, theater performances, parades, carnivals,
museum shows, and more. Check the weekly notification box to stay
informed when you don't have time to boot up the browser.

entertainment

CartoonNetwork.com

www.cartoonnetwork.com

Here's where *Space Ghost, Cow and Chicken,* and *Sailor Moon* hang out when they're not being played in an endless loop on the Cartoon Network. Dial up this site to play games, win prizes, buy cool stuff, and find out exactly when your favorite funny will air. You can also check out series premieres and find out background information on such aging 'toon stars as Elroy Jetson and Pebbles Flintstone.

Comics.com www.comics.com

Something like a comic potluck, Comics.com lets you move from one comic to another, serving up little tastes with the option of dishing up more when a strip suits you. The menu is made up of 90 of United Media's syndicated comics, including *For Better or For Worse, Dilbert, Peanuts,* and *Bizarro.* You'll be surprised how many titles aren't in your local newspaper.

Fametracker www.fametracker.com

For the opinionated verdict on who's hot in Hollywood, Fametracker takes no prisoners. The site's Fame Audit section mercilessly dissects the merits of certain celebs, and user comments in the Forum aren't exactly gushing either. (Gwyneth: "snobby," "skinny," and "washed out.") But credit where credit is due: the site often elevates a star who's been toiling in the shadows. The entire Hey! It's That Guy section is devoted to semi-stars whose faces we know but whose names we never remember.

jokeswap.com www.jokeswap.com

The jokes come fast and furious at jokeswap.com, a popular site where anyone with a funny bone can read—or submit—a joke. The site sports a great interface (we love the way colorful circles trail your mouse arrow around the page), but the knock-knocks, love jokes, animal jokes, sports jokes, and (of course) sex jokes here aren't always as hilarious as we'd hope.

eHobbies.com www.ehobbies.com

Keep yourself from gluing your fingers together by checking eHobbies.com before you build that wee plane, train, or automobile. The site has starter guides on the aforementioned three hobbies (as well as rocketry and radio control), and FAQs to answer questions that arise mid-model. There is also a store and an online zine for the hobbyist community, with articles on building a collection, kit reviews, and must-have tools.

Girls On www.girlson.com

Here's an old favorite that's been subsumed into the Oxygen Network. No worries—the opinionated Girls On movie reviews are still here, along with expanded coverage of TV shows, books, and music—but the focus now is on user opinions, which are highlighted in a window right next to the staff review. Our verdict? The site's better than ever.

Humor.com www.humor.com

Running to a lunch meeting and need something to break the ice? Slam your cursor down on Humor.com's Joke-a-matic for some funny (albeit often tasteless) material. Surfing this site will also get you hilarious Flash-enhanced comics, stranger-than-fiction news snippets, chat, and a joke database. But don't linger long at the buggy Comedian Links—when we visited, Pauly Shore linked up, but Paula Poundstone and others didn't.

Darwin Awards www.darwinawards.com

The stuff urban legends are made of. The Darwin Award goes to individuals so witless that their demises actually improve the gene pool. Browse the news articles here (confirmed true by the site) for details on the most recent person to play footsie with a landmine or "water" an electric fence. With archives that go back to 1995, you'll be laughing nervously for quite some time.

Mr. Showbiz www.mrshowbiz.go.com

Mr. Showbiz has made a habit of using his wicked sense of humor to slip the pedestals out from under this season's hit celebrities. The site scours sources from *People* to *The Stranger* (Seattle's indie newspaper) to generate reports on Hollywood's latest dirt (taking none of it too seriously of course). But while you'll come here for the insider info, you'll stay for the reviews, interviews and games; the Surgery Lab is a cool Flash game that lets you slice and dice the faces of the casts of *Star Wars* and *ER*, supermodels, and more.

AstrologyGuide.com www.astrologyguide.com

Whether or not you buy into scientific explanations of astrology, you'll enjoy this site's approach. The interface is elegant, the monthly horoscopes clear and concise, and the sign explanations right on target. The reference section has a complete glossary and a tool for creating your personal biorhythm chart (with the physical, emotional, intellectual, and intuitive cycles in your life). There's always the lively chat forum if you're more likely to trust strangers than the stars.

The Smoking Gun www.thesmokinggun.com

Thanks to the Freedom of Information Act, you can read police reports, legal documents, and other incriminating evidence on naughty celebrities (and others) at the clever The Smoking Gun. The editors have uncovered some real gems here—Frank Sinatra's prostitute parties in Vegas, confidentiality measures at Oprah's Harpo Productions, even John F. Kennedy Jr.'s last will. But celebrities aren't the only ones subjected to this site's prying eyes: hazing at college frats and a stripper's breast augmentation suit also make the list.

Collectors Universe www.collectors.com

Launch a hobby or keep your current one at cruising altitude: Collectors Universe is the destination for tracking autographs, coins, stamps, and sports memorabilia. The site adds new articles every few days, and the archive is huge (181 on baseball cards alone). You'll be able to get to almost every part of the site without registering, though if you're looking to shop in the stores or auction, you must become a member.

Entertaindom www.entertaindom.com

The entertainment information department store with the amusement park name, Entertaindom offers a one-stop dollop of online fun. Screen short films in the Cine Minis area, be the first to read the latest gossip in Hot Topic, or take the Daily Quiz. The site is distinguished by a few exceptionally user-friendly tools, such as the extensive FAQ page and a Looney Toones Teach the Internet program.

craft.com www.craft.com

Homemade crafts are not all glitter and hot glue. craft.com offers a sophisticated take on do-at-home projects, countering its e-commerce end with well-written and interesting feature articles. A glossary breaks down tricky jargon and the Tips and Techniques help ensure you won't find yourself on the bad end of a Bedazzler. Register for an account to stow promising ideas in the personalized My Studio.

Ticketmaster.com www.ticketmaster.com

Ticketmaster remains the biggest ticketing agency in the U.S. That's both good and bad. On the upside, you can get tickets to nearly any large event in the nation in music, sports, and the arts. On the downside, you'll have to pay Ticketmaster's considerable "convenience" charge every time. Still, for selection and reliability, the site can't be outdone.

Joe Cartoon www.joecartoon.com ⓓ ⓞ

Thankfully, there are sites like Joe Cartoon around to remind us how fun technology can become in the hands of the truly twisted. Joe Shields' animated shorts bring to life classic fourth-grade jokes like the frog in a blender or microwaved gerbil, as well as some new favorites like the SuperFly. Don't say we didn't warn you.

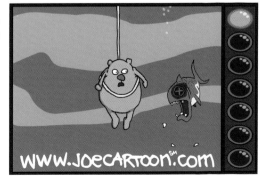

Entertainment Sleuth www.entertainmentsleuth.com

Why waste time sifting through entertainment news when Entertainment Sleuth can deliver only the dirt you want directly to you? A simple selection process lets you customize the site to get info on bands like 'N Sync or The Beatles, plus images and other multimedia from 1,000 sources. Then sit back and bask in the glow of the Fab Five, or Four, as the case may be.

ShowBizwire www.showbizwire.com

Here's a cool idea—ShowBizwire collects vital entertainment news headlines from a gaggle of sources (like E! Online, RollingStone.com, People.com, and Playbill) and displays them in one simple, clean interface that's updated every 20 minutes. You'll get all the day's breaking news on music, books, film, television, and celebrities, without glitz and graphics—just simple, no-frills, top-notch information.

Tickets.com www.tickets.com

Whether you're willing to fly halfway around the world to see Barbara Streisand or are just too lazy to drag your butt over to the local ticket kiosk, this Web site can help. It has tickets to sporting events, cruises, concerts, and museums. If you don't see what you want, head for the auction page, where you can do battle for the last two Macy Gray seats in the entire Midwest.

MyVirtuaLife.com
www.myvirtualife.com

One of the cool (but scary) things about the virtual world is the way you can take on a different identity at will. This site takes that idea one step further, offering a choose-your-own-adventure style interactive sitcom called *My Life Today*. Each day you'll find a new episode of the show, which lets you decide what you want your virtual doppelganger to do.

Voice Chasers www.voicechasers.org

Did you know Nancy Cartwright, the voice behind Bart Simpson, also did Mindy on *Animaniacs* and Daffney on *The Snorks*? The Voice Chaser's site reveals the actors behind the voices in animated films, cartoons, puppet shows, and more. Search for a specific character or just browse and be baffled (Minnie Driver, Glenn Close, and Rosie O'Donnell all in Disney's *Tarzan*!). Graphically, the site is bare bones, but content-wise, it packs a punch.

astrology.com www.astrology.com

You probably know what your sign is, but what about your Karmic sign? astrology.com gives you much more than your basic horoscope—it tells you what planets rule your love life, your finances, and even your summer vacation. Click on free charts to get a full work-up of your personality, or have your horoscope emailed to you daily.

StampsOnline www.stampsonline.com

Say you break a leg and have a lot of time to write letters. Thanks to StampsOnline, you won't have to hobble to the post office for stamps. This U.S. Postal Service site will sell you hundreds of different kinds of stamps, including collectibles and holiday-themed postage. There's even a useful list of philatelic societies across the U.S. for collectors.

FedEx www.fedex.com

The first name in fast shipping, FedEx brings all its services to the Web. Enter your package's destination and weight to have the cost calculated, or search for the nearest FedEx office or drop-off. For the virtually inclined, FedEx offers the whole shebang—have boxes and envelopes dropped off and picked up within hours—without ever having to leave the house.

Evite www.evite.com

Paper invitations may be going by the wayside with email around, but that doesn't mean that all social etiquette is lost. Evite is an online invitation service that helps organize the time, date, place, and RSVPs for your business or casual event. You enter the guests' email addresses; they get a note directing them to an Evite page with all the info. It's free, but registration is required.

iPrint.com www.iprint.com

Don't point your browser here unless you have 30 minutes to spare—the site's products and interface are tough to resist. iPrint.com is a fully interactive online design shop that lets you personalize greeting cards, clocks, mouse pads, magnets, and more. Their step-by-step guidelines take you from choosing card stock to arranging text and graphics to entering a print order. Need business cards? This is the place for professional-looking results at a price that won't break the bank.

Stamps.com www.stamps.com

It may be one of the best kept Internet secrets that you can actually buy and print U.S. Mail postage at home. Go to Stamps.com, which is officially approved by the U.S. Postal Service, to download the free software you'll need. The site requires you to pay a small fee (just as you would for a postage meter), but once you've set it up, you can print postage as often as you need. You can also pick up more traditional mailing supplies here, including labels, envelopes, and scales.

UPS www.ups.com

If you've been waiting to see those matching brown trucks and shorts go the way of the wooly mammoth, wait no longer! Catering to e-business managers, the UPS Web site takes the guesswork out of shipping, just like the offline service. Use the address validation software to make sure your package ends up in Paris, France, rather than Paris, Texas, and let your customer choose his own rates using the Online Rate Selection Tool.

Dialpad.com www.dialpad.com

Even the cheapest 10-10-whatever won't get you long distance for free. Dialpad.com's free calling service requires no software installation or download—just a microphone, speakers, and a Java-enabled browser like Netscape 4.5 or later. You can place calls online, receive voice mail through the eVoice service, and request a notification when someone leaves you a new message. The catch: Dialpad.com only works with PCs, so Mac users can't play.

DoDots www.dodots.com

Like a toolbox full of e-services for your computer desktop, DoDots give you instant access to helpful online content like dictionaries, personal shoppers, news tickers, and MP3 search engines. Each little dot sits in its own window on your desktop and updates itself, regardless of whether your browser is booted up or not.
Download the HomeDot organizer from the site and start collecting.

DoDots™

Ofoto www.ofoto.com

Free digital photos. That worked, didn't it? Upload digital images directly from your browser or send in your 35 mm film and they'll develop it free the first time you register. Once you're uploaded, use Ofoto's tools to add captions and organize photos in an album on the site. If you want a print of a picture, Ofoto guarantees high-quality Kodak shots delivered straight to your door.

PhotoPoint.com www.photopoint.com

An easy way to share photos and safeguard them at the same time, PhotoPoint.com lets its members keep an unlimited number of images

in their online photo albums. But instead of stopping there, the site has turned the service into the focal point for an online community that also includes huge galleries, contests, and chat forums. See the Photowall for a smattering of the best photos from the public albums.

eFax.com www.efax.com

Don't have a fax machine at home? Head for eFax.com, the originator of the fax/email interface. Not sure how it works? Here are the fax: Sign up at the site to receive a personal fax number. When friends or colleagues send you a fax, it is transformed into an image and sent to your email address, where you can view it as an attachment. Oh, did we mention that the service is advertiser-supported and entirely free to you?

eFridge www.efridge.com

The refrigerator's secondary function as household message board is taken online at eFridge. Although there's no ice cream here, there are virtual calendars to share with others—or just keep to yourself. Post events, keep track of your schedule, and check it from any computer with Internet access.

MyEvents.com
www.myevents.com

All dressed up and no place to go? There's no excuse when you have the services of MyEvents.com at your fingertips. It's a calendar, Rolodex, and social scene rolled in one. This ingenious site provides the venue for any online community you can imagine, from families to news groups to support groups. Log on to organize your daily activities, or to accept invitations and share photo albums, calendars, bulletin boards, and private chat. Both personal and group pages are available.

e-zines

Salon.com www.salon.com © ⓓ

Sleek, intelligent, and addictive, Salon.com collects hundreds of commentaries, comics, critiques, snippets, and stories, from writers as diverse as Camille Paglia and Garrison Keillor. For instant dispatches from the worlds of high tech, pop culture, travel, and the arts, subscribe to one of the site's dozen e-newsletters.

Suck.com www.suck.com

Suck.com takes the serious sarcastically, offering a clever blend of thumb-on-pulse and tongue-in-cheek writing. The daily features here are full of trap doors, random links, and audio clips (you'll often wonder what you just inadvertently downloaded). But the real gem is the comic strip *Filler*, a bit like *Dilbert* but edgier and much more neurotic.

e-zines

Atlantic Unbound www.theatlantic.com

 Culture, politics, and the arts captured in liberal form; Atlantic Unbound is *Atlantic Monthly*'s complete print magazine and then some. The extensive archives and search features invite readers to browse through political reportage, literary works, poems, columns, and interactive features (such as polls and online roundtables). Be sure to check out the Food and Travels sections for *Atlantic*-quality writing on the lighter side of life.

FEED www.feedmag.com

The source for "wisdom from raw information," FEED is a virtual reservoir of events, issues, and cultural coverage extracted from sources both online and off. A laissez-faire approach to cultural commentary defines the features on media, culture, and technology; FEED provides the fodder, you form your own opinion.

Utne Reader Online www.utne.com ©

Here's an eclectic e-zine that asks "Can war be fought for humanitarian reasons?" in one article and celebrates the renaissance of bowling in the next. Utne Reader Online gives a fresh, alternative spin on current events and culture with an emphasis on progressive issues. Articles like "Can you spot a sellout?" give away their grassroots, left-of-center origins, but don't be too quick to stick them in a political box; the critiques here spare no viewpoint.

Journal E www.journale.com © *d*

If a picture is worth a thousand words, then Journal E is a veritable tome. The site's definition of "story" goes beyond mere text to include top-quality photo essays, Shockwave-enhanced features, and QuickTime pieces on subjects that range from artificial body parts to the White House press corps. Even when the subject seems mundane, the artistry behind the lens reveals beauty in unexpected places.

smug www.smug.com *d*

If you're a webzine this smart and sexy, you can be as smug as you want to be. We love monthly features like Bumping Uglies and Smoking Jacket, which spin media, technology, and pretty much anything else relating to our current cultural climate with writing that isn't afraid to be irreverent. Subscribe to Smug's email fan club for advance notice of new postings.

Colors www.colorsmagazine.com © *d*

Life doesn't stop for naps—neither do issues of political, social, and humanitarian import, according to Benetton's print and online zine, Colors. The premise? "Diversity is good." The issues? All the goodies that get the blood a boilin'—religion, war, politics, capitalist culture, and the like. The elegant design and stunning Shockwave animations here are among the best on the Web. Definitely worth a stop.

MoJo Wire www.mojones.com ©

The electronic version of *Mother Jones* magazine, MoJo Wire has articles for independent thinkers. Recent stories include "The planet loves SUVs," "I was a dressmaker for the CIA," and "Senator Strangelove." Look here for news that corporate-sponsored papers are too afraid to report as well as "Must reads from around the Web . . . fresh daily."

Smithsonian Magazine www.smithsonianmag.si.edu ©

Pirates, gargoyles, Paderewski's Piano, and other cooler-than-fiction features come in heaping portions at the Smithsonian Institution's monthly Web magazine. Each article is accompanied by a list of related articles from the magazine's archive. You won't get the full text online, but the abridged versions are satisfying in and of themselves. Don't leave without visiting the image gallery—its breathtaking photographs and amusing illustrations are just icing on the cake.

Boulevards www.boulevards.com ©

Bored with the *New York Times*? Think the New World Order owns the *Washington Post*? Boulevards puts the alternative press—magazines, newspapers, and e-zines—front and center with a wide selection of articles from outlets ranging from the *Village Voice* to SheWire, *Mother Jones* to Salon. The design is somewhat static, but the stories and extras ("essential" links, astrology, nightlife guides to 35 U.S. cities) make it worth a cruise.

National Review Online www.nationalreview.com ©

With the same quality of reporting as *The New Republic*, but from a very different perspective, the *National Review* is perhaps the most respected conservative political publication in the United States. The online version is stellar, with articles written exclusively for the Web, as well as town-hall chats and excerpts from the print magazine. There are even hefty archives, one case of conservative generosity.

WORD www.word.com ⓓ

This cutting edge e-zine of issues and culture hasn't quite broken into the public awareness in the same way that similar sites have, and that's a shame. Daily pages cover an eclectic array of topics that simply can't be tucked neatly into a particular category; our visit turned up articles like "Where are the SnoBalls of Yesteryear?" and "Mark Trail Kidnapped." Hours of entertainment, information, and time-wasting, plus cool animation and design.

Wired www.wired.com/wired

Wired's comprehensive daily coverage of the business, culture, technology, and politics of information makes it the quintessential site for citizens of the digital age. Pieces from the current print edition of the magazine are posted to the site several weeks after publication. There's also a browsable archive of back issues (through its debut in 1993), regularly scheduled chats, and message boards.

iDetour www.idetour.com

Heavy on the sizzle, light on the meat. The Web spin-off of the L.A.-based magazine is pretty to look at and packs in a lot of content about its native Hollywood (including weather reports and horoscopes). But many entries, except those from the newswires (AP, UPI), run only a paragraph or two, so invest in the paper version to get any depth.

Brill's Content www.brillscontent.com

Brill's Content was founded on the notion that if journalists are not held accountable for their words, our basic freedoms are threatened. With the overwhelming glut of information out there, this is one place that's keeping a critical eye on where it's all coming from. *Brill's Content* serves up what it's known for in print: quality writing and an insider's in-depth look at the media industry.

fashion

Models.com www.models.com

Who needs content? Models.com is like a fashion magazine with all of the articles ripped out; all you get is picture upon picture of the season's lanky it girls. For wannabes and admirers this will probably suffice. Check out the Top 50 for a countdown of the most popular models, and click on their images to vote and log your own comments.

ELLE.com www.elle.com

Yes, we like it all: fashion, beauty, health, men, travel, and shopping (not necessarily in that order). There are plenty of things to keep you clicking through ELLE.com, from style lessons to runway photos to ask-an-expert-anything. Kudos go to *Elle* for providing content that's smarter and a bit more worldly than the usual women's magazine fare. For those who find it a little confusing to navigate, the site map should help simplify your stay.

FashionLive.com www.fashionlive.com

To find out what combination of feathers and poly-fill is strutting down Milan's catwalks this month, log on to FashionLive.com, the site with the scoop on all things *haute*. The site profiles the latest collections shown in New York, London, Paris, and Milan, with links to designer bios for a little background. Click through to the Fashion Live Channel for video clips of some hot, hot runway action.

Lucire www.lucire.com

Hemlines may go up and down faster than browser scrollbars, but Lucire can keep dedicated followers of fashion in step with the latest global trends. Jetsetters will love the travel guide, Volante, while virtual globetrotters can click through features on the hottest designers, models, and shows from London, New York, New Delhi, and Tokyo. The images are sadly low-resolution, but the global Shopping Guide, with discounts on designer fashions, makes up for the fuzzy pictures.

Vogue.com www.vogue.com

Vogue without the ads? Almost. At Vogue.com, you get direct access to the fashion scene in Milan, Paris, and New York. The fun part is peeking in on all the chaos that goes on behind the scenes—watch a model go from plain to Prada in five easy strokes of a makeup brush. You'll still need to subscribe to the magazine to read all the features, but when it comes to pictures, as they say, if it's in fashion, it's in Vogue.com.

Jean Paul Gaultier www.jpgaultier.fr

Just what is it that makes Gaultier so hot? Whatever it is, we want some. Stunning design and slick Flash animation provide a fitting backdrop for the designer's funky French fashions. The site showcases Gaultier's ready-to-wear collection, some fabulous and unaffordable couture, and his spin-off line, Mondino. Most of the text is in French, so here's a little primer to get you started: *chargement* means loading, *les pubs* means ads, and *pret-a-porter* means clothing so cool it'll make you suck in your cheekbones just thinking about it.

Gucci www.gucci.com

Gaze in awe at models decked head-to-toe in Gucci's glamour. Garb from the men's and women's haute and ready-to-wear collections is presented for looking (take advantage of the excellent zoom feature) but unfortunately you can't touch—Gucci doesn't yet offer online ordering. So enjoy the Windows shopping, hit the culture section for the company history, and strut your way to the Gucci zone nearest you.

Fashiontrip.com www.fashiontrip.com

What is it about Tom Cruise and Josh Harnett that makes hearts throb? How do you keep from getting freckles while sunbathing? And where can you find the coolest summer jobs? Fashiontrip.com has more than just fashion, including the answers to these questions, celebrity gossip, chick-flick movie reviews, a Beauty Guru, secure shopping, and, yes, links to employment resources (how else are you going to pay for all those fashionable frocks?).

DailyFashion.com
www.dailyfashion.com

Don't be thrown by the Barbie day-glo colors. This preteen fashion site offers some funny twists on everyday basics (e.g., trends and how to stop them). Ask the Resident Experts for the best tips on accessories, bargains, and vintage finds. They're no *Vogue* stylists, so if the "wrap a sweater around your waist" trick just doesn't do it for you, click over to fashion chat for a good old blabfest.

Ntouch ntouch.linst.ac.uk

The trans-global underground goes digital with this fashion e-zine hailing from Cool Britannia. For the people at Ntouch, fashionable refers to more than clothes—music, cult trends, global hot spots, and serious shopping are part of their cool world. Clicking through this e-zine is like committing to the ultra-chic "nu mod" generation. With horizontal scrolling, Flash enhancement, house beats, and lush images, the presentation is as impressive as the content.

fashionuk www.fuk.co.uk

The Beauty and Fashion sections at fashionuk read like fun magazine sidebars, showing you how to wear this season's body jewelry or paint on some sultry eyes. Head to the Daily Highlights section for deeper fare (like a piece on beauty and aging). Our only complaint is that the site is a little heavy on the "Buy! Win! Buy! Win!"

film

All Movie Guide www.allmovie.com

All Movie Guide lists what's new in theaters and out on video—helpful whether you're raring to go out or set on just sitting. Each movie comes with a plot summary, viewer ratings, production and cast credits, and links to related works. If you need some time to gather yourself together, browse the previews of coming attractions— listings stretch ahead as far as three months. A clean, easy-to-use site that is light on ads and heavy on substance.

The Internet Movie Database www.imdb.com

IMDb seeks to provide comprehensive, up-to-date movie information on nearly 200,000 flicks, with profiles on 500,000 actors, actresses, and directors that are constantly being updated. Look up movies by title, actor, plot line, or even quote. That's right—type in "Show me the money!" and IMDb lets you know which character said it in which film. Surfers will also find daily news articles, previews of films opening this week, and vote charts, which give recommendations on what movie to rent based on gender, genre, or decade.

Premiere Online www.premiere.com

An online peek at its print counterpart, Premiere Online's got a fresh and fun view of Hollywood that's endlessly entertaining. Surf around to learn about the hottest celebrity parties, up-and-coming stars, and the latest video releases. You won't be able to access all the articles promoted here, but for gosh sakes, these folks need to make money, after all.

Film.com www.film.com

Besides the standard reviews, news, and trailers found at every other major movie site, Film.com has a few gems that make it worth a bookmark. Look here for The Best Films You've Never Seen, Short Movies of the Week, Kid Picks, and Art Film Suggestions. Clever and well-organized, the site can save you valuable time and energy when trying to find a movie to match your mood. There's also a fabulous section with in-depth coverage of movie festivals from around the world.

Ain't It Cool News www.aint-it-cool-news.com

For hardcore cinema buffs who couldn't care less about the private lives of movie stars (but pine for the test-screening results of a yet-to-be-released film), there's Ain't It Cool News. Mine here to unearth such diverse gems as an account of a 10-day film festival hosted by Quentin Tarantino and a virtual tour of Father Geek's Movie Memorabilia Museum.

Roughcut.com www.roughcut.com ⓓ

Finally, a movie rating system that cuts to the chase: Roughcut.com tells you how much of a movie ticket any given flick is actually worth, so you'll know whether to rush to the theater ($7.50) or wait for cable ($1.00). Disagree with a rating? Flip to the Talk forum for chat and Q & As with the columnists. The site also has interviews with big-ticket stars (think Leonardo, Denzel, Chlöe) and a free weekly email newsletter to keep you abreast of all things celluloid.

IFILM www.ifilm.com ©

Cutting-edge, engaging, and not always polite, IFILM houses a bank of indie films you can watch on your computer. Selections fall under every conceivable genre, include both professional and student pictures, and generally run under a half an hour. Use Windows Media or RealPlayer to view them (though we had better luck with the former); you'll find the downloads quite speedy. If you're at all intimidated by the volume of choices, check the Most Viewed and Highest Rated hit lists for a solid place to start.

Moviefone.com www.moviefone.com ©

Wait in line for hours to get tickets to the new Scorcese picture? Fuhgettaboutit. You're better off visiting Moviefone.com, where you can purchase tickets in advance and catch up on movie news—you'll even save the $1.50 that using the phone service would cost you. If you're still torn between that romantic comedy and the space-voyage-turned-slaughter choice, download a trailer or read a review here.

Oscar.com www.oscar.com

Why endure four more hours of agonizing acceptance speeches when you can log on to Oscar.com? The site offers video clips of everything from the glitterati parade to backstage antics. The History section could certainly stand to be beefed up with photographs, but Oscar.com gets a nod for considerably improving this once scanty site.

CinemaNow www.cinemanow.com

A film site with a split personality, CinemaNow caters to viewers and filmmakers alike. The Watch area includes a Screening Room with free, feature length movies (if your connection can take it) and indie short films (if it can't). Alternately, the Make section makes it easy to submit work, gain exposure, and gather criticism—register and the site will give you a page of your own to stream a film, put up some still shots, or post an MP3 of your work.

The Astounding B Monster www.bmonster.com ⓓ ⓞ

"The Internet's coolest cult movie resource," The Astounding B Monster is sure to evoke nostalgic sighs from fans of beach party films and grade Z horror flicks. Surf here to discover 10 B-movie names you should know, behind-the-screams interviews, and profiles of sci-fi sirens. Perfect for filling time between *MST3K* screenings.

The Film 100 www.film100.com

A simple ranking of the 100 most influential people in film from 1890 to 1990, Film 100 pegs profiles of cinematic giants like Orson Welles and Greta Garbo alongside history-making lesser-knowns. Each biography includes an analysis of the person's career, a list of his or her best films, and related links. The quotes are particularly illuminating; for example, Vincent Sherman on Bette Davis: "That sexual suppression you see on screen, that nervous hysterical energy, was not acting."

Movieline.com www.movieline.com

Cinema buffs will love Movieline.com, the movie news e-zine that includes such tantalizing features as "Bad Movies We Love," "Greatish Performances," "Movie Jail," and "Trailer Park." Articles are delightfully dishy, with tidbits like, "Just how hated is that icy, terrifyingly ambitious, marginally attractive young lady? So hated that many likely male co-stars have practically told their agents they'd rather do Sally Struthers infomercials than go near her." Ouch.

Netflix www.netflix.com ⓒ ⓢ

If you've been wary about buying a DVD player for fear you won't be able to find the titles you want, hem and haw no longer. Netflix will send you any of its 4,700 movies via U.S. mail. Two-day delivery makes it tough to pick films according to your exact mood, but you do get the flick for a whole week, with the option to extend for just 99 cents. They even give you a prepaid mailer to send it back in.

bigstar.com www.bigstar.com ⓒ

For celebrity-obsessed fans, there's only one place to buy videos and DVDs: bigstar.com. In addition to the requisite comedies, dramas, and new releases, this site features a large archive of celebrity interviews to answer all your burning questions. Sign up for video alert and the site will automatically send you an email message when a long-anticipated movie is released on video or DVD.

POP.com www.pop.com

The two 500-pound gorillas who are Imagine Entertainment and DreamWorks SKG have joined forces on the Net (pregnant pause) to bring you Internet-only programming like films and live-action broadcasts. The good news is, these guys want raw talent. Independent filmmakers can enter to get some of their shorts onto the site. It's a big wave, but if you can surf with these guys ...

Zap2it.com www.zap2it.com

If there's not a newspaper in sight and you want to know what's playing at a theater near you, Zap2it.com has the solution. Provide your zip code and they tell you which theaters are showing what. It lists not only major movies at big theaters but also smaller movies showing at libraries and independent venues. The site follows up with their own reviews as well as reviews from critics at your local newspapers.

24framespersecond www.24framespersecond.com

Some sites claim to be for film buffs. 24framespersecond actually is.

Not only does it feature well-written and occasionally academic essays, it offers interviews with directors like Kieth Gordon and Mike Leigh and personal reactions to films by site users. Submit your own list of films or peruse others' favorites; film lovers will appreciate the site's fresh, independent voice.

Images www.imagesjournal.com

A well-designed online academic journal, complete with footnotes, video stills, and pictures, Images has many articles on all aspects of popular film. Its focus is historical, but it reviews contemporary films as well. Most of the writing here seems to have been done by the publisher, but it accepts manuscripts on a variety of topics, including television and comic books. A nice site for the media-inclined intellectual.

TapeHead www.tapehead.com

The huge, ugly underbelly of the film industry is what you'll find at TapeHead: namely, made-for-video flicks. The reviewers here provide gritty insider information and highly entertaining reviews on the flip side of mainstream movies, covering titles closer to *Clash of the Titans* than *Titanic*. Films win these critics over by including demonic nuns in the cast, or having teenagers play teenagers (instead of short actors pushing thirty). Smart, honest, and worth surfing.

Westerns.com www.westerns.com

With all the hokey wood paneling and branding-iron style writing you'd expect from the Wild West, Westerns.com rustles up the dirt on movies like *Fighting Caravans* and old TV episodes of *Bonanza* starring Lorne Greene. You can actually watch movies on the site, read biographies of actors (including the illustrious Mr. Greene), and test your knowledge in the trivia quizzes.

moviesthatsuck.com www.moviesthatsuck.com

The thing these guys do best—and they're clearly guys—is churn out silly, crude, sophomorically critical reviews of new movies. Their aim is to show you the stinkers before you buy the tickets, so you don't leave the theater thinking "feel-good movie my bunghole." Check the homepage for current movies, the Sucky Vault for previous reviews, or the Hall of Lame for flicks that live on in infamy.

FamilyStyle Movie Guide www.familystyle.com

A film site dedicated to separating the wheat (wholesome movies) from the chaff (naughty movies). The criteria? You guessed it: profanity, violence, drug use, nudity, etc. The site is good for parents who want to screen out violent or racy movies before heading to the theater. The question, of course, is whether there are any movies anymore that aren't violent or racy. The site offers a few.

Blaxploitation.com www.blaxploitation.com

This thoughtful and exhaustive tribute to blaxploitation movies promises hours of surfing for those wanting to catch up with Coffy, John Shaft, and Blackbelt Jones. In addition to the movies, books, soundtracks, and posters that pepper this site, there's a roster of informative articles and actor bios that would impress even experts on the genre. If you want to lift any images from the site (and you definitely will), you'll have to discuss it with The Man. Tell him Dolemite sent you.

finance & investing

finance & investing

TheStreet.com www.thestreet.com

What started as a site for investors who love to invest has blossomed into a wide-spanning network. You can still get the free, unbiased market commentary TheStreet.com has offered since 1996, but for the hardcore, subscription-based services you'll want to link through to its new wing, RealMoney.com. ipoPros.com and TheStreetPros.com sections offer deep coverage for finance professionals.

Quicken.com www.quicken.com

Fans of Quicken's popular personal finance software will be thrilled with its online component. In addition to providing the full range of online investment and personal finance information, Quicken.com allows users to download checking, savings, ATM, and credit card information directly from their bank into their personal Quicken files. You can even pay your bills online—though the convenience will cost you around two bucks a bill.

Morningstar.com www.morningstar.com ©

Morningstar.com earned its stripes with concise financial reporting, making it the top rung of mutual fund news and research providers. Still the industry leader, Morningstar.com now provides guidance for the faint of heart as well, with informative chats, interactive tools and Morningstar University, a self-professed "plain-language, no-nonsense guide to investing's basics." As the site doesn't own or manage any funds or stocks itself, you can count on information without bias.

The Wall Street Journal Interactive Edition www.wsj.com ©

Expect the same top-flight business news coverage that you get in the print version, with a twist: WSJ online is custom-tailored to your needs and is updated around the clock. This powerful site lets you search the WSJ archives and tailor the news to fit your personal investment portfolio. But it costs: $59 per year, $29 for print subscribers.

The Motley Fool www.fool.com ©

If any investment site can be described as jovial, The Motley Fool is it.

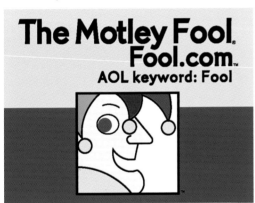

With a mission to "educate, amuse, and enrich," the Fool empowers average Joes with the information they need to make any financial decision: buy a house, invest in the stock market, and manage credit cards responsibly. The Fool's liveliness mostly comes from the discussions on everything from stock picks to online investing. But be warned: its contributors aren't necessarily experts, and aren't prohibited from investing in the stocks they discuss.

Bloomberg www.bloomberg.com

The big fish in the big pond of financial publications, Bloomberg online is even better than its print twin. The site is divided into three sections: Markets, with domestic and international news and financial figures; Money, with interviews, advice and personalized mutual fund centers; and Life, covering the finer ways to enjoy money and leisure time. Full access requires a subscription, but many sections are gratis.

Multex.com www.multex.com ©

It may not be a beginner's first choice, but award-winning Multex.com offers no-nonsense research and news for the avid investor. Discover how much risk your portfolio and perhaps your psyche can handle, or what analysts are saying about that stock your son's little league coach recommended. Once you've mastered the basics, move on to the impressive personalized stock screen and start tracking like a pro.

DLJdirect www.dljdirect.com

It's among the *crème de la crème* of Web brokers and DLJdirect has numerous awards to prove it. Trading is quick and easy, with a simple demo to show how the trading interface works. Also, there's no transaction fee for certain funds, trading over the phone is free, and investors with portfolios above the basic membership can access wireless information.

MetaMarkets.com www.metamarkets.com

A smart, witty, but deadly serious financial planning site. Any site that posts essays critical of AT&T by *Stupid Network* author David Isenberg will give you the straight, irreverent scoop on the markets. The best part: the site allows members to comment on articles, creating a kind of extremely well-informed chat room.

CNNfn www.cnnfn.com

Feel like even your grandmother is racing past you in the online trading frenzy? CNNfn—living proof that it's never too late to start—doles out general investing news and market updates that nearly anyone can understand. Authoritative but not heady, CNNfn tells beginners how to scope out mutual funds for long-term growth, and shows intermediates the who, what, and when of retirement planning and IPOs.

U.S. Securities and Exchange Commission www.sec.gov

If you stick to basic stock trading, you're unlikely to run afoul of the SEC, but anyone who has a hand in the pot should benefit from knowing the rules. The SEC Web page lets investors know what's legal, and offers info about the benefits and pitfalls of investing. The site also breaks down financial topics like mutual funds and margin trading for anyone who needs an impartial primer.

4freequotes.com www.4freequotes.com

Want to find the best car insurance rate possible? Look up 4freequotes.com, which enables you to submit a quote form to up to 10 companies at one time. List your state and the kind of policy you're interested in to see what local companies can do for you. This site also has a FAQ page about auto insurance, with links to top insurance companies.

National Discount Brokers www.ndb.com

It's time to do something with the pocket change that's been accumulating in your piggy bank. This highly reputable online brokerage and financial service firm offers the same investing services as other big name firms, but at a discounted rate. If you're a wary beginner, NDB University will serve as a helpful resource to bring you up to speed.

SmartMoney.com www.smartmoney.com

The *Wall Street Journal*'s foray into personal finance has moved from the racks to the little screen with everything from the print mag plus the kitchen sink. There seems to be no limit to the resources offered at this one-stop portfolio/market/investing/features hub. Hourly stock updates and cool visual "market maps" are searchable and neatly organized. SmartMoney.com is as compact and useful as a site can get.

American Bankruptcy Institute www.abiworld.org

The source for all possible information and news about bankruptcy. It's definitely worth a visit if you're curious (or ultracautious), but calling up this site is mandatory if you're in serious debt. Little life preserver icons direct you to general information and counseling, as well as to resources to keep you afloat once you've decided to take the bankruptcy plunge.

www.abiworld.org

The premier site for bankruptcy information on the Web.

National Foundation for Credit Counseling www.nfcc.org

Went a little overboard with the credit cards last month? A lot overboard? The NFCC is the place to start rebuilding your credit. Its 1,450 offices across the country provide confidential financial counseling and debt repayment plans, and this user-friendly site is also the place to find out how to get a copy of your credit report directly from the credit reporting agencies.

CBS Market Watch www.marketwatch.com ©

Exhaustive, extensive, comprehensive. And comprehensible. Market Watch offers some of the best market data, tools, and news (with real-time headline updates) on the Net. Visitors can discuss financial topics in the Wealth Club, or use the customizable Portfolio Tracker to follow the performance of almost 200 securites. A power-hitting lineup of commentators complements the impressive interview offerings for broadband users. Can't be beat as a personal finance resource.

H&R Block www.hrblock.com

You don't have to wait for tax time to visit the H&R Block site. The Tax Center is open year-round to answer questions or calculate next year's withholding, and extensive information on mortgages and investments is here as well. But mid-March is probably when you'll end up logging on here; file taxes online for $9.95 with the free assistance of a tax FAQ and glossary.

Charles Schwab www.schwab.com

Got a wad of cash and don't know what to do with it? Mr. Schwab, who actually appears in videos accessible on this site, can help you out. The site for this 26-year veteran of the discount brokerage world offers tips and schemes to help you maximize your earning potential, whether planning your retirement or investing funds for college. Step-by-step instructions, pop-up lists, and a financial glossary score points for user-friendliness *sans* condescension.

finance & investing

InsWeb www.insweb.com

If you want to insure your car, motorcycle, house, whatever, you can give InsWeb your info (your state, the value of the thing, who owns it) and the site will give you a list of insurance companies and their various charges. You can then contact a company and request coverage, right from the site. Some states are missing from the databank—Massachusetts notably—but most are there.

worldlyinvestor.com www.worldlyinvestor.com

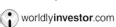 worldlyinvestor.com

Pundits. Mandarins. Gurus. Guys with thinning hair in dark suits who know more about the markets than Alan Greenspan. With columns like "Meanwhile In Canada" and "Biotech Stocks," worldlyinvestor.com is written by specialists who serve up the stock market on a very complicated, info-heavy platter. The site is perfect for those in the know, sort of like a racing sheet for brokers, with info on European stocks, global Internet stocks, and the like.

Redherring.com www.redherring.com

The computer nerd's *Forbes*. Claiming an email audience of more than 250,000 business leaders and investors, Redherring.com is devoted to emerging high-technology companies and markets. More a magazine than a stat sheet, the site contains articles on everything from the uses of military technology in civilian life to Microsoft's latest Machiavellian maneuver. How will all this affect your business and your portfolio? Subscribe to find out.

E*TRADE www.etrade.com

The premier online brokerage site, E*TRADE is slick, ultra-convenient, and offers competitive pricing as low as $4.95 per trade. Open a cash account and trade stocks, bonds, options, and mutual funds while enjoying the site's hallmark speed (crucial for online investing) and accessible customer service. For beginners: E*TRADE's risk-free market simulation game lets you create an imaginary portfolio and see how your stocks fare. Each month, the most successful make-believe investors win prizes.

Yahoo! Finance finance.yahoo.com ©

Don't think that Yahoo!'s finance site is just a bunch of links sucked from the search engine that mothered it. While you do get the same ultra-streamlined design and comprehensive content, Yahoo! Finance has some special features you won't find elsewhere. Hit Finance Vision to be patched through to webcast interviews with traditional and new economy bigwigs, or download the instant messenger software to track stocks while you chat.

PayMyBills.com www.paymybills.com

For those of us who keep our telephone, gas, and (ugh!) school loan bills in a shoe box, this site could be the savior. Send in your paper bills and PayMyBills.com will scan them in, post them on the Web for your review, and allow you to choose how (which bank account) and when to pay them. Strong encryption, insurance against unauthorized transactions, and the first three months free are a few incentives to sign up.

Internal Revenue Service www.irs.gov

There's something undeniably annoying about the IRS's attempts of late to become more user-friendly, like a burglar leaving a thank-you card after robbing your house. But this Web site is a welcome addition—you can download forms and read tax regulations in plain English. For true tax mavens: Keep up with changes in collection procedures! Read tax conventions, legislation, and court decisions! Subscribe to the Digital Daily for updates!

S&P Personal Wealth www.personalwealth.com

Personalized features backed by the clout of the Standard & Poor brand name make S&P Personal Wealth a heavy player in the online finance league. Subscribe to the site for $10/month to get access to the company's huge database of research—11,000 companies and 10,000 mutual funds for starters—as well as tailored tools like your own home page, stock ticker, and investment recommendations. A 30-day trial is free, though you'll have to call the toll-free number if you decide to subscribe.

Netstock www.netstockdirect.com

Tired of listening to the so-called financial whizzes? Never quite know why or how they're spending your money? This site allows you to buy stock directly from the company, cutting out the middle man entirely. Its free service offers information on all sorts of stocks and lets beginners start small, spending a few hundred bucks at a time. Perfect for getting your feet wet with blue-chip stocks.

BowieBanc www.bowiebanc.com

Why would anyone want to put their money in the hands of a lamé-wearing, spiky-haired super celeb? Free checking, free bill paying, and a credit card with David Bowie's face on it. BowieBanc is a division of USABancShares.com that offers these perks as well as everything else a typical online bank does: savings and credit accounts, credit cards, loans. Transactions are all performed on the bank's secure server, and BowieBanc is FDIC insured up to $100,000 per account.

Mortgagebot.com www.mortgagebot.com

If conversations can be virtual, why not business deals too? Those once painful processes of mortgage and home equity loan approval have been simplified and taken online. Though "instant approval" really means instant pre-approval, you can't beat the simple 20-minute form, handy rate calculator, and glossary of terms for first-timers.

WingspanBank.com www.wingspan.com

Separate companies handling your investments, banking, bill payment, and loans ... Who needs it? This division of First USA Bank solves the modern-day dilemma by housing a plethora of personal services under one roof. Not impressed? WingspanBank.com also offers award-winning educational info for novices and a handy ATM locator to boot.

MSN MoneyCentral www.moneycentral.com

Death and taxes. You may not be able to avoid them, but with a little advice from Microsoft's MoneyCentral, you may be able to make the latter slightly more bearable. Though loaded with ads and lacking in original content, MoneyCentral's intuitive set-up and breadth of topics make it worth a whirl for anyone trying to find that special mutual fund, plan college financing for their family of five, draft a will, or just catch up on market news.

ResponsibilityInc.com www.responsibilityinc.com

Money talks, and if you want your money to be well spoken, check out ResponsibilityInc.com. This online magazine reports on the importance of corporate social responsibility and its relationship to success with employees, consumers, and investors. Coverage includes news, human rights, reputation management, public relations, environmental issues, consumer changes and much more.

401Kafé www.401kafe.com

Prefer Fiji to Fort Lauderdale but not certain if your retirement portfolio will ever get you there? 401Kafé, a favorite in the financial community, serves up some of the best advice on the Web for those thinking ahead. Sit down and learn more than you ever thought possible about your 401k and legislation that may be affecting it, chat with fellow investors, or play with one of the site's handy interactive tools.

food & drink

Epicurious Food www.epicurious.com

"For people who eat" (that means you), Epicurious Food is one of the Web's best-known food sites. Over 9,000 recipes, articles from *Bon Appétit* and *Gourmet* magazines, cooking tips, and a food term dictionary with more than 4,000 entries make it a one-stop resource for foodies. The most delectable tidbits? The Playing with Your Food section, which teaches dining etiquette like how to crack a lobster and where to hide sugar packet wrappers, and the exhaustive wine list.

Zagat.com www.zagat.com ©

The guide we depend on when dining out is also an easy-to-use Web site featuring 20,000 reviews for restaurants in 30 cities worldwide. Search by location, price, cuisine, decor, or food ratings, or use one of the quirky "uniquely Zagat" lists like "Teflons" (restaurants with qualities that keep criticism from sticking). Be sure to vote on your favorite spots as well; users' critiques are the basis for the reviews.

FoodTV.Com www.foodtv.com

If you haven't had enough of Emeril Lagasse screaming at you, simply dial up FoodTV.Com. Featuring a recipe file that makes grandma look like a short-order cook, you're sure to find something delicious and innovative to serve up here, whether you're in the mood for a hedonistic porcini risotto or a calorie-conscious couscous salad. Less ambitious cooks need not despair, though; there are also some wonderfully quick dinners that take less than 30 minutes to prepare.

Cooking Light Online www.cookinglight.com

The print standard for healthy eating and living is online. Food ideas and cooking tips stand alongside recipes with full nutritional information, while the Healthy Living section provides even more tips for eating right and keeping fit. The excellent search feature here allows users to hunt for their favorite dishes by such criteria as calories, sodium content, or fat grams per serving.

StarChefs www.starchefs.com

Imagine Paul Prudhomme, Jean-Georges Vongerichten, Jacques Torres, and Emeril Lagasse in one virtual kitchen. At StarChefs, the eager cook can get tips from the masters, visit their restaurants, read their bios, order cookbooks, and copy recipes. Culinary hopefuls should check out the links to schools and job listings, or the Rumbles and Rumors section for mini-courses taught by the pros.

Cooking.com www.cooking.com © Ⓓ Ⓢ

Weekly menu planners, holiday menus at a glance, recipes for international food, and feature articles are just the tip of the iceberg at Cooking.com, which is also a giant kitchen accessory superstore. Find everything from tablecloths to barbeques to cake pans and food processors in the great shopping section, which features searches by product, brand name, or price range. The site could inspire even the cooking-impaired to slip on some oven mitts and get baking.

PlanetVeggie.com www.planetveggie.com

Hand over that ham hock, mister. Visiting PlanetVeggie.com is almost enough to convince any meat eater to go green. This Internet mecca for the vegetarian lifestyle has everything the modern herbivore needs, be it affirmation, information, or a homeopathic virtual storefront. The best part, however, is the cooking section, chock-full of tasty dishes and culinary tips—even an online cooking show. Iron Chef, eat your artichoke heart out.

Divina Cucina www.divinacucina.com

Judy Witts Francini, bona fide diva of Italian cuisine, brings her renowned cooking institute to the Net with Divina Cucina. You'll find a few recipes and cooking tips for her Tuscan dishes, but the real attraction here is the guide to fine dining in the Florence area. If you ever spend any time in such a beautiful city, it's a good thing to know where to get food that will complement the view.

Allrecipes.com www.allrecipes.com

Start with an insanely large database of recipes, toss in a hearty helping of useful cooking tips, and click liberally to enjoy Allrecipes.com. This site's user-supported recipe exchange allows visitors to add their own concoctions and share ideas online. Each subsection of the site has its own domain, so if you want a recipe for peanut butter chocolate chip cookies, you can go directly to Cookierecipe.com. See the icons along the bottom of the page for the full group of subsites.

Dean & Deluca www.deandeluca.com

Astronomically priced (but gastronomically unparalleled) food from the SoHo grocer of legend. The site peddles luxury basics like truffles, chocolate, caviar, and fine cheeses, as well as D & D's own specialty items (almond flour and dried Morel mushrooms, among others). Nothing can stop your mouth from watering, but the price tags will keep you from splurging (balsamic vinegar for $175?). Can't afford the lifestyle? A new section of articles on food and entertaining lets you read about it instead.

The Real Beer Page www.realbeer.com

Much cleaner and a lot less smoky than the local bar, The Real Beer Page has more information about beer than you could ever imagine. News, health information, shopping, games, brewery guides, events, city guides, book reviews, and even an incredibly extensive online beer library are all documented, linked, and archived here. Join your local brewers' association, brew your own at home, or select the perfect beer for your barbeque.

NetGrocer.com www.netgrocer.com

Finding items in the grocery store can make you feel like the object of the stock boy's personal vendetta. End the insanity with NetGrocer.com's ShopFast feature. You enter your shopping list, the site matches it with items that are in stock (indicating which items are on sale), then ships them to you by Federal Express. The site even saves your list to make your next shopping trip easier. Victory is yours.

Food.com www.food.com ©

Welcome to the Internet's takeout and delivery service. At Food.com, you can access menus from restaurants in your area and order dinner for delivery in an hour or less. Though the selection varies from city to city, you're sure to find a refreshing alternative to pizza and Chinese among the 12,000 restaurants listed.

Tavolo www.tavolo.com ©

Have a special occasion coming up? Here's our advice: preheat your oven, dial up Tavolo, and try not to get batter on the iMac. With cookbooks, kitchenware, and buying guides, you won't find a better resource for cooking gourmet. Use the recipe channel for meal suggestions, preparation instructions, and a categorized shopping list. Then shop their specialty foods to buy the ingredients you'll need. Apricot and White Chocolate Brownies are only minutes away.

Liquor.com www.liquor.com

Want to impress at your next cocktail party? Liquor.com lets you personalize a bottle of champagne by putting your own message on the label. The site is full of quirky offerings like this, plus links to the Libation Library and Ask the Bartender . . . He Knows. Of course, an enormous range of booze is available, from a $14 bottle of tequila to a $799 bottle of Dom Perignon. Just be sure to scroll down when shopping; prices are listed in descending order.

Candy Direct www.candydirect.com

Four out of five dentists recommend not going anywhere near Candy Direct, but don't let a little thing like cavities stop you. Candy Direct has your fix of Jujyfruits, Butterfingers, and more, plus specialty candy like Gummi Pet Rats and violet-flavored mints. You'll be buying in bulk, but the prices are roughly what they would be at the corner store ($24.93 for 24 King Size Baby Ruths). Stock your pantry for Halloweens to come.

WineToday.com
www.winetoday.com

For educated wine enthusiasts, WineToday.com packs in reviews on hundreds of varieties and vineyards, plus a unique and delightful section on wine-related events. You don't need loads of money to enjoy the selections here. A wine-of-the-day program for your Palm Pilot lets you see what wine to order right from the restaurant table.

Onlinefood.com www.onlinefood.com

Culinary adventures await at Onlinefood.com, where Middle Eastern, German, Italian, Asian, kosher, and Spanish foods share the shelves. With more than 50,000 items from around the globe (baklava to bamboo leaves), you can plan a theme dinner or mix and match. Who says marinated cactus doesn't go with udon?

foodline.com www.foodline.com

If you're drowning in a sea of restaurants, grab the foodline.com for the best in dining choices. This zany-looking site can help you make reservations at restaurants in select cities and offers fresh perspectives on the experience of eating out, along with a frequently updated (if unlikely) recipe archive. It's up to you whether you trust the Zagat restaurant ratings or the testimonies of fellow users more. Either way, you'll get a customer's eye view of the best and worst in dining out.

Winebid www.winebid.com

Fine vintages from around the world are sent to the auction block at Winebid. Not necessarily for novices, the site also boasts an "Auto-Bid" service. If you tell it the highest price you'll pay for a certain wine, it will automatically bid for you in response to any competing bids until either others stop bidding, or the bidding goes above your ceiling price. It also offers auction strategies and a subscription newsletter outlining the best time to buy.

Adagio Teas www.adagioteas.com

Fancy coffees may be all the rage, but tea cuts cancer risk, comes in far more flavors, and makes 200 cups per pound. Adagio Teas puts a modern spin on the age-old beverage and breaks down distinctions between green, iced, black, herbal, and other varieties. For the novice, the site offers super-cheap samples with a money-back guarantee, and for the connoisseur, the Tea Alchemy section lets a user blend his own flavor. Let's see, 30% caramel, 30% currant, and 40% orange ...

Coffee Review www.coffeereview.com

The idea was blissfully simple: conduct expert taste-testing of various kinds of coffee and report the findings in a 100-point review. Since its founding in 1997, Coffee Review has become an enormous and well-respected coffee buying guide, breaking down the subtle aroma, acidity, and aftertaste for hundreds of kinds of joe. Regular coffee, decaf, organics, and exotic blends—as well as java-related topics like home roasters and the oft-baffling biscotti—are all covered here.

games & gambling

The Station@sony.com www.station.sony.com

The answer: Trivial Pursuit, Wheel of Fortune, Backgammon, Keno, and Spades (among others). The question: What games can you find on The Station@sony.com? Tune in to play on your own or with others at this virtual cornucopia of game shows and classic games. If Alex Trebec doesn't put the gravy on your turkey, check out role-playing games like EverQuest and Tanarus, which let you battle with as many as 1,000 online enemies. Players beware: not all role-playing games are free.

Gamestop www.gamestop.com

Carpal tunnel factor: 10. You'll wish you'd worn a wrist brace after visiting Gamestop, home of more PC and video games than you can shake a joystick at. There are separate areas for PCs, Sega Dreamcast, Nintendo 64, Sony PlayStation, and Game Boy, and there's even a respectable Mac section (hallelujah!). Downloadable demos will help you decide if a game is worth getting, and should you get your Diddy Kong stuck in a tree, one of the many official strategy guides can help you out.

ClassicGaming.com www.classicgaming.com

This site is a shrine to game systems of old (such as Atari) and offers hosting and links to sites that show you how to play classic games on your PC. The tone here is fun, accessible, and easy for newbies to understand; the museum section is particularly funny (if taken with a grain of salt), providing blow-by-blow histories of the rise and fall of 80s game systems like Pong and ColecoVision. Go straight to the Vault to download ROM games like Pulirula and Pacman.

Adrenaline Vault www.avault.com

Gamers, start your engines. You can't play tournaments at the Adrenaline Vault, but it is a stellar source for game demos, patches, and previews of PC and console favorites like Tomb Raider and Duke Nukem 3D. Catch up on the latest with daily news updates, and stay abreast of the industry's best with AV's hardware reviews and monthly review wrap-ups.

Games Domain www.gamesdomain.com

Whoever said that cheaters don't prosper never visited Games Domain's ever-growing bank of game cheats—tricks guaranteed to get you ahead faster than skill will. This U.K.-based site also has an impressive array of concise reviews that include a pros and cons summary of each game; you'll find out that the new edition of Risk has better preference settings than the first and a lackluster soundtrack (for starters).

Electronic Arts www.ea.com

Ever dream of designing the world's scariest roller coaster? Build your own at Electronic Arts' radical "Sim Theme Park World," and see how many people you can make barf. This is just a small part of EA's powerful site, which compiles feature articles, reviews, interviews with game developers, and a shop where you can buy (or demo) all the hottest shoot-em-ups.

Internet Chess Club www.chessclub.com

Who's the Master? If you think you are, then try your hand against one of the several International Masters and Grandmasters who compete here every week. If you're not feeling so bold, try the Loser's League tournaments for novices, and then work your way up to higher challenges. Live team tournaments are organized each week.

ZDNet GameSpot www.gamespot.com

With all the adolescent alien-blasting games online, sites that showcase titles like Wall Street Trader2000 are a rare and precious find. Proving that gaming isn't just for kids, ZDNet GameSpot offers more sophisticated fare along with the usual game reviews and player hints. You'll find ratings and rankings of the latest releases and hardware, downloadable trailers, and feature-length animated movies starring your favorite digital characters.

The MUD Connector www.mudconnector.com

Bid goodbye to one more baffling acronym: MUD actually stands for Multi-User Domain, a text-based environment for online role-playing games. With a no-frills design and no-stone-unturned listings, The MUD Connector gets players the skinny on the constantly growing number of domains, including information on which MUDs are popular, which have a graphic interface, and which are now defunct. The site also provides a Resource Area for improving your gaming skills.

IGN.com www.ign.com

Imagine a gaming site that's three parts Sony PlayStation and one part *Maxim* magazine and you've got the idea behind IGN.com, a virtual boys club that holds considerable sway in the gaming world. IGN.com offers codes for more than 12,000 games (and growing) on its Game Sages channel, as well strategy guides to help you master any slice-'em, dice-'em favorite. Other testosterone-friendly features include wrestling, sex tips (in the For Men section), and movie reviews.

CNET Gamecenter.com www.gamecenter.com

Macintosh users feeling left out of the gaming brotherhood will appreciate how Gamecenter.com's democratic coverage treats Macs, PCs, and consoles equally. For each, Gamecenter.com provides editors' picks, strategy guides, product reviews, and Game Grabs (pre-release screen shots of hot, upcoming games). If you're in the market, this is also a great place to shop for games.

GameSpy.Com www.gamespy.com

Any site can give you free sneak previews of games, but how many gaming sites also offer recipes? For the connoisseur of the digital and culinary arts, GameSpy.Com's crass cooks create recipes based on video and computer games. Of course, there is the standard gaming fare here: reviews, downloads, freebies, a guide to gaming basics for novices, and some hilarious articles. A word to the weak of stomach: Half-Life Headcrab Delight is as good as it sounds.

Casino.com www.casino.com

This online gambling hub has a ton of resources to help you hedge your bets. The site's bi-weekly newsletter offers articles, industry news, gambling horoscopes and columns written by the pros to help you "Play Better." There is also an entire menu of links to gambling sites and tutorials, but if the closest you want to come to financial ruin is losing your virtual shirt, fun.casino.com has Shockwave versions of craps, poker, slots, and other Vegas favorites.

lottery.com www.lottery.com

Which games currently offer the highest jackpot? What are the best strategies for playing lotteries? What's it like to be a winner? And most importantly, did your numbers come up last night? The answer to these questions and more can be found on lottery.com, where beating the odds can mean retirement at 30. In the words of one recent winner, "I don't plan on going back to work for now because it's a headache."

WON.net www.won.net

Despite its ominous name, WON.net (aka World Opponent Network) features some exceedingly friendly games, like spades, checkers, dominoes, and others, all of which are free and can be played immediately. Additional games include Leisure Suit Larry's Casino, You Don't Know Jack, Trophy Bass, Roach Invaders, and Lords of Magic, as well as hundreds of free video game downloads. (Note: These are only demos, not the actual games.) It's pretty plain-looking for a gaming site, but the respectable content and easy-to-follow instructions make up for it.

Happy Puppy www.happypuppy.com

Sit! Stay! Play! These are the commands anyone can learn at Happy Puppy, a site dedicated to playing games. This site is so friendly to navigate, even the newest newbie can download demos, read reviews, and find cheats to new, popular, and classic games for many different systems. Games have ratings and stats and you can buy them if you like what you read.

eGames www.egames.com

Parents can rest easy with this site's exclusively family-friendly selection of games. The puzzles, classic games, shooting galleries, and adventure games here focus on strategy rather than guts and gore, with graphics that rival their more violent counterparts. Some are available at a discount by download, others come in software packs or on CD-ROM. Keep an eye out for special offerings like the Games for Girls pack.

Lycos Gamesville www.gamesville.com

For online wagering made easy, go to Lycos Gamesville, where relatively low stakes and games ranging from poker to virtual slots await the bored and unmonitored 9-to-5er. Or, if you'd prefer, relax with a low-pressure game from the collection of classic titles. All the personalization that goes with most Lycos subnetworks can be found here, but the real attractions are the diversions. Its slogan, "Wasting your time since 1996," says it all.

OneAcross www.oneacross.com   ⓞ

Racking your brains for the answers to the last couple of clues in the crossword? Check out OneAcross. Using a database compiled from user contributions, the site lets you search for words corresponding to any clue or pattern of letters. No payment is required for this frustration-easing service, other than return contributions to help expand the database. Oh, and just for kicks, they've thrown in solutions for anagrams and cryptograms, too.

WinnerOnline.com www.winneronline.com

The bright lights of the Web gambling scene can be dazzling to new-comers, but sites like WinnerOnline.com can help cut through the glare. A place to go for the latest news and views in online casino gaming, the site offers reviews, strategies, and tips on winning big money. Insightful interviews with the major players can be very educational, too. If you tire of all this strategy and seriousness, kick back with a few free games of poker or roulette.

Puzz.com www.puzz.com

Flex your mental muscle with trivia, puzzles, brain teasers, and IQ tests—non-tech games seemingly from the days of yore. Some are for fun, while others serve as true evaluations of your cerebral prowess. If you're particularly proud of your scores, there are links to high-IQ societies where you can congregate with other members of the community. Or join others at Puzz.com in getting news of the latest in contests, free stuff, and even, as a strange detour, MP3s.

Lotteries.com www.lotteries.com

If you're in the market for some happiness, here's the money to buy it—$40 billion cash is up for grabs in the international lotteries accessible through this site. You can purchase entries by ordering online, by fax, by mail, or with an agent over the phone. The site also lists past winning numbers, should you want to attempt a calculation at which will come up next. *Bon chance!*

health

drkoop.com www.drkoop.com ©

What's going on in the chat room called Saturday Night Friends? Only members get to peek into these forums officiated by health experts. Other resources at drkoop.com, like the medical encyclopedia, drug checker, and alternative medicine center, won't intimidate even doctor-phobic patients. We like the emphasis on preventative as well as curative techniques, even if we're baffled by the chat room names.

Phys.com www.phys.com ⓓ

Phys.com is physical fitness for women that covers the gamut from weight loss to nutrition and exercise. Lots of advice here on eating healthy and sculpting your bod into bikini-worthy perfection (whatever happened to being active for fun?). Skip the "Snack Bandit" virtual slot machine and go straight to the Nutritional Rx page for sound advice on how to prevent illness. Cool calculators let you figure out your ideal body weight, body fat percentage (yikes), or daily carbohydrate needs in a couple clicks of the mouse.

drugstore.com www.drugstore.com

Take a peek inside your medicine cabinet—then head for the Web. drugstore.com will ship you all the bathroom basics, from cotton swabs and rubbing alcohol to surprisingly good brands of makeup, shampoos, and bath products. Compare items by brand and price, or get your prescriptions filled—the site has a huge drug index for drug info and prices.

Ask Dr. Weil www.drweil.com

The cure to whatever ails you? Simplicity and balance, says Dr. Weil, the first name in America's alternative medicine community. His homey site doles out tools to enable healthy living, like a farmers' market locator, an herbal medicine chest (Ginkgo, anyone?), and reams of sage advice. If you don't see the answer you're seeking in the Q & A archive, you can always contact the doctor directly through the site.

PlanetRx.com www.planetrx.com

Gone are the days of the friendly corner pharmacist, so why venture out for your medicine at all? PlanetRx.com will take your prescription, fill it, ship it for free, and remind you when you're due for a refill. Need some dental floss, Vitamin E, or waterproof mascara? Order it along with your prescription and it'll get shipped for free as well. PlanetRx.com also provides health news, topic-driven weekly chats, and a staff pharmacist who can answer questions within 24 hours.

Go Ask Alice! www.goaskalice.columbia.edu

Am I normal if I ...? Answers to all varieties of this question come to you from Alice, Columbia University's health education Q & A site. From fitness and nutrition to emotional health to sexuality, Alice has answered more than 1,700 questions and continues to answer more each week. Search the archives to see if your question has been answered, or submit a new inquiry in one of seven categories.

SelfCare.com www.selfcare.com

Healer, heal thyself. This site's Health Centers, SelfCare Stores, Community, and Latest Health News offer some unique options for taking better care of yourself. Information on Acupressure, Aromatherapy, Light and Sound Therapy, and Magnets can be found within the Alternative Therapies section, which also offers products to get you started. And the category on traditional products, including fitness equipment and nutritional supplements, will round out any regimen.

MedicineNet.com www.medicinenet.com

A huge anthology of articles written by doctors and scientists for consumers, MedicineNet.com provides excellent, current medical information in easy-to-understand language. The wide range of topics, from diseases to drug breakthroughs to first aid procedures, is easily navigated using their new search engine and dictionary. The information is fairly general, so the site is better used as a guide than a database.

eNutrition www.enutrition.com

The name may be cyber-trendy but the contents of eNutrition are solid. Each of its categories (Weight Management, Your Health, Sports Nutrition, Vitamins & More, Body & Senses) is backed by a comprehensive group of products that will help you slim down, de-stress, or just get healthier. Breaking health news, gift baskets for fitness fanatics, and a glossary of terms from "absorption" to "yeast" round out the offerings. Shipping specials change weekly, so check back often.

Sexual Health infoCenter www.sexhealth.org/infocenter

While some of the information on this site reads like *Cosmo* (sex tip of the week!), the Sexual Health info-Center also contains loads of serious data and advice on topics such as sex and aging, safe sex, sexual dysfunction, and sexual orientation. Two more useful features: one guide to the use and effectiveness of certain birth control methods and another to the symptoms and health risks of various STDs.

The American Anorexia Bulimia Organization www.aabainc.org

An informative site dedicated to the disorders that affect more than five million Americans. Look here for advice from the professionals on symptoms and medical consequences of anorexia, bulimia, and binging, causes and risk factors, and how to find help. Sufferers, friends, and family will find it a worthwhile resource.

Planned Parenthood www.plannedparenthood.org

plannedparenthood•org

A virtual clinic and activist site rolled into one, Planned Parenthood online gives advice on safe sex and sexual health, family planning, pregnancy, parenting, abortion, and more—and the key word is more. Articles on how to talk about sex with children, men's parenting responsibilities, congressional debates on reproductive issues, and the politics of the word "slut" turn this medical insight spot into an interesting and informative news site.

GYN 101 www.gyn101.com

Do you shiver when you imagine those cold, metal gyno-gadgets? Ever wonder what they are? GYN 101 offers a complete guide to the most dreaded doctor visit of the year, including the reasons for going, what happens on the table, the patient's rights, and how to find a doctor. The relaxation techniques are really useful.

Gazoontite.com www.gazoontite.com

Gazoontite.com fills a long-empty niche by offering products for asthma and allergy sufferers. Order items like hypo-allergenic bedding, a dust mite detection kit, and an auto air purifier to make your commute a lot less sniffly. Or treat asthmatic kids to inhaler holders in the shapes of Bart Simpson and Casper. The help of a live nurse between 9 a.m. and noon on weekdays is nothing to turn your nose up at either.

Vitamins.com www.vitamins.com

Vitamin specials, vitamin experts, vitamin encyclopedia. The sheer volume of vitamin-related content here may leave you feeling like you've ODed on C. A helpful beginner's guide starts you off right, with explanations of which pills to take for better energy, immunity, and health. If you find the same vitamins at a lower price from another online vendor, Vitamins.com will give them to you for free.

HealingPeople.com www.healingpeople.com

Whether it's herbs for your ailments or shiatsu for your mental state, HealingPeople.com will lead you to alternative therapies and practitioners for any concern, physical or spiritual. The assortment of articles here is organized into categories like homeopathy, western herbalism, and aromatherapy, with extensive descriptions of treatments for different afflictions and an online store to buy them.

Athealth.com www.athealth.com

Straightforward, useful resources about and serving the mental health community—both practitioners and consumers. This site gives pretty basic information on dozens of disorders and conditions, but does provide a list of mental health professionals located near you. Other categories include recommended reading, a self-help store, a treatment directory, and a "medicine cabinet" that describes medications used for different disorders.

Floss.com www.floss.com

As the saying goes, be true to your teeth lest they be false to you. The folks at Floss.com have finessed the potentially dull topic of dental care into a rather interesting and educational site. Tips cover daily maintainence and oral hygiene, while features explore topics like tooth news, bad breath, and dental emergencies. Take one of the dozen self-tests to see how your choppers stack up.

OnHealth www.onhealth.com

"Has your cough started recently?" From there, it's a choose-your-own-adventure through a series of questions, until the Symptom Checker determines your course of action. Other terrific tools include a myriad of articles, advice centers, and forums, mostly geared toward women. The information is solid, if somewhat alarmist—we're guessing the Harvard doctors who wrote it prefer to err on the side of caution.

MedicineOnline.com www.medicineonline.com

How much would you pay to get those crow's feet removed? MedicineOnline.com actually allows users to bid on surgery on the site. Learn everything you ever wanted to know about cosmetic, plastic, and vision surgeries, then check out detailed before and after pictures and place a bid. Not sure how much a tummy tuck is worth? The site includes fee ranges along with risk factors, side effects, and surgery durations.

WebMD www.webmd.com

If Shirley Maclaine's discussion of her pilgrimage to Spain doesn't interest you, tune in later to the live, professionally facilitated conversations on topics like raising twins, or living with anorexia or arthritis. This eclectic mix of topics makes the Live Events Channel at WebMD worth visiting. But the site also offers a broad variety of health-related advice and practical services such as "My Health Record," a place where families can safely and conveniently store their medical records online.

CBSHealthWatch www.healthwatch.com

For those of us who can't remember when we last visited the doctor, CBSHealthWatch.com offers a unique tool called the Daily Diary that lets you track medication, doctor visits, diet, and exercise. But while the Daily Diary even allows users to graph their records, it doesn't come with clear written instructions; users may also get confused by the icons that look deceptively like links.

American Psychological Association www.apa.org

If your kid's online 24/7 and it's beginning to worry you, take the Inter-net-addiction quiz at the American Psychological Association's Web site. Though geared more toward professional psy-chologists and psych students, (so easy answers are rare and quizzes aren't the focus), newcomers will find information on mental health, lists of APA books for sale, and resources to help them find local psychologists.

Mental Health InfoSource www.mhsource.com

The experts at Mental Health InfoSource will tell you whether you are really manic or just a garden-variety narcissist. Intended for the general public and mental health professionals, this comprehensive site allows users to search its vault of articles and frequently asked questions by symptom. While not a flashy or commercial site, Mental Health InfoSource provides tools to find mental health professionals, ask the expert services, chat rooms, and online continuing education.

health

The Body www.thebody.com ©

Exhaustive and well-organized information on HIV and AIDS in a format so unlike your HMO—straight up. The Body tackles the technical and emotional aspects of HIV and AIDS, with great links to the latest research, government and activist groups, and online advice from top MDs. Click here for easily accessible answers to the questions you're too embarrassed to ask your doctor as well as the ones you haven't even considered.

eDiets.com www.ediets.com

Don't know the difference between a crunch and a squat? Let the animated fitness instructor at eDiets.com show you exactly how to get the most out of your exercise routine. The licensed dieticians and counselors here will also supply you with meal plans, shopping lists, and motivation specifically tailored to your personalized diet profile. But while the profile is free, the program is not—although eDiets.com says that its approach costs about half as much as traditional diet programs.

HealthGrades.com www.healthgrades.com ©

Find out why you look like you're 26 but feel like you're 40. While HealthGrades.com's primary purpose is to help you find a four-star cardiologist or a five-star orthodontist within 50 miles of your home, this comprehensive site also offers individualized health report cards. Use the calculators to find out your "real age" and peruse personalized wellness tips at the site's Wellness Manager.

The International Council on Infertility Information Dissemination www.inciid.com

Don't let the formal sounding name fool you—this site is nothing but user-friendly when dispensing information on fertility and reproductive health. It breaks down what you need to know in simple, topical articles and cultivates a community feel with chat forums where couples can connect and relate. An online pharmacy, glossary of fertility jargon, and list of offline specialists in all 50 states make it a comprehensive resource as well.

MedicalRecord.com www.medicalrecord.com ©

No need to worry about scorpion stings during your upcoming trip to Morocco. If your doctor has access to the Internet he can retrieve your medical records through MedicalRecord.com and choose the correct medication to fix you up. The no-nonsense site dispenses with frills like chat rooms, medical articles, or doctor's advice.

Oncology.com www.oncology.com

With articles ranging from descriptions of cancer to talks about
acupuncture and cancer therapy, Oncology.com is informative for both
patients and those just learning about the disease. Research highlights
include a database of alternative treatments and an online library of
oncology resources. The site's best feature, however, is its ability to balance the practical and the personal. There's a journal to record doctor
appointments as well as touching stories about cancer survivors.

HerbVigor.com www.herbvigor.com

Conventional medicine meets herbal alternatives in this wellness zine,
where viewers can check out the latest in health research or bone up on
herbal remedies. Experts offer tips on natural medicine treatments for
everything from skin ailments to oily hair, while special corners tailor
info for men, women, and children. There are a few big words here (like
pycnogenol), but overall, it's an easy to understand reference.

CenterWatch www.centerwatch.com

At CenterWatch, the general public and pharma-
ceutical industry professionals can find in-depth
information on the latest drug therapies
approved by the FDA and track news on the development of clinical
trials. The site is an important resource for patients (or their loved
ones) looking for innovative treatments; register your email address for
periodic updates.

National Institute on Drug Abuse www.drugabuse.gov

Drugs A to Z. This site has an impressive listing of drugs—along with
abuse information—and comes complete with articles, glossaries, and
references. There's info on the drugs we've been warned about since
junior high as well as the lesser-known club drugs and steroids. It lists
details for upcoming conferences and projects that educators and parents can check out for kids.

kidsDoctor www.kidsdoctor.com

Since 1996, thousands of questions have been submitted to kidsDoctor,
a wonderful site hosted by Lewis A. Coffin, M.D. Although the information here is not meant to replace the advice of your real-life doc, the
site does provide a rather remarkable collection of timely articles dealing with your kids and their health. There are dozens of topics,
including calcium intake, fever, growing pains, newborns, sleeping trou-
bles, and much more.

home & living

HomeArts www.homearts.com

HomeArts is an excellent resource for people who've turned their
home into a hobby. Less manic than Martha Stewart but more exacting
than Peg Bundy, the site invites searchers to discover information on
everything from performing heavy-duty repairs to adding the occasional
light decorative touch. As a part of women.com, it also has the
community vibe, with chats and bulletin boards.

Better Homes and Gardens Online www.bhglive.com © ⓓ

A Web portal on par with the magazine and television program, Better Homes and Gardens Online aims to turn hearth and yard into showcases of domestic expertise. It brings together banks of resources on cooking, decorating, craft projects, and family time—click on any topic to get articles, online tools, and doorways to discussion groups. The how-to encyclopedia is especially valuable, with step-by-step instructions on common repair topics like plumbing and painting.

Garden.com www.garden.com © ⓢ

Whether you have an urban window box or a full-scale rose garden, Garden.com has products and solutions for you. The site offers a full selection of seeds and bulbs (shipped overnight), plus accessories, gardening tips, and a community of other gardeners with whom you can share strategies. The extensive Design a Garden feature takes your existing light and climate considerations into account to help you choose flowers and plants to suit any patch of green.

marthastewart.com www.marthastewart.com

Cooking, gardening, entertaining ... does this woman ever sleep? After silently eating your heart out over that gorgeous Connecticut farmhouse that Martha calls home, do yourself a favor and check out her Web site. You'll wonder how you made it all these years without the crafts, canapés, and assorted Good Things you'll find there. Martha's line of everyday basics (linens, towels, silverware drawer liners) is also available for purchase. Admit it, the woman could turn a motor home into Buckingham Palace on her lunch hour.

Geomancy.Net www.geomancy.net

Anyone interested in feng-shui, the ancient art of placement, will love this beautiful site. It is a highly informative reference guide that can help you design your home so that it will look terrific, feel welcoming, and (some say) be more attractive to luck. Learn how to assess the landscape, survey your home, and interpret the intangible forces that affect your living space. You can also buy reports, books, software, or apply for courses here.

YardMart.com www.yardmart.com ©

From planting to pruning to patio partying, this site has nearly every outdoor need covered. Check out the selection of lawnmowers, clippers, and assorted tools to whip your weed patch into shape. Once you're finished, buy a barbecue, choose any of a dozen hammocks, grab a mint julep, and invite over the neighbors. What to do if you've picked the wrong shears? Call within ten days of receiving the item to get an authorization code for credit upon return.

Crate & Barrel www.crateandbarrel.com

Rattan storage baskets, scissor-cut centerpiece bowls, Cuisinart frozen yogurt machines ... this, my fellow Americans, is what we fought the Cold War for. Get all this classic Crate & Barrel merchandise at their great-looking e-store, which opts for a manageable selection of well-photographed products rather than hundreds of tiny pictures. Purchases are backed by solid customer service and yes, you can return merchandise to the brick-and-mortar store. Ain't capitalism grand?

Windowbox.com www.windowbox.com

You don't have to have a backyard to have a garden, and with the help of Floracle, the gardening oracle, you can find the right plants for your own little bed of loam. Describe your gardening style (devoted to negligent), the container, where you live, and the type of plant you're seeking, and she'll hand you back a combination that would suit you. Clicking through any of the names gets you the info you'll need to know to make the plant grow, with the option to buy it online.

Smith & Hawken www.smithandhawken.com

If most of your friends are of the fine and feathered type, Smith & Hawken's amazing bird feeders will have them flocking. (A corncob windmill! A millet wishing well!) The site also has beautiful home accessories, quality garden supplies, and clothes that will make you want to get out and weed. While you're shopping, be sure to stop by the resources link for great how-tos on topics like cooking from your garden and forcing bulbs.

living.com www.living.com

Hands down one of the most practical interior design sources on the Net—and living.com has a store to boot. After you've finished choosing a dining set, patio table, china cabinet, or night table, head over to the Room Designer, where you can virtually arrange (and rearrange) your buys in a customized floor plan. The selection mingles classic and more contemporary pieces. Also, check living.com's magazine for heaps of advice, how-tos, and trends.

Furniture.com www.furniture.com

With more than 50,000 affordable home furnishings on offer here, there's bound to be something for your kitchen, bath, bedroom, or home office. Want to throw together a refined sitting room? Head for the Traditional corner. Going for a Bauhaus feel? Check out the Modern selections. Furniture.com's commitment to customer service is obvious everywhere; they provide substantial information about each piece before purchase, send email updates after purchase, and even call you on the day of delivery to ensure that someone will be home.

GoodHome.com www.goodhome.com ©

A virtual house for voyeristic decorators: GoodHome.com lets you browse through fully decorated dining rooms, bedrooms, living rooms and more, each with a different style like urban or rustic. Click on the one you like the best to get a zoomable picture and a list of its contents—everything is available through the site, right down to the candles. You can also customize the wall colors and fabrics of rooms in the decorating studio. An impressive tool that's totally fun to use.

myhome.com www.myhome.com

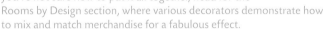

myhome.com is simply bursting with accessories to turn your shabby studio into a cozy hideaway. There's no furniture here, just small accessories like vanity shelves for your bathroom and decorative boxes for your desk. If you're not sure how to put it all together, head for the Rooms by Design section, where various decorators demonstrate how to mix and match merchandise for a fabulous effect.

HomePortfolio www.homeportfolio.com ©

Wonder what your dream house could look like? With HomePortfolio, you'll never have trouble explaining what you want to interior decorators again. While the number of items for sale online is small, you can browse images of some of the most stylish home furnishings we've ever seen, rate them ("love it," "like it," "not my style"), and save them to your own personal portfolio. Nearly everything here is decidedly upscale—wingchairs start at around $1,000.

eZiba www.eziba.com ©

What's a home without Moroccan filigree screens or Thai porcelain

stools? You'll be asking yourself that very question when you find eZiba (Persian for "beautiful"), an online catalogue of irresistible artifacts, furniture, and garden supplies from every corner of the world. Items have thorough descriptions, clear pictures, and are searchable by region and category, making browsing a breeze.

Additional perks include themed online auctions and the stories of selected artists.

DoItYourself.com www.doityourself.com ©

A site that unites the how-to community, DoItYourself.com amasses advice on small home repairs, large home improvements, decorating, and other areas of Sunday puttering. The guide is both comprehensive and easy to use, with information that is universally applicable rather than tailored to a specific state. How much space is required between the hearth and the combustible area of a fireplace? How do you clean a gas range? This site can tell you.

Homestore.com www.homestore.com ©

Everything and especially the kitchen sink is addressed by this massive index of domicile data. Home improvement, realty, mortgages, gardening, and decoration each receive a separate section of how-tos, advice, and links, so it's easy to find a house or improve a current one (or pay someone else to). The only thing we didn't like: the high number of sponsors masquerading as site services.

Williams-Sonoma www.williams-sonoma.com ⓓ ⓢ

What started as a small neighborhood French cookware shop is now, well, Williams-Sonoma, the chain and catalog of upscale kitchenware and gifts. Shop their online store for top-quality cutlery, appliances, glassware, cookbooks, and furniture. The beautiful site provides some thoughtful touches to make shopping easier like letting users specify whether they would like each item in their cart shipped to them or to someone else—ideal for purchasing gifts.

Party411 www.party411.com ©

Party gone out of bounds? Prevent a repeat performance by visiting Party411 before the fact. The site has tons of tools for the detail-oriented host: guest list planners, seating arrangement charts, drink mixers, and an archive of tips, dips, and jokes. For expert advice, PartyGirl, PartyDoctor, and the Etiquette Queen have pages of past answers and columns, and can be queried through their respective forums if they haven't covered your concern before.

party411.com™
Your Party. Your Success.

homedepot.com www.homedepot.com

The house, like the human body, requires doctoring. For absolutely anything you need to do in terms of repairing your house or installing something new, this site has the info. It provides easy-to-follow, step-by-step "how to" pages on everything from replacing a door to replacing a wall—with great advice. And, of course, you can buy stuff online and find out more about the company itself.

RoommateFind.com www.roommatefind.com

The roommate who never showered and drank from the milk carton has moved out, but now you've got to replace him—or foot his share of the rent. RoommateFind.com is a personals service for roomies that uses preferences like age, smoking, and pets to match people. Only compatible members can get contact info on each other, and the site provides an email service so no one has to give out personal information. Post and browse for free; pay to contact a listing you like.

iCastle www.icastle.com

Not an unwieldy compendium of how to fix every inch of your house, but rather a refreshingly basic tool for finding local contractors who can. The site lists carpenters, roofers, and assorted other craftspeople in your area, and guarantees that you don't pay for any part of the work that doesn't satisfy you. On-site content includes how to fix typical problem areas—windows, doors, roofs, carpets, and fencing.

Pets.com www.pets.com © ⓓ

A simple way to buy supplies, food, toys, and gifts for anything with fur, feathers, or fins. You'll find the usual selection of pet products here, as well as some unique items like ferret hammocks, gourmet doggie treats, and freeze-dried fish food. All kinds of resident experts are on call to answer burning questions on products (What *is* a Booda Velvet?), pet health (cures for persistent vomiting), even animal law.

PETsMART.com www.petsmart.com

PETsMART's Web site adds a community angle to the pet supplies it's known for offline, profiling pets in the news, hosting bulletin boards,

and discussing the roles that animals fill in society. Naturally, you can get a whole host of supplies here, as well as useful e-tools—the dog food calculator and Ask a Vet will help current pet owners, while the breed guides and pet adoption info will assist prospective ones.

Umbra www.umbra.com © ⓓ

Umbra's first product was a printed-paper window shade but they've come a long way since then, moving on to translucent trash receptacles and gyro wall clocks. A collection of consumer-friendly products with intelligent design at its heart, Umbra offers a wide range of surprisingly practical household items ideal for more than just the minimalist urbanite. Reasonable prices and lifestyle consultants mean any aspiring hipster can join in the fun too.

real estate

Rent.Net www.rent.net

Tons of resources for every kind of renter—corporate and short-term, seniors, and vacationers, as well as standard apartment seekers. The search feature locates apartments by price range and locale (U.S. and Canada), often providing a "360° Virtual Walk-Through," that lets you poke around the floor plan. Pre- and post-move resources like job finders and moving services are also at your fingertips here.

Owners.com www.owners.com
Why pay a realtor when you can check out home listings yourself online? Owners.com makes it a reality. Buyers can use the competent search engine to choose from a surprising number of properties, all without having to pay the standard 7-8% commission; sellers in all 50 states can list their home on the site for $99.

move.com www.move.com
move.com streamlines the traumatic relocation process—as much as it can—by offering top-notch advice for dealing with everyone from the mover to your mother-in-law. Use one of their interactive calculators to help you define the cost of the move, peruse rentals and properties for sale, then hop over to their Move Manager to plan each step of the way. Got an aching feeling you've forgotten something? Use one of the site's checklists for reminders as you go.

FSBON www.forsalebyownernetwork.com
The For Sale By Owner Network helps people who want to buy and sell cut to the chase. Its foundation is home listings organized according to zip code and style of home, but the site also offers discounted property signage and T-shirts for becoming a human billboard. Although it suffers from a lack of listings, it does allow users to list their homes and apartments for only $50, and people can look at the listings for free.

Homes.com www.homes.com
Homes.com takes on Barbara Corcoran in full force at this mecca for all that is real estate. Like many other sites, Homes.com can brief you on mortgage rates, help you apply for one online, and connect you with recent property listings, but what makes this site shine is its easily searchable neighborhood info. Curious buyers may search via zip code for such stats as average seasonal temperature, dollars spent per student and SAT scores at area schools.

Domania.com www.domania.com
A site that gives whole new meaning to the phrase "keeping up with the Joneses." Just type in your neighbor's address to find out the market value of their home or the plots right around it; the site includes info on sale price, property value, taxes, mortgage, and a host of other facts to feed the neighborhood gossip mill.

.com domania
DO YOUR **HOME** WORK HERE

NearMyHome.com www.nearmyhome.com
Air pollution, land fills, fault lines, and assorted natural disasters: all important factors when planning a move that may not be taken into account by a realtor. Enter NearMyHome.com, a site that takes your zip code and hands back a map of the surrounding area with details on potential hazards. Additional information on child safety and schools is accessible as well, all for free.

The Tenants Resource Directory directory.tenantsunion.org

If your landlady won't return your security deposit because of "cat scratches on the walls" (but you never had a cat), this cut-and-dry directory has links to tenants' rights groups all over the country. The number and quality of links varies from state to state—California, obviously, has more links than Wyoming, and other states with fewer resources, such as South Dakota, simply link to the state government's site—but it's a good first step toward settling any rental dispute.

kids

Nick.com www.nick.com

Milk Bossie's musical udder, make hand shadow monsters, or help Chuckie find the missing Rugrats. Over 40 different Shockwave games almost make up for the fact that Nick.com is basically one big commercial for the channel. The site also has a hefty interactive forum where kids can send in drawings (which the site will animate), submit a funny joke, or make up a new Nicktionary word.

Cyberkids www.cyberkids.com ⓓ

How do you spell your name in ancient Egyptian hieroglyphics? Find out at Cyberkids, a virtual home for kids ages seven through 12. Funny Bone jokes, animations, and games pepper this super-colorful site, which aims to give kids a voice by showcasing their creative work and letting them connect at monitored chat rooms. Well-wrought and easy to navigate, the site offers links to online tutoring and homework help as well as shopping.

Yahooligans! www.yahooligans.com ⓞ

Yahoo! for kids has all the power and breadth of its parent directory but screens out any material that's inappropriate, making it easy for younger surfers to explore the gentler side of the Web. Like adult Yahoo!, Yahooligans! has other services too, like news, sports, and Net events, all kid-safe. To get started, hit the super Help section or look for the listings with sunglasses icons—the best of the bunch.

FunBrain.com www.funbrain.com ©

Mrs. Weagle at Calvin Coolidge School would have loved FunBrain.com's range of educational games. Math problems, word games, and historical trivia are the specialty here, all built to give kids in K-8 extra school help in a fun, online format. Separate sections for parents and teachers supply activity planning advice and games to play along with youngsters—there are even printable flash cards.

The Yuckiest Site on the Internet www.yucky.com
A science education resource cleverly disguised as a catalog of all things gross, the Yuckiest Site is loaded with simple instructions for rainy day activities, like changing milk into slime, making soap bleed, or turning a penny green. There are also trivia quizzes that answer burning questions like "What is snot made of?"

Disney.com www.disney.go.com
Mickey, Donald, and other beloved characters host the many activities this site offers, from arts and crafts to interactive comics and stories. One word of warning: the Disney Blast arcade requires a parent's credit card, which automatically gets charged after the free month-long trial.

MaMaMedia.com www.mamamedia.com
A bright, kid-friendly design and a buffet of activity choices entice kids to design an e-card for a friend, paint a picture, play with sound stamps, or view what others have created. MaMaMedia.com offers special perks for parents, too: the site sends an email notice when your child registers on the site, and labels which links are advertisements.

Funology.com www.funology.com
Ever wonder how to make a homemade lava lamp? Find a smorgasbord of wacky facts, simple craft projects, and magic tricks at Funology.com. While there is plenty to do online here, the focus is on offline activities that turn the computer into an activity book (and the kitchen into a war zone). Blend some gummy worms into a Doodle Bug Shake, or create a lava eruption; it's like third-grade science fair's greatest hits.

Sports Illustrated For Kids www.sikids.com
For any Little Leaguer who's ever wanted to draft his own major league team, SI For Kids comes through. The Bat-o-Matic gives kids four million virtual dollars to draft a team, and scores it according to real stats. SI Kids also has advice, sports news, and video clips of cool plays, making this site a quality junior version of the grown-up magazine. Be sure to click on Toons for fun animated shorts.

Bonus.com www.bonus.com
Following any of Bonus.com's multi-colored CyberWays will lead you to information and activities for kids ages three to 15. Click on the Green link for exploration, like virtual fieldtrips to Westminster Abbey or the Washington Monument. Yellow leads to art, with a step-by-step guide to drawing, and Purple gives you recipes and craft projects for imaginative play.

Crayola.com www.crayola.com

Build a birdbath, play recipe roulette, or grow a winter kitchen gar-den—Crayola's online activity resource is an incredible store of offline project ideas for creative kids. Art projects, birthday party ideas, games, science experiments, and nature adventures are just some of the categories offered, with databases searchable by age, skill, or loca-tion. Parents will love the car trip games and couch potato cures.

HomeworkCentral.com www.homeworkcentral.com

Much more than just the place to go for homework help, HomeworkCentral.com is an award-winning education portal that rolls information for students, parents and teachers into one indispensable resource. The students section spans kindergarten to college, while the teachers and parents sections link to online learning resources and ways to integrate the Web into lessons. What happened to the "work" in homework? It seems to have gone the way of ye olde Trapper Keeper.

BrainPOP www.brainpop.com

With its animated mice, robotic tour guide, and bright design, award-winning BrainPOP presents kids with a way to learn about science, technology, and health that is easily more engaging than TV. The site's primary draw is a collection of animated educational movies that cover topics like digestion, photography, and photosynthesis with humor and imaginative illustration. We won't be the first to tout its charms, but it's just so explosively good that we had to add our two cents.

Ask Jeeves for Kids www.ajkids.com

Where can I learn about gross body topics? Where can I see pictures of dinosaurs, or just have my spelling checked? Ask Jeeves and he'll go scouting around the Web to answer all the questions that kids love to pester grown-ups with. All the results are kid-appropriate, of course.

healthwindows for kids www.healthwindows.org

Kids ages nine to 15 can learn about all things delicious, nutritious, and health-promoting at this commercial-free portal devoted to the health and well-being of children. Healthwindows provides extensive links and should be a first stop for kids, parents, and teachers seeking inter-active educational games on health (from nutrition basics to cancer and ADD) and safety information (bike helmets to child abduction).

Sesame Workshop Online www.sesamestreet.com

E-stickers? Check. Tickle Me Elmo? Check. Web page builder for pre-schoolers? You bet. The whole Sesame Street gang is breaking in the concept of "col-laborative family edutainment" (translation: cool things for par-ents and kids to do together). There are separate activity sec-tions for babies, preschoolers, and older kids, as well as a link to the games and stories on the Sesame Street page.

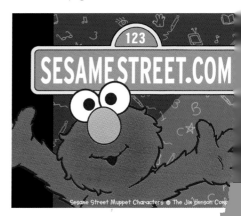

Blipz www.blipz.com

How much is that doggie on the Web page? At the Best Little Internet PetZ, it's free to adopt and care for any of the doggies, cats, horses, unicorns, or dinosaurs on the site. We're talking virtual pets here—the kind that don't wet the carpet or shed on the furniture. Excellent graphics make the furry ones in the Pound hard to resist, but beware: you still have to clean out the (virtual) litter box.

Time for Kids www.timeforkids.com

The online version of the magazine read by 2.2 million kids is actually two magazines: the News Scoop edition for grades two to three, and a more content-rich World Report for grades four through six. The weekly articles cover kid-friendly topics like space travel and animals of Antarctica, with an archive that goes back to 1995. Other features include Kids' Views on the News, and Kids Talk Back, a message board of surprisingly sophisticated young opinions on everything from Kosovo to homework.

toys

eToys www.etoys.com

eToys is designed for parents in panic; this is the place to go when you absolutely must find your child the latest, greatest action figure, computer game, or monster truck. For anyone who's clueless on what exactly a Renkly Space Ball is, there's also an information section at the bottom of the page that defines the popular toys of the moment.

AreYouGame.com www.areyougame.com

Remember Clue, Uno, Cootie, and Operation? This site's got all your favorite rainy day games and puzzles, as well as some newfangled titles like Who Wants to be a Millionaire? Prices are slightly cheaper than other online stores, saving customers anywhere from one cent to five dollars. And serious gamesters can pick up essential accessories like the Monopoly calculator or another batch of poker chips.

SmarterKids.com www.smarterkids.com

Kids grow out of books faster than shoes—get the right fit from preschool to high school at SmarterKids.com. Parents and teachers offer their insights on the best tools for tots, with an emphasis on books and printed learning matter. Special features for supplemental instruction can be found in the zine-like Parents Center, which is full of advice, articles, and activities.

FamilyWonder.com www.familywonder.com Ⓢ

Yes, you can control what your kids watch on TV! Go to FamilyWonder.com to find fun videos tailored to your child's age group. The site also offers music and toys, deals under $10, and articles on how to turn video time into quality time. Satisfaction is guaranteed, and returns can be made for up to 30 days.

The smarter way to shop for kids.™

Barbie.com www.barbie.com
The famed femme with the infamous proportions has a spot in cyberspace where you can preview upcoming Barbie collections, shop for Barbie software, and check out the latest additions to the Barbie empire. (Did you know she has a jet?) Of course, a huge variety of dolls are available for purchase, from the vintage Spring in Tokyo Barbie (around $50) to the Jewel Essence Barbie, with designer duds courtesy of Bob Mackie (at a cool $400).

Noodle Kidoodle www.noodlekidoodle.com © Ⓢ
Selling only non-violent and gender-neutral games and toys for kids from ages 0 to 12+, Noodle Kidoodle lets you browse by age, category, brand, or character (Scooby-Doo, Barney, Elmo, etc.) for toys both parents and kids can live with. The fabulous selection here includes CDs, puzzles, and nature toys as well.

law . . .. .

Internet Legal Resource Guide www.ilrg.com ©
Winner of many accolades, including a few from the American Bar Association and the National Law Journal, the Internet Legal Resource Guide is a comprehensive source of information on law schools and the legal profession, with research tools, federal cases, law school rankings, and links to firms and journals. For lawyers and scholars only, the archive of more than 80 legal forms is searchable, but tough to browse.

NetLitigation www.netlitigation.com
Cutting-edge legal info for citizens of the digital age. NetLitigation provides information about legal issues related to the Internet, such as antitrust legislation, e-commerce laws, the First Amendment, privacy, and trademarks and copyrights. Each section comes with an overview, details of past cases, and a helpful bank of related links at the bottom. Headline news articles are also posted on a regular basis.

Supreme Court Collection supct.law.cornell.edu/supct
While somewhat complicated to navigate, this massive site is an invaluable resource for info on current cases and major court decisions. Rabid for the results of a particular case? The site will email you a synopsis of the decision the day it's made. Also check here for landmark decisions, biographical info on the justices, and a glossary for "those who don't speak legalese."

law

FindLaw www.findlaw.com

If you're sweating through first-year law school (or just a glutton for intellectual punishment), FindLaw is for you. This site has got it all: listings of law schools, firms, and attorneys; cases and codes; federal and state resources for the United States; foreign and international legal information; a legal subject index; and much more.

Law.com www.law.com

Law.com offers superb coverage of the legal media for lawyers and law students. Promising to "cut through the clutter," the site delivers current and extensive legal news, links to law journals, and access to a massive online bookstore. The site might be a bit dry for the layperson, but how many non-lawyers would want to delve into legal vagaries anyway? (Unless checking a fact from *The Practice*, of course.)

Lawyers.com www.lawyers.com

For consumer-oriented legal information, surf no further than Lawyers.com. The site covers a diverse range of law specialties, including family, employment, bankruptcy, and civil rights. It also profiles 420,000 lawyers worldwide and supplies pages of advice on selecting one. If you can't find the answer to your legal conundrum in the articles or 10,000-term glossary, take advantage of the Ask a Lawyer forum.

Law School Admission Council www.lsac.org

What's worse: being tortured slowly and deliberately to the tune of a looped Backstreet Boys single, or first-year law school? We're betting on law school. Brave souls willing to go should consult the Law School Admission Council's page, which houses advice on how to prepare for school, when to take the LSAT, where to apply, and how to pay for it if you get in. Though not a comprehensive resource, the site can head you in the right direction—if you're sure you want to go.

Nolo.com www.nolo.com

Although lawyers may be the only people who call 10,000-word documents "briefs," Nolo.com keeps its legal advice short and simple. Its encyclopedia rewards research with concise explanations, and its advice persona, Auntie Nolo, specializes in commonsense answers to legal dilemmas. Sign up for the monthly email newsletter and grab a new Lawyer Joke while you're there (Ambrose Bierce's definition of a lawyer? "One skilled in circumvention of the law").

love & sex

Playboy.com www.playboy.com

We come here for the articles, but discerning gentlemen might also enjoy some of the other things this magazine and men's hub has to offer. The site boasts the same big bag of lifestyle features that made Hefner's original publication the cultural giant that it is, along with streaming video and live webcams. For a subscription fee, the Playboy Cyber Club offers exclusive photos and chat for members. But if you're a penny-pinching voyeur, the answer to your question is yes.

CollegeDates.com www.collegedates.com

 If you're a college kid who spends Saturday nights cuddled up to a cup of Ramen, put down your fork and head to CollegeDates.com. Designed to set you up with another student at your university, the site matches you based on a profile that describes you and your potential mate right down to your eyewear. Just be careful—a search for a curly-haired, gray-eyed love interest may turn up your professor's name!

Swoon.com www.swoon.com

A decidedly girly take on "dating, mating, and relating." Swoon.com offers an abundance of love horoscopes, quizzes (Measure your Mojo), and dream interpretation up front, but to get to any substantial articles, you'll need to click through to the table of contents. There you'll find recent features on why a quickie beats marathon sex, what cohabitation is really like, and how to plan a foolproof seduction.

Matchmaker.com www.matchmaker.com

With more than four million members worldwide—and online communities for everyone, be they straight, gay, nudist, or "over 40"—Matchmaker.com guarantees you're not alone. And, covering more than 80 cities (most in the U.S., but some international), there's someone here for almost everyone. A free 14-day trial membership makes it easy to join; you'll have to fork over $13 per month after that.

eCRUSH.com www.ecrush.com

Who loves ya, baby? eCRUSH can help you find out. Here's how it works: you fill out a questionnaire and give the folks at eCRUSH the email address of your secret heartthrob. eCRUSH sends them a message

 that they have an admirer and only reveals your name if they complete the questionnaire listing you as someone they're eyeing as well. The next step is up to you … eCRUSH can't do everything!

Nerve www.nerve.com ©

The self-billed e-zine of "literate smut," Nerve serves up tasteful tidbits, pictures, articles, and stories for the sexually enlightened. Occupying a cool middle ground, the site is careful not to offend passersby with huge displays of flesh, but titillates nonetheless with an extensive library and links to suit any taste from delicate to dominatrix. Check out the shop for digital prints of the art on the site, or hook up to Nerve Radio to listen to sexy tunes while you surf.

Lovingyou.com www.lovingyou.com

Cynics, no need visit here. Lovingyou.com is for people who love to love, whether or not there's someone right now. The tone of the site is positive, affirming, and above all, helpful. Getting bored in the bedroom? Here are 10 tips for better sex. Don't know how to set the mood for dinner? Start with throwing pillows all around the living room. Lovingyou.com conveys that love is not enough—you still need communication and creativity, and they've got plenty to share.

Match.com www.match.com

Having a tough time finding that special someone? The Internet is teeming with potential mates, and two million of them are members of Match.com. Search for specific qualities in appearance, lifestyle, education, and location or just browse. The free trial offers a peek at the millions (did we say millions?) of personals. Be sure to take a look at their monthly e-zine Mix 'n' Match for dating anecdotes, success stories, funny flops, and advice.

CleanSheets www.cleansheets.com

Not a site for new linens, but an online erotica magazine, CleanSheets "showcases intelligent and sexy erotic fiction, poetry, and art," while commenting on sexuality and society. Particularly good are the searchable archive of book and Web site reviews and the gallery of erotic pictures (closer to Mapplethorpe than *Playboy*).

Good Vibrations www.goodvibes.com ⑤

Treating hysteria among housewives was the original function of the vibrator when it was invented in 1869. Since then, better technology and broader minds have done away with the eggbeater-like contraptions of yore, and Good Vibrations has become the place to buy them. The site also packs in info among the products—FAQs, columns, and an eye-widening vibrator museum.

GOOD VIBRATIONS

SocialNet.com www.relationships.com

What's the point of all this manic (cat and) mouse play if you can't connect with anyone? Find fellow netizens you click with at SocialNet.com, a hub of social relations that matches people for social activities, networking, and dating. The site's specialty is privacy: you have ultimate control over who can contact you and what happens to information you submit. Plus, when you register, you're given an email account that you can set to show your user name, or no name at all.

Edwina www.edwina.com

Vanilla, adventurous, or kinky: where do you fall on the sliding scale of bedroom demeanor? No need to blush—it's easy to reveal intimate details to Edwina, the liaison extraordinaire at this charming singles site for gays and lesbians. Upon registration (free), Edwina equips you with your own little black book and sends you off to contact promising ads. The five dollar monthly fee comes in when you decide you want to access notes other members have sent you.

VirtualKiss.com www.virtualkiss.com

The soul kiss, the butterfly kiss, and other variations on the lip lock of love fuel this quirky romance site. VirtualKiss.com teaches the basics in Kissing 101 ("Don't bite."), shares stories of smooches gone wrong, and offers the directions for kissing games that go beyond mere Spin the Bottle. The site also provides a variety of computer fun, like print-able kiss coupons, a kissing cursor download, and e-kiss cards.

Anthologia www.anthologia.com

High-class erotica for both men and women is the order of the day at Anthologia, an exceptional site that caters to the sexual tastes of both genders. The main attraction is Phantasia, a repository for reader-sub-mitted sexual fantasies to titillate the mind. But it doesn't stop there—you'll also find the finer points of the Kama Sutra and how-tos on the maintenance of sexual well-being. Definitely adults only as nude photos accompany many of the features.

Dating911 www.dating911.com

Dating911 is: (a) an entertaining response to the culture of dating, (b) "mouth-to-mouth for your comatose love life," or (c) all of the above? The answer is in the advice, anecdotes, and Fortune Cookies of Love provided by the site. While it won't get you a date (no personals here), it will teach you dating basics, let you peek into writers' dating diaries, and provide shriek-worthy horror stories you'll be glad you're only reading about.

Intimategifts.com www.intimategifts.com   © ⓢ

Shopping online means never having to explain that you're buying for "a friend." If that's not reason enough, Intimategifts.com tenders toys, videos, and books, priced to sell and easy to browse. The stock is complemented by buying guides, informative FAQs, gift suggestions, and a return policy that guarantees your satisfaction with your purchase (if not your love life). If you're stuck, the online advisor, Alexa, fields email questions and recom-mends products in her on-site forum.

love & sex

The Cyrano Server www.cyranoserver.com

Don't know the right words to tell that special (or not-so-special) someone how you feel? The Cyrano Server does, and it's offering to do all the composition for you. It has different Mad Libs-style forms for Valentines, love letters, and break-up kiss-offs—you plug in the personal details and it spits out the completed text. Add some graphics or sound clips and hit send; the only email address the recipient will see is the one you chose to enter.

Sexilicious.com www.sexilicious.com

Women of the new millennium are tossing aside inhibitions like used towelettes, and they want to talk about it. Sexilicious.com, a community for the sexually liberated female netizen, offers a lot of original content, from feature stories on important issues to reviews of the hottest sexual aids. Discussions take place in forums and chat; be sure to leave your timidity at the door.

Tantra.com www.tantra.com

Want to get your chakras humming? Log on and learn the "Soaring Butterfly Position" and the secrets to energy orgasms. Absolute pros who don't need the Ask Suzie section can go directly to the online catalog of books, videos, and e-sensuals (e.g., Bawdy Butter) to put them in the mood. The site offers a weekly discussion forum as well as directory listings of teachers and workshops. If you don't want to go it alone, peruse their personals for your perfect tantric buddy.

XseeksY.com www.xseeksy.com

XseeksY.com is all about matching people up with their next true love, but it's also a community site with tailor-made advice for men and women of all sexual preferences. Their Personal Writer will draft an ad for you if you're tripped up by the abbreviations and salesman tone of the personals. And if you should find your love only to lose her, visit The Healing Room, or just rant and rave on the message boards.

Condom Sense www.condoms.net

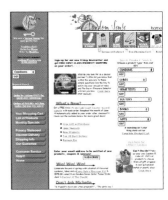

If there was ever a site that needed one-hour delivery ... Nevertheless, Condom Sense is a one-stop shop for sex aids, adult gifts, advice and, of course, condoms. It's easy to find what you want with a comprehensive search engine and the staff's own recommendations. The site even displays pictures of the rubbers in various stages of inflation for full evaluation. For tough questions that must be answered immediately, try the customer service ICQ account.

The Purity Test www.puritytest.com

The morality quiz you passed around on paper in high school has gone high-tech, with surprisingly amusing results. It's simply a matter of answering yes or no to a list of questions about past experiences. You can even save your answers and finish later. Questions escalate quickly from holding hands to more explicit thoughts and actions and while the results may not be scientific, they're indisputably entertaining.

Split-Up.com www.split-up.com

Divorce, like breaking up, is hard to do. But with the help of Split-Up.com, it doesn't have to be a nightmare. All sorts of financial calculation software is featured and for sale, but casual visitors may be more interested in features contained in categories like Law, Lifestyle, and Finance. You can even get information specific to your state of residence. What's more, future divorcés can consult the directory of professionals to find more personalized, experienced help in smoothing the split-up process.

Cherrybomb.com www.cherrybomb.com

Girls want to have more than just fun and nobody knows this better than the ladies at Cherrybomb.com. An all-woman staff makes this one of the best of the rare breed that is women-oriented erotica sites. Light on text and heavy on streaming audio and video, users must have the latest media gear to fully enjoy Cherrybomb's live webcasts, interactive shows, advice, and erotic bedtime stories.

KingLove www.kinglove.com

Sauce for vanilla sex lives comes in the form of KingLove, an e-tailer that wraps a clean-cut design around its fur massage gloves, naughty party games, edible finger paint, and other erotica. While you're window-shopping, see the Entertainment area for columns on the dating ritual or the FAQ for such helpful gems as "The largest reason for returns of battery operated products is that the batteries are not in correctly."

weddings

The Knot www.theknot.com

A wedding hub with advice and products for every aspect of your nuptials from "Will you ... ?" to "I do." Choose a gown, pick a ring, register for goodies—then, once you've covered the basics, find a DJ, feather your love nest, and decide on your cake topper. For the finishing touch, don't leave without visiting the Knot Shop for accessories that are both serious (ring pillows) and lighthearted (church-shaped bubbles).

The Nearly-Wed Handbook www.nearlywed.com

The definitive guide on "How to Survive the Happiest Day of Your Life," the Nearly-Wed Handbook takes a refreshingly funny look at the difference between getting married and putting on a wedding. This practical, no-holds-barred site for wedding planning provides useful information on finding the right photographer, dress, caterer, and registry, with a wry sense of humor.

ModernBride.com www.modernbride.com

The name speaks for itself. ModernBride.com incorporates everything the print magazine offers with the convenience of the Web, providing online registries, honeymoon hot spots, fashion tips, and general advice on how to make this much-anticipated day go smoothly. See the Wedding Planning section for an interactive calendar, a groom's checklist, and online tools that address easily-forgotten details.

Della Weddings www.dellaweddings.com

From the basic truth that 12 toasters is 11 too many came the wedding registry. Della Weddings offers a cool way to bring all of your registries together in one online interface. Register on the site (or in any of the separate brick-and-mortar stores) for gifts from Dillard's, Crate & Barrel, REI, and 35 others. Della Weddings will send email to your guests to let them know how to purchase the items online.

theweddinglist.com www.theweddinglist.com

The site where prospective newlyweds who would have registered at Tiffany's or an upscale department store go when they decide to register online. Browse the catalogue for gorgeous, top-quality housewares like a Simon Pierce vase or a silver-plated caviar server. Consultants are available during business hours to hold your hand through the entire process of registering and breaking the news to your guests.

MarryingMan.com www.marryingman.com

The bachelor party—that bacchanalian festival of pre-wedding insanity—is only one part of the nuptial process that gets the treatment at MarryingMan.com. With previously independent sites unGROOM'd and BachelorParty411 under its wing, the hub covers every aspect of being a groom from proposal to toast to honeymoon. Don't miss the Bachelor Party Guidebook, where best men can find the best bars, diversions, and—ahem—attractions in a specific city.

men

Esquire www.esquiremag.com

Kudos to Esquire for not succumbing (completely) to coverage of bulging biceps and bodacious babes; there are always plenty of intelligent reads here, on everything from Cuba to golf to the NASDAQ. Then again, there is the perennially popular Women We Love Gallery for hot pics of beauties like Gisele and Daljit Dhaliwal; go ahead and Talk Back to Esquire's editors if there's someone new you'd like to see.

Rouze.com www.rouze.com

"Unapologetically male" and proud to keep a lowbrow, Rouze.com is a basic testosterone cocktail of nude pictorials, articles on sports, finance, sex, and video games, and a shopping zone of gadgets and magazines. Simply designed, updated daily, Rouze.com should speak to men ages 21-35 going on 14.

TheMan.com www.theman.com

 Got a date? Need the perfect scenario for that first encounter? For that romantic getaway? For that "other woman?" Fill out a survey and out comes a series of possibilities: a beach picnic, a jazz club, a mountain hike, ready made for your ideal evening. Aptly named, TheMan.com has some good ideas but limits itself by self-stereotyping and coming off like a department store, linking every page to its store and making a visit seem like a call from TheSalesMan.

FHM www.fhm.com

A woman saving up "to pay for a reef mapping course in Honduras" promises to show her breasts at a certain price (Honduran geography ain't cheap)—this and other forms of goofy kink personify FHM, a British "lad" mag about sex, sex, soccer, bar jokes, and sex. It's well done, with plenty of video clips, notes on gadgets and sports, sex advice, sexy pictures of women (who are assumedly recognizable in England), and links to U.S. and French versions of the same.

Guyville.com www.guyville.com

There's the rebel who a girl dates to upset her father. Then there's Guyville.com, the boy who charms your mom and has an edge. Guyville.com is a community for guys that covers the normal "guy" categories, with QuickTime videos, an in-progress shopping area, and boards that read like sex and relationship support groups. But unlike some, this site never implies that you're a loser if you don't date a model or jump out of helicopters fortnightly.

MaximOnline.com www.maximonline.com

 Maxim, the success story of the publishing industry, has brought its babes and its really-short-story attitude to the Web. You'll find everything here that you love in the maga-zine: lots of content (mostly humorous, though the archive is skimpy), and plenty of half dressed, air-brushed starlets. Impress your friends and sign up for MaximOnline.com email, which attaches pictures of "The Girls of Maxim" or "grotesque sports injuries" to your correspondence.

Men's Fitness www.mensfitness.com

For a magazine that's all about sweat and working hard and feeling the burn and all that good stuff, they certainly didn't put too much into their Web site. It looks like the clothing racks after a sale, a few things here, a few there. But if you work at it, you can piece together the remains and find enough work-out tips to get "legendary" abs, tight glutes, and strong arms.

music

All Music Guide www.allmusic.com ©

Hands down the most comprehensive source of music info online. Go to All Music Guide when you want the low down on the latest smash hits, or need to find the answer to an obscure piece of trivia. The selection is mind-bogglingly vast: 430,000 albums, 150,000 album reviews (even out-of-print favorites), 40,000 musician bios, plus audio samples, reviews, and recommendations—all searchable in six languages.

RollingStone.com www.rollingstone.com ©

Like the magazine, RollingStone.com is intelligent and well designed, offering interactive versions of its cover stories complete with video interviews. To get all the articles, you'll have to subscribe to the print version, but the site is worth a look for artist bios and discographies, album reviews (in QuickTime video), and the browsable gallery of *Rolling Stone* magazine covers, which features rock and celebrity icons from John Lennon to Kurt Cobain—practically a visual history of music over the past three decades.

MP3now.com www.mp3now.com ©

Sure, you know how to download and play MP3s. But have you mastered the delicacies of accessing Napster on a blocked network? For an advanced MP3 education, log on to MP3now.com. For beginners, hints explain how to play, find, and record MP3s; for pros, experts elucidate which players work best; for scientists, technical explanations detail how MP3 works; for philosophers, essays discuss its legality.

Billboard Online www.billboard.com

It's all about the charts at Billboard Online: log on here to find the top albums, songs, and videos in all the mainstream genres (R&B, country, and pop). A catchall for concert updates, album releases schedules, and artist interviews, Billboard Online may take some time to sort through, but is nicely organized and easy to follow, with some unique features like This Day in Music.

Vibe Online www.vibe.com ©

Hip-hop's number one print rag for music news and album reviews holds nothing back on its Web site. The online features section covers the stars and the industry that makes, breaks, or bows down to them; check out Vibe A/V for music video clips and live interviews with the likes of Ving Rhames and De La Soul. Smart, solid writing and a strong grasp of what's happening online and off make Vibe Online a hit with readers.

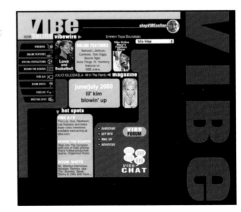

harmony-central.com www.harmonycentral.com ©

Got your licks down, but can't get a gig to save your life? harmony-central.com is teacher, agent, and rodie rolled into one, putting an exhaustive collection of online resources for drummers, bassists, and guitar players at your fingerpics, er, tips. You'll find product reviews, FAQs, links to manufacturers, and the ever-helpful job listings.

ARTISTdirect.com www.artistdirect.com

ARTISTdirect.com holds the reigns for a network of musicians' own sites, making it easy to tune in for a Cher webcast, attend a Matchbox 20 fanfest online, or buy the Beastie Boys' new release right off their own home page. Head to the UBL link (short for Ultimate Band List) for a huge index of popular MP3s. Samples of everyone from Ozzy to Eminem can be had for free and the full versions purchased directly.

MusicMatch www.musicmatch.com

Unanimously voted the best ripping (CD tracks to MP3s) software available on the Net and selected as one of the top 100 products of the year by *PC Magazine*, MusicMatch and its unique CD jukebox help users create MP3 files and organize them into playlists. A basic version is free, while a smarter, faster edition costs $30. The site also offers links to concert schedules from around the world.

All About Jazz www.allaboutjazz.com

All About Jazz is an all-volunteer site run by people with a love for jazz music. There are feature articles on famous faces, unsung heroes, and up-and-coming jazz musicians in the pages here. To search for information on specific types of jazz (like fusion or dixieland), visit the Styles page. Lighter fare includes jazz slang, and a bulletin board where musicians post their worst playing experiences, aptly titled "Gigs from Hell."

AudioFind.com www.audiofind.com ©

OK, so AudioFind.com might not be the most visually appealing site out there, but sifting through the clumsy interface does get you one of the largest master artist directories available on the Web. You can search by song title or artist to find the gems in the MP3 rough, or hit the New Files link to see recent additions. The 45 most searched terms are also available on the homepage, if your taste runs mainstream.

MP3.com www.mp3.com

How can you sum up MP3.com in one word? Try "controversial." The site's features change often, as the hot issue of digital music is still very much in flux. Regardless, this a great place for a newbie to get in on the MP3 action; the site has a Getting Started page that teaches how to download the free music files and make playlists (digital mix tapes).

CountryCool.com www.countrycool.com

E-bumpkins will flip their ten-gallon lids over CountryCool.com, an extensive site devoted to the music that made Nashville what it is. This site is packed with content: webcast coverage of the American Country Music Awards, artist interviews, and even a name-that-tune game called Fastest Ears in the West. You can also purchase CDs; RealAudio previews are available for many of the artists.

Soul Strut Online www.soulstrut.com

Get up for the down stroke and bring in the funk. Soul strut is dedicated to old school 70s funk, with little morsels of rap and soul mixed in for flavor. Check out featured artists like Dennis Coffey, Harlem Underground Band, and the Mountain Brothers, or see how 70s porno accompaniment funk fits into our musical heritage. The site is a little confusing to navigate and some of the listening links don't work, but most of the offerings funk-tion smoothly.

CDNOW www.cdnow.com

What do you get when you cross Sheryl Crow, INXS, and Brahms? CDNOW's Album Advisor takes three titles you like and suggests other music you might enjoy, making it easy to discover new favorites. The site's focus on personalized content simply blows the competition out of the water; after browsing CDNOW's sizable assortment of reviews, clips, and CDs, click on My CDNOW for a tailored start page that includes your order history, wishlist, and some more recommendations. (By the way, the answer is Jimi Hendrix.)

SecondSpin.com www.secondspin.com

CDs, videos, and DVDs may not improve with age, but their prices certainly do. SecondSpin.com, the self-proclaimed "Largest Buyer and Seller" of used music and videos in the world, has so much cheap stock, the boast just might fit. Surf here for great deals on obscure oldies, as well as picks so recently released, you won't believe they're used. To get the goods that go fast, browse the Just In Bin, which is full of items added in the last 24 hours.

Songfile.com www.songfile.com

Although not on its way to winning a Webby, Songfile.com is one of few substantial sites for serious musicians on the Web. In fact, it's the only way on the Internet to get in touch with music licensing organizations like BMI and ASCAP. The site also has links to the International Lyrics Server, companies like Fender and Steinway, and a massive sheet music search engine that can help you find and buy anything from Notorious B.I.G. to Burt Bacharach.

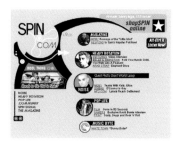

Spin.com www.spin.com

Spin's super-navigable site leaves no tune unturned. It has the latest music news and reviews, video and audio clips, and even advice on what to wear to that Cyndi Lauper concert. Also included: movie and book reviews, features from the print magazine, and an Ask Monkey column that's sure to baffle and amuse.

Farmclub.com www.farmclub.com

Mixing the best of MP3 and MTV, this site brings control of the music industry to the fans. Watch live performances of unsigned rock, pop, and garage bands and cast your vote for the best—the winners score a recording contract. The site also has resources to help aspiring musicians, legal MP3s to download, and a rapidly growing (though currently limited) music video archive.

Ink Blot www.inkblotmagazine.com

Versatility is Ink Blot's middle name. Where else are you going to find reviews of a 1946 Charlie Parker show alongside a rare Pink Floyd album pick and the scoop on Prodigy's latest? The site is geared toward mainstream listeners looking to branch out a bit, so you're likely to find bands who are in MTV rotation. One could question this choice, but we'll take the site at its fresh and uncluttered face value.

Tourdates.com www.tourdates.com

Dead-heads have been doing it for years; now the rest of us can follow the tours of our favorite bands or score tickets to local shows. This site makes it easy to see where musical groups are playing locally and across the country. It's also a place to buy a ticket, get a map to the show, or see if anyone wants to swap your seat for a spot in the pit.

LiveDaily.com www.livedaily.com

Learn who's opening for Pearl Jam on their next tour, what bands are playing at the summer country music festival, even why Napster paid for Limp Bizkit's last tour. With both articles and blurbs, general music news, and regional lists of concerts, LiveDaily.com is live music heaven. The name may be something of a misnomer (Friday's stories were still up when we checked in on a Monday), but for uncluttered concert briefs, this is a geat source.

Platform Network www.platform.net ⓓ

Load up Platform Network and slide on in; the site posits itself as the digital source for urban survival. Packed into this sleek silver interface are hip-hop album reviews (KRS-One, Ghost Face Killa), dispatches from the sports and skate scenes, style tips, and links to 27 of Platform's subsites. It's all about attitude, kids, and man does PN have it.

MTV Online www.mtv.com

I want my, I want my MTV ... online? That's right: fans of the channel will flip for the site. The news, live chat, and band information here are top-notch, but what sets the site apart from other musical wannabes are hundreds of 30-second video clips for every act from the Beastie Boys to Beth Orton. Naturally, there are glossy promos for the channel's many shows, including the Internet game show, webRIOT.

Global Music Network www.gmn.com

Global Music Network is an in-depth journal, live webcast site, and music e-tailer that spins classical, jazz, and opera for your reading pleasure. You'll be impressed with the wealth of information here—from interviews and reviews of performers to educational articles, like a page detailing the roots of jazz—and with their concert lineup, which features a new show about every other week.

Launch.com www.launch.com ⓒ ⓓ

Cleanly organized, updated daily, Launch.com is the place to go for nitty-gritty music news. Album release info, tour dates, arrests (surprisingly common), marriages, births, and deaths of anyone who's anybody in the music industry—this site knows its stuff. When informational overload sets in, chill with some MP3s, videos, or live chat. By the time you're ready for more news, it's probably been updated.

RadioSpy.com www.radiospy.com

When the Top 40 gets tired, log on to RadioSpy.com and be your own DJ. The site offers a free shareware program that allows you to broadcast your own online radio station to any point on the globe. If you'd rather listen, the site connects to hundreds of streaming audio stations and lets you know which ones play music by your preferred artists.

The New York Times on the Web www.nytimes.com   ©

Tired of those musty unread papers piling up in the corner? Then take out a free electronic subscription to the *New York Times*; it gives you access to the day's entire paper, including the Sunday edition and the Book Review. Unparalleled news reporting that's absolutely free, with a solid search feature to boot. Archived articles do cost, though.

USAToday.com www.usatoday.com

Look at America, right there on any newspaper's front page, big and messy, lots of ads, lots going on all the time. It's almost frightening. Fear not. USAToday.com takes that heaping plate of information and cuts it into bite-sized chunks. It seasons it with eternally active message boards and a host of career and shopping links, and allows you to search way back to 1994 for free.

ABCNews.com www.abcnews.go.com   ©

It's heartening to see that ABCNews.com has everything you expect (the presidential campaign, the latest headlines, live and recorded video clips) as well as things you don't (a story on kangaroos that live in trees?). Whether or not you want a personalized email from Peter Jennings is your call, but while deciding, catch up on all the news—or *20/20* and *Nightline*—by watching and reading well-crafted, well-laid-out, and thoroughly archived reports.

CNN.com www.cnn.com   ©

Yes, it's primarily a news network, but CNN.com's got a lot of entertaining programming, too. Whether it's Larry King dodging kisses and anti-Semitic comments from Marlon Brando or Elsa Klensch extolling the virtues of the catwalk, you're sure to find plenty of items to distract you from the day's issues. Naturally, the news coverage is comprehensive and current, updated every half-hour.

MSNBC www.msnbc.com   ©

Don't let the overwhelming format and quantity of information overwhelm; MSNBC combines two well-established, can't-go-wrong brand names, Microsoft and NBC, and offers breaking news and features for the rabid news junkie. Enter your zip code and all that juicy news—from sports to weather—can even be personalized.

Weather by E-mail www.weatherbyemail.com   ◎

The URL says it all: enter an email address, choose a daily time of delivery, and sit back and wait for the weather report to come to your computer (or pager, if you prefer). Visit the homepage for more extensive weather information including national weather, forecasts for the coming days, storm watches and warnings, and an ultraviolet index.

Slate www.slate.msn.com

Yet another collection of big-time journalists and editors who love talking about each other. Slate covers enough serious news to make it interesting, but it can come across like a country-club roundtable after 18 holes, cliquey and self-important. We'll withstand the posturing for Slate's terrific features—like free summaries of the nation's newspapers delivered via early morning email—and political coverage that stands up to the most revered news outlets.

Newsweek www.newsweek.com

Devotees of *Newsweek* will find all that they dream of and more on this eye-catching, online version of the dependable old-timer. The latest news and commentary on domestic affairs, international politics, arts, business, and healthcare is available for free online. The catch? There isn't one. Although Web sites certainly aren't easy subway reads.

The Nation www.thenation.org

Founded in 1865, *The Nation* is one of America's oldest political, social, and cultural commentary magazines. The lefty weekly offers clean, intelligent writing on everything from the most current trends in pop culture to long-standing debates on the values that shape the nation. Look here for columns by Katha Pollit or Christopher Hitchens.

Newcity.com www.newcity.com

The news source for "Alternative America," Newcity.com digs into its

coast-to-coast affiliate network (ostensibly outside the mainstream media) to post daily salvos for the 18 to 34 demographic. The *San Francisco Bay Guardian* on World Trade Organization protests; the *Memphis Flyer* record reviews; sex advice from numerous columnists North and South—you're never sure what you'll find or where it will come from, and that makes the site all the more interesting.

The Washington Post Online www.washingtonpost.com

The Washington Post Online is an excellent resource, no doubt about that. It's also one of those sites where the home page seems to scroll on endlessly, with four columns and six screens worth of links, ads, and article teasers. Though it's tough to find what you want to read in this pile of content, the site's obvious pluses include access to the entire content of the paper and a Google search box at the top of every page.

APBnews.com www.apbnews.com

Whether cool (live police scanners) or creepy (a child killer's video-taped confession), APBnews.com covers crime without the sensationalism rampant in the tabloid rags. The Web-based reporting outlet's wide scope spans from celebrity news to personal safety tips to missing-person reports, getting particularly cloak-and-dagger in Crime Solvers, where it tracks serial killers and lists America's most wanted.

Individual.com www.individual.com

Individual.com customizes business and tech news to your needs, with hourly updates and information on specific companies and industries. The most popular topic, ahead of both politics and technology, is WeirdNuz, which recently featured "Top 10 Puke Scenes in Movie History." Its value compared to, say, global trade issues or market tips (they offer both) is debatable, but for livening up a stolid site, it's priceless.

TIME.com www.time.com ©

The weekly news standard, *TIME* covers celebrities and their turmoil, politicians and their turmoil, and everyday folk and their turmoil. Now it's daily and interactive on the Web, with a homepage that links to its many online permutations: TIME Digital for tech and Internet articles, TIME Kids for a younger slant, and Web Features for the online-only content. Just stay put to see the print mag's standard features.

AJR NewsLink ajr.newslink.org ©

So much media for the *America Journalism Review* to cover, so little time. Those interested in reading about the fourth estate can link up to major newspapers, magazines, and television and radio news, or read AJR's coverage of said outlets. Would-be journalists can skim the lengthy job boards or read up on the methods and/or ethics (we hope) of folks already in the field. A little dry at times, but overall a superior guide to this beast we know as the media.

CNET News.com www.news.com ©

All tech news, all the time. Very intense, very focused, News.com provides the latest on developments in tech and Web culture. You can read news headlines here, but if you like, it can send you instant updates by email, cell phone, or Palm Pilot. Once sufficiently geeked, check the job boards or click back to parent-site CNET to buy any and all of the tools necessary for the digital age.

International Herald Tribune www.iht.com

With bureaus around the world, the International Herald Tribune combines its own resources with the forces of dozens of respected papers to provide only the meatiest international events. Although the barebones layout is less authoritative than the classically designed print version, the information—including international travel tips, cultural calendars, and a list of medical facilities—takes up the slack.

Weather.com www.weather.com ©

There's so much more to weather than "partly cloudy with a chance of rain." So while The Weather Channel's Web site may start with daily forecasts, it also has deeper info on natural phenomena, a stunning photo gallery, and a weather glossary. Wireless weather updates are also available (if you somehow overlooked the raindrops on your cell phone).

Alternative Press Index www.altpress.org
Radical America, Hinduism Today, Gainesville Iguana, and Disgruntled
Housewife: these have in common their inclusion in the Alternative
Press Index, a listing of (mostly) liberal political and social journals and
zines that makes other so-called "alternative" sites look like *People*
magazine. Some journals have links, some don't, but there's enough
information to track them down if you're interested. The design is
decidedly low maintenance; it'll be the words that do it.

parenting

Family.com www.family.go.com ©
Disney does it again. Family.com, one of the company's many huge info
hubs, promotes family bonding with activities that parents and kids can
enjoy together: kids' cookbooks, craft projects, and family outings.
There are also tips for parents here, like how to help children make
friends and what to do with picky eaters. Links to other Disney sites
lead kids to safe activities and games on the Web.

Parent Soup www.parentsoup.com
A one-stop parenting community with info on every aspect of raising a
child, from grade-by-grade guides, developmental milestones, and cur-
riculum norms to expert Q & A on breastfeeding, bullying, and sibling
rivalry. Check out the Tools section for neat stuff like the baby name
finder, or join a parenting community and chat on just about any topic
relating to your little bundle of joy.

Connect for Kids www.connectforkids.org ©
Touting their site as "Guidance for Grown-ups," Connect For Kids
features news and advice to help parents become more active
guardians and members of their community. Whether you're searching
for recent product safety recalls, the latest talk on teen violence, or
local volunteering opportunities, it's worth a look.

BabyZone.com www.babyzone.com
A great site for new and expecting parents, BabyZone.com features a
week-by-week pregnancy planner to prepare moms and dads for each
new turn of their first nine months, plus a baby gear shopping guide
and loads of tips on everything from birthing to breastfeeding. A special fathering section treats the oft-neglected partner to financial and
emotional tips, and fun facts about baby fat and sex during pregnancy.

BabyCenter.com www.babycenter.com Ⓢ

Whether you're considering taking the big plunge
into parenthood or already have a playpen full of lil'
nippers, BabyCenter.com can help you navigate the
exhausting—er, uplifting—road of parenthood. The
site has tips on everything from when to conceive
to disciplining toddlers to starting a college fund.
Once you've got the basics down, head to the store
for fabulous products designed to distract parents
from their nonexistent sex lives.

ParenthoodWeb.com www.parenthoodweb.com

Ever heard of co-sleeping? Neither had we. How did parents ever make it through without expert child-raising advice? ParenthoodWeb.com offers insight into pressing issues like single-parent households, nutrition, and co-sleeping (infants sleeping in parents' beds) that actually comes from M.D. and PhD experts. You'll also find help with names, gum-friendly recipes, lots of recalled products, and advice for conquering the perennially sticky issue of potty training.

Myria www.myria.com ©

Myria is an e-mag designed to help belabored mothers find the balance between managing their children's lives and their own. While the tone of the self-esteem articles smacks of Richard Simmons, advice on health, pregnancy, parenting, and relationships is insightful and applicable. A community of members is available for chat and support, as is a bunch of sponsor sites like Land's End and PlanetRX. If you find the homepage too crowded to navigate, head for the site directory.

ePregnancy www.epregnancy.com ⓞ

 The, well, motherload for those expecting. ePregnancy is ground zero for pregnancy info and community on the Web. From before conception to after birth, ePregnancy provides articles, interactive features, forums, and other enlightened resources to keep you informed and inspired for the duration. Enter your due date to get day-by-day briefs and tips from the experts, and share birth stories and journals with others eating for two (or three, or four ...).

iBaby.com www.ibaby.com ⓢ

iBaby.com's got all the equipment and baby supplies a mom could want, from strollers and car seats to bassinets and breast pumps. While you're there, be sure to check out fun and informative features like the Baby Name Finder and the New Parent Checklist, which lists all the must-have stuff for your precious one.

babystyle.com www.babystyle.com ⓓ

For little ones whose first word was "DKNY," babystyle.com's got chic clothes (maternity, too!) from designers like Zutano, Hanna Andersson, and DKNYbaby. After you've maxed out your credit card, be sure to check out such features as Cindy's Corner, where supermodel Crawford shares her thoughts on "style, stardom, and the joys of bringing up baby."

Adoption.com www.adoption.com

Resources like Adoption.com remind us how truly useful the Internet can be. Remarkably well-organized and managed, Adoption.com provides listings for prospective parents and for children who are waiting to be adopted. The site lets users walk through the adoption process to see if it's the right choice, or search international adoption listings for a child overseas. Other resources include agencies, attorneys, adoption experts, and a reunion registry.

Moms Online www.momsonline.com

Trying to get pregnant? Having trouble with the babysitter? Looking for fun projects to do with your kids? Oxygen Network's Moms Online offers particularly good advice for women who are balancing career and family demands. Click over to the Dare I Say It? section for animated chat with some very opinioned moms from across the country. Among the 40 or so running boards you'll find discussions on bad hair days, true confessions, and welfare reform.

familydoctor.org www.familydoctor.org

Sometimes a nagging health problem like asthma or bronchitis can be remedied with a few simple tips. While your doctor is the best person to dispense this advice, anyone seeking further knowledge about an ailment should stop by familydoctor.org to glance at the daily tip or delve into the extensive archives. Easy-to-read handouts and health facts are presented alongside extremely intuitive self-care flowcharts.

Parents.com www.parents.com

A product of *McCalls* magazine, Parents.com is an exceptional guide to nearly all facets of raising children. Handy advice for cooking for lil' tikes of all ages and smart stuff like the "Ultimate Bug Bite Guide" will make you glad you found this basket on your doorstep. The New Parent Survival Guide reveals the merits of breast-feeding over bottle-feeding, plus other essential info.

Onna Maternity www.onnamaternity.com

Because maternity leave doesn't start until the ninth month, Onna Maternity helps busy women shop easily and efficiently for a professional wardrobe. A stylish selection of suits, blouses, skirts, and scarves is available, as well as expert advice on fitting, styling, and accessory options. The number of pieces is small, but each is made to work well with several others. Free shipping and returns and fabric samples upon request make shopping here a smart career move.

C-SPAN.org www.cspan.org

Tune in here when you tune out there, leaving the political filibustering on C-Span TV to visit C-SPAN.org. Here, the straightforward public affairs information cuts through the mumbo-jumbo. History buffs should check out the Historical Oral Arguments section and students should hop on the C-SPAN School Bus. If you're a glutton for details, scan the Congressional Votes Library or go to the Congressional glossary to find out exactly where "filibuster" comes from.

Politics.com www.politics.com

Darth Vader in 2000! Dan Quayle for Pope! The top 62 reasons why you should vote for David Letterman for President. Okay, these might not be for real, but Politics.com has plenty of serious news, too. This is the site for keeping up with Presidential goings-on. The format is a little busy and the content is limited mainly to electoral races, but the wicked sense of humor is much appreciated.

Town Hall www.townhall.com

Yes, the Rush Room is just what you think—a page dedicated to Mr. Limbaugh, the brash warhorse of the far Right. Listen to tapes of his radio shows or participate in a discussion about his ideas. Town Hall is the place for conservative news and discussion, complete with a shrine to Reagan's legacy and a Hall of Fame featuring Russell Kirk.

PollingReport.com www.pollingreport.com

Not sure what to think about a political candidate? If other people's opinions matter to you, log on to PollingReport.com. The site is a frequently updated, nonpartisan purveyor of public opinion, with the results of polls on everything from Ralph Nader's election standings to the percentage of Americans who secretly hate Valentine's Day. But it's not all stats and facts—it also has articles on public opinion trends and answers to questions like "How Come Pollsters Never Call ME?"

Voter.com www.voter.com

Voter.com empowers the people by bringing political facts and informed debate to a wide online audience. At times self-important, the site extends its coverage beyond the presidential race, also tracking regional politics in urban areas like New York and the latest boil-overs on controversial subjects like abortion. A heavy selection of personalizable features lets you sort politicians, issues, and news to see your particular causes from a multitude of angles—once you register.

Doonesbury Electronic Town Hall www.doonesbury.com

Gary Trudeau's brilliant brainchild, *Doonesbury*, has reached the ripened age of 28, logging more than 10,000 strips—all of which are available online. One peeve: to see today's strip, the site forces you to visit a newspaper that has syndicated it, and finding *Doonesbury* amongst the local news and movie listings requires persistent digging.

Mr. Smith E-mails Washington www.mrsmith.com

Having found the only way to improve on a concept this cool, Mr. Smith has doubled his site so that it now gives access to the email addresses of high-ranking press as well as government officials. The president, the VP, journalists, and magazine editors are all included on the list, as well as every member of Congress. Easy to use and terrifically helpful, Mr. Smith deserves another standing ovation.

National Charities Information Bureau www.give.org

Sponsored by the National Charities Information Bureau, this site's Quick Reference
Guide links to more than 400 charities
organized by issue (Relief Agencies and Environmental Organizations, for example) and
alphabet. A useful symbol system shows
readers how each of the organizations fare
by NCIB's strict standards of philanthropy. A
great guide for informed giving online.

The Jefferson Project www.capweb.net/classic/jefferson

This is one of the few Web sites that profiles political personalities as well as providing information on the executive, legislative, and judicial branches of the U.S. government. There are also links to international resources, political watchdog groups, activist organizations, and political humor. Nonpartisan and informative.

The White House www.whitehouse.gov

Here's your chance to tour the First Family's mansion without having to agonize over what to wear. After snooping around the Oval Office or Lincoln Bedroom, take a look at the impressive artwork scattered throughout what Jacqueline Kennedy called "La Maison Blanche," and read about the lives of the presidents and first ladies. Of course, more serious fare is here, including the President's speeches and news briefs.

Electronic Frontier Foundation www.eff.org

Want to know the Electronic Frontier Foundation's number one
recommendation for protecting
your online privacy? Use a pseudo-
nym in your Web browser's
preferences menu to avoid inadvertently disclosing your name and
email address. The Foundation was
founded in San Francisco in 1990 to
protect fundamental civil liberties
like privacy and freedom of expression on the Internet. Stop in here for
11 more tips on protecting your privacy, and for activities and member
services.

American Civil Liberties Union www.aclu.org

The ACLU has been busy saving the world, and they want you to know it! The site is chock-full of news stories and press releases, plus frequent updates on high and low profile cases involving the ACLU. Find out how to become an ACLU member here and check out your state's rating on the National Scorecard. This is the perfect jumpstart for your own activist career.

IntellectualCapital.com www.intellectualcapital.com

Here's a fantastic weekly public policy e-zine where bipartisan commentators (the likes of Nadine Strossen and Eric Alterman) chew the fat on issues like the Mideast peace talks or trade relations with China. Editor Pete duPont (a former Delaware governor and Congressman) relishes user postings and interaction, so don't be afraid to submit scathing letters if you like; nearly all get published on the site.

Institute for Global Communications www.igc.org

PeaceNet, EcoNet, LaborNet, WomensNet, ConflictNet, AntiRacism-Net ... if there's a social ill, IGC has it covered. Frequently updated alerts on everything from public policy to protests, related news headlines, and an extensive searchable database that pulls up links from around the globe are all available for free.

Grassroots.com www.grassroots.com

A nonpartisan political action network, Grassroots.com discusses the ins and outs of hot issues like gun control and animal rights. The site stresses involvement on a local level, explaining what you can do, where to donate funds, and how to contact representatives. While the issues are heavy, the approach is low-key—the proof is in the Fun Stuff section, where you'll find a mock video of Bill washing Hillary's limo.

reference . . .. .

Britannica.com www.britannica.com ©

Any dotcom PhD can design a Web site. Britannica.com plucks the dummies from the barrel and handpicks 125,000 engaging sites—from philosophy to travel and tech news—for their superior content and design. Search their site database, browse clips from the latest encyclopedia, or flip through selected features from *Discover,* the *Washington Post* or *The Economist*. Either way, you'll feel wiser for it.

Electric Library www.elibrary.com

Elibrary offers a remarkable collection of searchable resources for media-based research. Among the titles it searches are *USA Today,* the *L.A. Times, Fortune, Sports Illustrated*, and sessions of NPR's *All Things Considered*. You can even keep track of articles published after your search by signing up for the email update service, eLibrary Tracker. A 30-day free trial gets you access; $60 a year lets you keep it.

Internet Public Library www.ipl.org/ref

In keeping with the spirit of good public libraries, IPL's research collection is vast, its organization fluid, and its cost nothing. Check out the Ready Reference Collection for an overview of major subdivisions, or use IPL's Pathfinders—"home grown guides to get you started." A must-surf for teens doing research projects, the site includes a primer on researching and writing papers for the high school and college level.

The Argus Clearinghouse www.clearinghouse.net

Most Web research sites measure their value in quantity of results. At Argus, exclusivity is a virtue. Billed as a "selective collection of topical guides," Argus is one of the few research sites with truly discriminating taste, rating each of its selections based on design, organization, and the quality of its sources. And it's free.

Merriam-Webster OnLine www.m-w.com

THE HOT SITE
Merriam-Webster ®
FOR COOL WORDS

This isn't your parents' dictionary: Merriam-Webster OnLine has all the information in the old standby, plus a search engine, a thesaurus, and loads of great features. Dictionary and thesaurus search queries work even when you misspell a word, providing a list of close words. In addition to these standards, M-W's Word a Day feature includes example sentences and etymological explanations.

A Web of On-Line Dictionaries www.yourdictionary.com ©

Bucknell University's amazing site links to dictionaries for more than 220 different languages, from Hebrew to Eskimo to Klingon. It also connects to specialized dictionaries, grammar guides, and thesauri perusable by academics and laypeople alike. Log on to find the Czech word for computer (*pocitac*), or brush up on French or Esperanto.

Alta Vista Live!: Translation babelfish.altavista.digital.com ⓞ

For anyone who ever read the *Hitchhiker's Guide to the Galaxy*, Alta Vista's translation service is as close as modern technology has gotten to creating Babelfish. Type in a word, a phrase, or even a sentence and in a matter of seconds view your personal translation. You can even translate entire Web sites into English, French, German, Spanish, Portuguese, or Italian—just type in the URL. *C'est magnifique*!

The English Server www.eserver.org ©

With more than 20,000 files (including audio and video recordings) on every imaginable topic from Marxist theory to psycho-acoustics, The English Server is a remarkable research source. Created and maintained by the English department at Carnegie Mellon University, the site is a member-run cooperative and offers an interactive community for scholars or anyone interested in the humanities.

How Stuff Works www.howstuffworks.com

How Stuff Works is paradise for the nerd in all of us, perfect for those who wonder how their remote control functions or how it is that jet airplanes don't just fall out of the sky. Ask a question, browse the list of questions (such as: "How DO Pop Rocks candy work?"), or search by topic for the mysteries of everyday object science revealed.

HyperHistory Online www.hyperhistory.com

Only on the Web could the history of the world, with all its dates, facts, figures, and events, manageably unfold in one panoramic chart. Search by name (keyword), event, or map to access 1,400 files spanning the past 3,000 years of civilization. Amazingly easy to navigate considering the massive amount of information—go straight to the HyperHistory Online link on the homepage to begin.

Library of Congress www.loc.gov

Believe it or not, the Library of Congress started out as Thomas Jefferson's personal book collection. These days it's a bit bigger, offering more than 500 miles of shelved material. The Library's Web site features descriptions of special collections, access to films, interviews, and historical documents, and provides lots of information on copyrights. Oh, yeah—it's a great resource for congressional materials, too.

Infoplease.com www.infoplease.com

Did you know that more people speak Javanese than French? That

Denmark is the least corrupt country in the world? That Dr. Seuss originated the word nerd? Information Please is good for quick statistic retrieval, but it's also worth wandering around its almanac, dictionary, and news for interesting trivia bits. What it lacks in absolute comprehensiveness it makes up in currency.

Encarta Learning Zone www.encarta.msn.com

Microsoft's comprehensive and meticulously organized encyclopedia is the student's best friend. MSN offers two freebie samplers: an abridged Encyclopedia, with Cliff's Notes-like summaries on everything from existentialism to the history of the Muppets, and the seven-day free trial to the Deluxe Edition, which is where the site's elaborately cross-referenced organization really shows its stuff.

Researchpaper.com www.researchpaper.com

While this site may look like it's just for students, Researchpaper.com is great for anyone who needs their brain jogged. The Idea Directory offers fresh angles on possible paper topics (such as how inflation has affected the arts) as well as the standard issues discussed in the humanities. Links to both Elibrary (a subscription-based service) and Net Info (a free one) accompany each question.

U.S. Census Bureau www.census.gov

America's population monitors do much more than just count people. Their online repository of statistics is invaluable for anyone seeking facts on demographics, business, economy, and geography. Site navigation can be tricky, so for specific statistics, consider multiple search queries or the drop-down state menu.

Maps.com www.maps.com

Was I supposed to make a right at Santa Fe? Or was that a left at Albuquerque? Maps.com has some remarkably innovative maps, globes, and atlases. Buy a traveler's map that shows the best hiking spots in the Rockies; download a high-quality digital map for your Web site; or pick up a laminated road map. Maps.com will even customize a map to suit your needs if you're willing to foot the bill.

eHow www.ehow.com

Want to camouflage a hickey or a tattoo? eHow suggests using two different shades of concealer. This is just one of the topics in this massive and often giggle-inducing site, which explains stuff like how to change the oil in your car, how to get over a breakup, or where to find a job. Search by keyword for a specific project, or browse through their more than 20 centers for inspiration.

Refdesk.com www.refdesk.com

From the father of the founder of the Drudge Report comes a singular destination for facts available online. Refdesk.com rounds up hundreds of brand name links from sources like *Roget's Thesaurus*, *Britannica*, the *New York Times*, and Yahoo!. We counted nine different dictionaries on the home page alone. The only snag is the cluttered layout—use the Facts Search Desk or head right for the Index to get started.

Poets.org www.poets.org

You know that poem about the roads that diverged? In the woods? No more fumbling for a name and author. The Academy of American Poets Web site has a search engine that allows you to look for poems by keyword. Plug in "roads diverged" to find "The Road Not Taken" by Robert Frost, or check out the poetry exhibits for special essays, poems, photos, and RealAudio samples.

World Book Online www.worldbookonline.com

$50 a year awards you access to pre-revolutionary France, insects of the world, Beethoven's biography, and everything else covered within the Web pages of World Book Online. When you subscribe to the electronic edition, you get all the articles from the recent print volumes, plus links to thousands of additional articles, periodicals, photos, and animations. A month pass costs $10, and the 30-day trial is free.

E-Conflict World Encyclopedia www.emulateme.com ©

What color is the Japanese flag? (Red) What's the capital of Afghanistan? (Kabul) How well can you dredge up your seventh grade geography lesson? The E-Conflict World Encyclopedia is a compendium of information on every country on the globe. Though the information doesn't go as deep for each listing as we'd like, you can't beat the breadth.

TimeTicker www.timeticker.com ⓓ

Though it may sound like a ticking time bomb, TimeTicker is elegance in motion. Move your cursor across time zones or choose a country from the scroll-down list to get the real time in any area of the globe. Then, hit the Set Computer Time to synchronize your system clock to the global time based in Greenwich. Note: the site is only compatible with PCs, or Macs running Netscape.

Bartleby.com www.bartleby.com

Who said "Knowledge is power"? Bartleby.com can tell you it was Francis Bacon in no time. This site makes classic fiction, nonfiction, poetry, and reference works available for the English major in all of us. More than 20 famous authors are represented, including Shakespeare, Woolf, Whitman, and Agatha Christie, as well as timeless tomes like *Bartlett's Familiar Quotations* and Strunk's *Elements of Style*.

farmersalmanac.com www.farmersalmanac.com

Like The Weather Channel and the Psychic Friends Network rolled into one, farmersalmanac.com contains a mish-mash of weather reports, gardening tips, and livestock rearing information. As you might guess, their focus is on fields and crops, but many details are adaptable to the small-scale gardener (what day is best to plant your leafy vegetables, when to mow the lawn).

Oxford English Dictionary www.oed.com

The Oxford English Dictionary has long been the ultimate authority on the history and development of the English language. Scholars and laymen alike will find the online version similarly useful and simple to use; anyone who's seen the miniscule font in the print edition will appreciate the easy-on-the-eyes typeface here. A subscription is not cheap, however—an individual license costs $550 per year.

AskMe.com www.askme.com

A custom answer from a real person to just about any question you might dream up. Browse the extensive list of categories, choose an expert from a selection of bios, and fire your query at him or her. You'll receive a quick answer in your inbox, or on the site if you choose to remain anonymous. Of course, you don't always have to ask to get an answer—thousands of past questions are easily accessible already.

HistoryChannel.com www.historychannel.com © ⓓ

Hindsight is 20/20, and nowhere is this more obvious than at HistoryChannel.com. You can surf your way through a growing bank of download-able speeches (like Lou Gehrig's farewell to base-ball), learn the history of a famous object (like the lantern from Paul Revere's famous midnight ride), or follow one of the site's

museum-style theme exhibits. The site can also tell you what historical events took place on any given day—a fun function to try with your birthday.

religion

Digital Theologian theos.webprovider.com

Amassing content from publications like Catholic World News, Salon.com, and Philosopher's Web, Digital Theologian presents a straightforward way to stay on top of worldwide religious news. Articles run the gamut of topics from Holocaust studies to a Methodist panel on gay marriage to the Catholic stance on Vietnam. The editor also chooses a surf-worthy selection of religious Web sites each month to round out this well constructed and growing resource.

Beliefnet www.beliefnet.com

Multi-faith and independent, Beliefnet covers the basics of 20 different religions and then branches out to topics like the importance of bowing Buddhism and Hindu wedding traditions. Members are encouraged to join in the online community, which includes both discussion boards and prayer circles.

Hindu Universe www.hindunet.org ©

A busy, tightly knit portal site about Hinduism and India, Hindu Universe creates a community through thousands of news and resource links. A favorite category is God, Sages & Gurus, which teaches the many avatars (or forms) Lord Vishnu may take. Also packed in here is news of India, explanations of Hindu traditions and festivals, online stores, classifieds, a glossary, and even a list of baby names.

OU.ORG www.ou.org ©

Want to discover your Jewish IQ? Take one of the Orthodox Union's dozen online quizzes and see how you do. Do you know what the Jewish Supreme Court was called? Or when to light Chanukah candles? How about which direction to kindle the flames? All of the answers to these questions and more can be found on the site, so if you don't know, you can certainly learn the answers here. *Behatzlacha*!

Internet Sacred Text Archive www.sacred-texts.com

Almost entirely graphics-free, the Internet Sacred Text Archive is an enormous collection of sacred texts both religious and mythological, eastern and western, traditional and modern. From the *Tao Te Ching* to Darwin's *Origin of Species*, the site provides the primary texts in English, and in some cases the original language as well.

Gospel Communications Network www.gospelcom.net

The widest online gateway to Christian Web sites, the Gospel Communications Network links to pages on every facet of the faith. Prayers, counseling, guidance, and mission news are among the more prominent features. The Bible Gateway is especially useful, a foot-noted, cross-referenced, and easily searchable Bible in nine languages. But while the site amply addresses Christianity's serious side, the selection isn't bland—there are various bits of sheer entertainment mixed in, such as movie reviews and the daily cartoon.

The Holy See www.vatican.va

As graphically refined as they come, The Holy See is chock full of news and wisdom from the center of Roman Catholicism. Read, listen, or watch the pope deliver speeches in five languages; search the letters, constitutions, and exhortations of the last four popes; or browse infor-mation about the Vatican libraries and museums. The Holy See also offers explanations of the church's hierarchy and offices.

The Secular Web www.infidels.org

The largest and most heavily visited atheist site on the Web, The Secular Web attempts to provide a community for users interested in the existence of a god, science and philosophy of religion, and a number of other religion-related issues. The library contains more than 6,000 expert documents on various aspects of nontheistic and theistic philosophies, and it features a monthly Web scan that scours the Internet to expose erroneous religious claims and schemes.

tricycle.com www.tricycle.com

This online version of the well-known nonprofit Buddhist quarterly is, like many online magazines, sparse in content, saving the full-text articles for the paper version. But tricycle.com makes up for this with other features: meditation how-tos, an extensive history and explanation on the ABCs of the faith, a regional source directory, and even a personals section where Buddhists can meet and become one.

IslamiCity www.islam.org

IslamiCity is a vast collection of Internet resources for the worldwide Muslim community, with news from and about Islamic nations, radio and TV broadcasts in a number of languages, and cultural and eco-nomic information. The site also includes a large section on the religion's tenets and activities, prayers and prayer times, and a search-able Qu'ran.

Jewish Community Online www.jewish.com
Jewish Community Online provides followers of Judaism with a convenient way to keep up on the details of their faith. The Introduction to Judaism section lists important holidays and explains the history behind them, while Ask a Rabbi holds a bank of 4,050 past questions on complex issues like kosher foods, Bat Mitzvahs, God, and interfaith relationships. A personals section is also provided to help "warm, spirited Orthodox" Jews meet their "independent, humorous" mates.

science & nature

nationalgeographic.com www.nationalgeographic.com

 The classic magazine has filled its online version with a slew of interactive stories more vivid than the print version; you'll find that reading about Chinese Dragons, Timbuktu, or a Congo trek is a truly immersive experience. Don't leave without visiting the photography gallery, which features breathtaking images in signature *National Geographic* style.

Discovery.com www.discovery.com
Inquiring minds have a friend in Discovery.com, which allows surfers to take live peeks at a pair of newborn gorillas or check in with explorers hiking all over Antarctica. This is an excellent site for getting kids interested in science or for fueling your own curiosity; it's got stories on both cutting-edge technologies and ancient civilizations, plus a dazzling array of photographs that are a feast for the eyes.

explorezone.com www.explorezone.com

 What do genetic warfare and flying trains have in common? They both make headline news at explorezone.com. While the drab homepage of this science magazine will leave non-scientists cold, users who dig deeper will find a wealth of exciting information on everything from microscopic bacteria to sun spots. Amateur scientists and junior Einsteins will appreciate the short, clear explorezone.com articles.

The Exploratorium www.exploratorium.edu
The celebrated museum of "science, art, and human perception" nestled in San Francisco's Palace of Fine Art stretches out online with an impressive collection of exhibits, games, and webcasts whose archives include solar eclipses and the science of skateboarding in RealVideo. Stare at the dot on a Web page and it disappears. Why? You'll learn this and more science-related stuff as you explore.

popsci.com www.popsci.com

Some scientists predict that every one of our kitchen appliances will soon be Web-enabled, but until you can browse from your toaster, keep a window on your PC pointed here. You'll get articles from *Popular Science* and a great selection of stuff that's not in the print mag, like an interactive map of the earth, the annual list of the 50 best science and tech sites, and the Q & A forum. The place to go to be in the know about serious (and not so serious) science breakthroughs.

NASA Human Spaceflight
www.spaceflight.nasa.gov

If launch videos and pre-flight images don't impress you, the NASA virtual tour of the International Space Station will blow you away. Electronic still imagery is now available, so be sure to check out the Gallery for links to videos, imagery, and audio clips from STS-101 and Mars. Real-time stats keep you up to date on current missions, and their Astronaut 101 pages won't disappoint.

Scientific American www.sciam.com

Scientific American will keep you abreast of all happenings on the frontier of the mind with sophisticated but readable features on physics, mathematics, astronomy, computing, and even philosophy. Ask their experts, "What's the origin of zero?" or any other question you're losing sleep over. Colorful articles and images allow you to be a part of the next superconductor breakthrough—or just enhance your knowledge.

The Natural History Museum www.nhm.ac.uk

The interactive floor plan and a panoramic view of the gallery take visitors through dozens of earth and life exhibits that showcase 78 million specimens in Britain's 250-year-old Natural History Museum. In the Life Galleries, you'll find yourself face-to-face with the Diplodocus skeleton, with other intrigues like 3D virtual fossils, simulated solar eclipses, and ancient teapots turning up as you go.

PBS Science & Technology www.pbs.org/science

Home of such long-running series as *NOVA*, *Newton's Apple,* and *Stephen Hawking's Universe,* PBS is the educational source for the natural and physical sciences. PBS Science's archives feature articles from the channel's family of programs and Web sites, touching on archaeology, digitechnology, and science mysteries. The beautiful graphics and engaging full-text stories like "Curse of T. Rex," and "Ice Mummies of the Inca" are reason enough to visit.

The Tech Museum of Innovation www.thetech.org

The Tech Museum's virtual presence is as instructional and hands-on as its physical counterpart in the heart of Silicon Valley. Build a satellite, pet a robotic rhino, get an up-close look at DNA, or simply browse articles detailing the technological innovations that got you online in the first place.

Zoological Society of San Diego www.sandiegozoo.org

Meet the world-famous zoo's new babies, take a cybertour of recently opened exhibits, or guess which footprints go with which animal. The San Diego Zoo Web site hosts news, information, and games about the zoo and wildlife park as well as its related research facilities for endangered species. With beautiful photos illustrating its virtual exhibits, the site is almost as vibrant as the zoo itself.

Monterey Bay Aquarium E-Quarium www.mbayaq.org

Sea otters, abalones, and crabs, oh my! The E-quarium offers a peek into its "Mysteries of the Deep," the world's largest living exhibit of deep-sea animals. Viewers make their way through the Monterey Canyon by clicking on images of the different flora and fauna and reading descriptions of how they live. Younger kids will like the E-quarium Kids' Guides, which include explorable habitats and printable coloring pages.

The Last Word www.last-word.com

For anyone who's ever wondered why penguins' feet don't freeze or when the next ice age will hit, there's The Last Word. This simple compilation of reader questions from *New Scientist* magazine offers answers to everyday science questions from actual scientists, physicians, and engineers around the world. Though written by experts, the responses are still comprehensible enough to the kitchen chemist.

SPACE.com www.space.com ⓒ ⓓ

Battle androids, take a tour of Mars, or kick back and peruse the latest science and astronomy-related news. Brainchild of media icon Lou Dobbs, SPACE.com is dedicated to the popularization of space and offers a fresh approach to a once-neglected topic. The site is updated daily with news, educational links, and games, making it an ideal go-to for curious kids of all ages.

seniors

ThirdAge.com www.thirdage.com ⓒ

An all-around community for active seniors, ThirdAge.com covers work, technology, family, and romance for those in their "third age of life." Features include "Beautiful at 50+," "The Summer 'Do: Long and Lovely," and "Looking for Love." Chat, communities, forums, and free homepages for users round out a vibrant community experience.

SeniorResource.com www.seniorresource.com

SeniorResource.com is a simple, information-oriented site that gives the elderly a hand in managing big life issues like housing options, finances, and estate planning. The site explains options in easy-to-understand language and offers links to online resources. There are no graphics or chats or fancy features here—just straight-up information on issues that matter.

SeniorNet www.seniornet.org

The greatest generation is speaking all right, to each other at SeniorNet. No smart-aleck dotcom kids here—just a diverse group of adults aged 50 and up tuning in to the Internet experience. SeniorNet features excellent computer education resources, a Scams and Fraud Center for safe surfing, and a virtual art gallery (for visiting or contributing). There are literally hundreds of discussions to jump into, on topics ranging from World War II to computer shopping.

HealthandAge.com www.healthandage.com

HealthandAge.com is an easily navigable gateway to senior health information. The Health Center has separate sections for a variety of later-life ailments, like Alzheimer's and impaired mobility, and a risk assessment tool to see if you're a candidate for any of them. Other community-oriented sections include the Senior Meeting Place discussion forum, Learning message boards, and a special portion devoted to caregivers.

American Association of Retired Persons www.aarp.org

The AARP site is partly an advertisement for the services provided by the association, including travel discounts and special insurance rates. But the site also offers info that other senior sites neglect, like legislative coverage and advice for older drivers. With content from its *Modern Maturity* magazine on life transitions, leisure, and health, AARP is a great resource for retired folks.

iGrandparents www.igrandparents.com

Recognizing the important role grandparents can play in children's growth, this seniors' hub aims to arm its members with new activities and answers each week. The site focuses on fun projects and places to go with the grandchildren, but doesn't neglect to tackle some of the harder issues like grandparent rights and values. The many message boards and chat forums keep a community feel throughout—registering will get you access to both.

The Alzheimer's Association www.alz.org

This sleek and useful site by the Alzheimer's Association covers the disease that affects more than four million Americans and their families. Learn about the causes and symptoms and explore treatment options here. Also, a special caregiver section helps the families of Alzheimer's patients find the care and support they need.

shopping

Amazon.com www.amazon.com ⓢ

Remember when Amazon.com was just a cool online bookseller? Now the gargantuan e-tailer has added music, DVDs, electronics, toys, software, auctions, and zShops to its staggering product line. We still love classic features like "Customers who bought this book also bought …," but there are some noteworthy innovations, like easy one-click shopping. Will Amazon.com lose its focus by trying to be everything to everyone? The jury's still out.

Wal-Mart.com www.walmart.com

Exactly what you'd expect from Wal-Mart.com. There are very few fancy graphics here, just tons of merchandise and some unusually helpful services—including realtors, a tire and lube locator service, and online photo developing. Even online, it's hard to imagine where they'll put it all.

macys.com www.macys.com

New York shoppers know it as the real miracle on 34th Street, but now everyone can access Macy's online. Where else can you find Movado watches, Calvin Klein khakis, DKNY jeans, and Borghese exfoliant all in one place? You can also take advantage of the online Perfect Gift for your next birthday or baby shower, or purchase a gift certificate. You'll have a full 60 days to return items by mail or to drop them by a brick-and-mortar store (should you enjoy battling the crowds).

dealnews.com www.dealnews.com ©

Want the latest in DVD, but don't know where to begin? dealnews.com does the work for you by scouring the Web for the best deals on high tech gadgetry, ranging from DVDs to the latest crazes for Macs and PCs. But the site isn't devoted to geek gear alone. Shopping and surfing tips can assist even the least tech-savvy among us, and simple links on the Top Reader Picks show you the latest bargains on clothes, travel, and even pet food.

dealnews.com™
When you care enough to spend the very least.

target.com www.target.com ⓓ ⓢ

Who ever said Target wasn't cool? The brand has had a makeover and it shows on their site, which sports a hip design and amazing product shots that rival the high-end department stores. Shop here for everything you usually shop here for: clothes, music, school supplies, housewares—you name it. The Web Clearance links in each section spell out exactly which items have been discounted for Net shoppers.

coolshopping.com www.coolshopping.com ⓓ

If finding cool shopping sites seems like searching for a needle in a haystack, consider coolshopping.com your metal detector. This site handpicks the best shopping sites across the board and breaks them into categories for easy browsing. Check out the What's New to see what they've just added, or hit the Site of the Day link for a random gem. The reviewers' tastes may not always match yours, but skim the reviewer bios anyway—you might find a kindred soul.

Sears.com www.sears.com

Sears deserves praise for putting together a Web site that's sleek, understated, and easy to surf, which is just what you'd want from a store of this magnitude. Not only is there plenty of well-priced merchandise for your home, car, yard, and wardrobe, there are also pages and pages of advice on doing all sorts of odd jobs. When worse comes to worst, hapless do-it-yourselfers can even call upon the repair specialists here.

Value America www.valueamerica.com

Instead of stocking a warehouse with electronics, computers, and appliances, Value America works through specific suppliers who take the orders and ship them directly. Translation: the same stuff found at slicker, specialty dealers but without the 800% mark-up. When you click on a product, Value America creates a chart showing models, prices, backorder status, and links to more detailed information. But wait, there's more: free shipping when you order right on the site.

Buyer's Index www.buyersindex.com

With more than 153 million products listed in its database, Buyer's Index can almost certainly find what you're looking for, be it Elvis memorabilia or a silk bathrobe. This is one of the most accurate shopping search engines we've found. Items are sorted by product, category, and brand; the more specific the keywords you enter, the better your search results will be.

CatalogCity.com www.catalogcity.com

Shop online from thousands of catalogs, ranging from the familiar (Neiman Marcus, Lane Bryant) to the obscure (Acme Lite Laser Pointers, ADD-IT Fertilizer Injectors). Or have one of 13,000 print catalogs delivered to your home. The simple search page here offers a good range of options, and the sheer volume of products is mind-boggling.

AltaVista: Shopping www.shopping.com

As overwhelming as waking up in a mall in the middle of the night, this site is what happens when a search engine (in this case AltaVista) takes on e-commerce. While the homepage can feel unfocused, the site does manage to cover just about every type of product sold online, with price comparisons handy at each turn. You may even want to try your hand at the rewards progam it pushes so persistently— even reading the articles wins you points to spend.

OnlineChoice.com www.onlinechoice.com

Stick it to the people who make you hate getting the mail.
OnlineChoice.com pools buyers and negotiates better rates for gas,
electricity, home security, and telephone service. Though you're under no obligation to use the services that submit quotes through the site, you may be hard pressed to refuse— 20% off natural gas and phone calls for less than five cents a minute are standards here.

BlueLight.com www.bluelight.com

Forget the flashing blue lights, the Rosie O'Donnell cameos, the "Attention Kmart shoppers." The best way to take advantage of Kmart's low prices is through its airy, new e-store. Toasters for $20, CDs for $12, and Martha's cheap yet chic line of linens can all be easily located, though no clothing is for sale online. BlueLight Rewards members get further savings, a speedy checkout option, and free shipping specials—become one by registering your billing information.

iGive.com www.igive.com

When shopping online you could: (a) spend shamelessly and feel guilty, or (b) spend shamelessly at iGive.com and feel virtuous. The first "online charity shopping mall" gives you the chance to indulge in your material ways guilt-free; as much as 33% of your purchase goes toward the charity of your choice. A great selection of products and charities makes this an excellent service all around.

Kozmo.com www.kozmo.com

Videos, CDs, books, beverages, and free cookies with every order make Kozmo.com the site to surf when you need something brought right to your doorstep. Enter a zip code to find out what stock the site's bike messengers can get for you—so far, only residents of 10 metro areas (like New York and Chicago) can get anything at all. Prices are comparable to Amazon.com, delivery takes less than an hour, and videos and games can be rented as well as bought.

Half.com www.half.com ©

Have you heard that Half.com persuaded the town of Halfway, Oregon to tack a ".com" onto its name? We understand their enthusiasm, having seen just how cheaply the site prices its music, books, and movies. Items listed are both used and new; used items are labeled "like new" or "good" and priced accordingly. $18 CDs for $5, $20 books for $2— while an ever-changing stock makes finding specific titles hit or miss, the prices more than compensate.

inshop.com www.inshop.com

It's like your own personal shopper, but better: 24 hours a day, 7 days a week, inshop.com is on call to keep you posted on the sales at your favorite stores and spas, from Barney's to Bloomies. Loads of great deals await—just select a city and the product, designer, or store you want; inshop.com gives you the lowdown on where and when to buy at discounts of up to 50%.

Harrods Online www.harrods.com

Recreating a time when people dressed up to go shopping, this site gives a taste of the famous Harrods ambiance with muted colors, moving images, and virtual tours of the store's antique and luxury items, clothes, and gifts. Customer service is similarly exemplary, with a toll-free help line always open. The only hitch worth noting is the sheer number of clicks it takes to get to individual products.

Overstock.com www.overstock.com

Let the bargain hunter beware: you may find yourself overstocking on everything from fax machines to fishing rods at this discount warehouse. Not the most sophisticated or interactive site, but with price cuts up to 70%, a decent return policy, and new items added every day, true bargain hunters will be more than happy to fend for themselves.

Volumebuy.com www.volumebuy.com

The bigger the group, the sweeter the deal: Volumebuy.com pools people according to the item or service they all want and then negotiates a group discount for them. The final price drop depends on the number of people who want it, how common the item is, and the amount of time a pool has been open. While it's best for travel and vacation services, computer products are the most popular pool. If you have trouble, an extensive help desk can answer any questions that arise.

Global Mart www.globe-mart.com

Consumers with foresight will appreciate the varied selection at Global Mart: where else can a parent buy an electric guitar for Janey's 16th birthday and a power saw as insurance against midnight jam sessions? In addition to the computers, camcorders, and kitchen appliances available at every electronics site, you'll find such diverse items as portable solar panels and high-powered metal detectors here.

ShoppingList.com
www.shoppinglist.com ©

If you love the convenience of online comparison shopping but aren't ready to start buying products via the Web, consider ShoppingList.com. Punch in your city or zip code and the site brings up a list of major stores in your area, including the departments and products within each. Compare brands and find deals on your favorite items without even hopping in the car.

Hagglers.com www.hagglers.com (d)

This site relies on the truism that some people like finding bargain prices and others like paying them. Members of Hagglers.com can post about products they need or point out deals they've seen on products that other members want. The deal listings are then rated by the members, and the best deals earn the poster "hagglers points" that can be exchanged for cash. A good option for shoppers who like to take time to hunt down good deals; bad for a quick shopping experience.

getCustom.com www.getcustom.com (d) (o)

Word on the street is that customizable products are the next big thing in the chameleon world of e-commerce. getCustom.com is ready for the craze, offering sportswear, clothing, and gifts that can be "configured" to a certain look. Pick the trim color of a pair of shoes or the length and fabric of a tie, and then save your creations in your own product catalog. Despite the tailoring, products are reasonably priced and returnable.

Wish-List.com www.wishlist.com

Not another pack of Daffy Duck trouser socks!? Wish-List.com spares recipients the grief of a bad gift by letting givers know exactly what is wanted. Once registered, the wisher has only to browse around—any product on any Web site is fair game. There is even a carry-along Wish-List that loads in another window and lets the user drag and drop potential presents directly. Givers can see the list and link through to buy the exact items online.

Netmarket.com www.netmarket.com

Blackbelt shoppers love the thrill of the chase, but regular people just want great prices, fast. Enter Netmarket.com, a supersite for electronics, clothes, books, etc. that guarantees its members the lowest prices on 800,000 products. You'll have to shell out a $70 annual membership fee, but if you find the product for less somewhere else, Netmarket.com will pay you the difference plus 35%. Guests have limited access to the deals here, so go ahead and browse before you join.

auctions & classifieds

eBay www.ebay.com © Ⓢ

Hold on to your wallet. Aside from the usual barrage of collectibles,
eBay lets you bid on Ginsu knives, secret lasagna recipes, power drills,
and even—get this—a new best friend. You must see it to believe it. Not
sure how auctions work? There's a thorough how-to section here
that'll start you off right. eBay even offers insurance (up to $200) on
items for sale, but we're not sure whether the policy will cover you if
that new best friend ditches you.

Excite Classifieds classifieds.excite.com

You can find anything from a car to a house to a roommate to a spouse
here. You can also place ads or create a hot list of other interesting ads
to consult after you've surfed. If you tell its Cool Notify feature what
you're looking for, it will email you when the item appears in the
classifieds. A great way to locate bargains, the love of your life, or both.

Bidder's Edge www.biddersedge.com

A fabulous auction metasearch site that
allows you to monitor many auctions at the
same time. It will find even the most obscure
item, quote market prices for it, and alert
you when it hits the auction block on any of
the 100 sites it tracks. There are more than 6
million items up for sale, so there's sure to be
something you think you desperately need—
that signed poster of Britney Spears,
perhaps?

i-Escrow www.iescrow.com

Online auctions have brought about a whole new way of doing business. Now folks are willing to plunk down money for items sight unseen
to merchants they'll never meet. If you're hesitant to do business this
way, then head to i-Escrow. The site provides a neutral place for buyers
and sellers to send money and merchandise; when both parties agree
that their demands have been fulfilled, i-Escrow sends on the goods.
There's a small fee involved, but it may be worth the peace of mind.

AuctionWatch.com www.auctionwatch.com ©

If you want a deal on Leo's autographed T-shirt, AuctionWatch.com
will find the best site to place your bid. The super user-friendly site
tracks several auctions simultaneously, letting you view the highest bids
and closing dates. Unique features like Auction Manager help you
manage, launch, and track all your dealings. And, for a fee, the site's
appraisers will evaluate your items to be auctioned.

clothing & accessories

Bluefly.com www.bluefly.com © ⑤

Everyone's buzzing about Bluefly.com these days, and for once, the hype is deserved. Three reasons why you must visit: top designers (Cynthia Rowley, Prada, and Calvin Klein), deep discounts (50% off on a Daryl K dress), and a 90-day return policy. Click on Flypaper for the latest news from the fashion world, or poke through their housewares if you have a small space to deck out.

jcrew.com www.jcrew.com ⓓ
Think about it: Who doesn't have a JCrew sweater tucked somewhere in their closet? The store-cum-catalog of cool and classy basics is online (of course) and totally simple to use. Why bother with the Web? Incentives include frequent 50% discounts, a clearance link, and for those with the catalog, direct ordering by product number.

Bachrach www.bachrach.com ⑤
Fraying blazers and clip-on ties do not a snappy dresser make. Bachrach carries great-looking clothes for when you want to look put together—jewel-tone ties, Merino wool mock turtlenecks, and flannel trousers are among the offerings here. Considering the quality, you'll find the reasonable prices a pleasant surprise. Web shopping perks include shipping deals, a store locator, and express catalog ordering.

Nordstrom.com www.nordstrom.com © ⑤
Some would say you haven't lived until you've huddled outside Nordstrom at daybreak, waiting with the herd for the Half Yearly Sale to start. We, however, prefer the more pleasant experience of shopping at this swank Web site. The same products are offered, and finding sale items requires no pushing or shoving. Nordstrom's notoriously courteous customer service is in evidence, too; to return an item, head to a local store or stick it in the postage-paid envelope they include.

Fashionmall.com www.fashionmall.com ⓓ

Shopping variety without the typical mall mayhem. Fashionmall.com is a massive clothing and accessory resource with something for every taste and price range. Choose the Madison "floor" for finer threads, SoHo for cutting edge clothes, Galleria for brand names, or Main Street for basics. You'll also find fashion advice and trends for every season. Before you buy, be sure to read the return policies for the individual sites Fashionmall.com has patched you through to.

FashionDig www.fashiondig.com

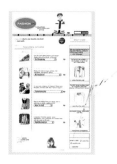

Total squares won't dig the groovy threads on the site that's carrying retro into the future. The "mod" crowd, however, will go way wild over the classic designs and rare accessories that go for a pretty, but worthwhile, penny. Even if you can't own an original Emilio Pucci dress, browse through the archives of clothes and designer's bios, or become a Fashion Digger and access the Secret Style Chamber.

alight www.alight.com

Cheetah pants in size 14 are a rare find, as is other plus-sized clothing that's not baggy, dowdy, and otherwise unfashionable. alight's got designer duds in sizes 14 to 22, along with a selection of fanciful intimates and accessories. Fashion advice comes in the form of feature articles like "Animal Magnetism," "Fanciful Feathers," and "Bra-la-la" that put a funny spin on current trends. To find the clothes among the mass of content, hit the Department Store link.

Nine West www.ninewest.com   ⓓ ⓢ

If you're a woman (or a freaky kind of guy), chances are you've got a pair of Nine West shoes in your closet. The prices at this online store are super-reasonable, considering the quality; for $70 dollars or less you can buy beaded sandals or classic loafers here. Register at Club Nine to get express ordering, a personal address book for sending gifts, and periodic email updates (if you so desire).

Victoria's Secret www.victoriassecret.com

What is Victoria's secret? Perhaps it's the fact that her catalog's readership is predominantly male. Ladies, however, will find the Web site a convenient way to buy the slinky bras and silky nighties the company is famous for. Additional Web features include a Bra Search (which helps overwhelmed shoppers select the level of push-up, padding, and wires they want) and the stunning selections in the Glam Lounge.

FigLeaves www.figleaves.com   ⓓ ⓢ

Do your wardrobe a favor and buy some underwear that doesn't come in a 10-pack. FigLeaves sells stylish underwear, hosiery, socks, and sleepwear for men and women, by popular labels like Wacoal and Ralph Lauren. For help on fit or selection, try chatting live with online intimate apparel experts Adam and Eve—they'll stock your personalized Top Drawer with custom-selected recommendations. Special sections also cover full figures and active wear.

dELiAs.cOm www.delias.com   ⓓ ⓢ

Shop dELiAs.cOm and you'll be the best-dressed teenager around, guaranteed. They've got everything from retro glasses ($8) to sundresses ($38) that are destined to make you the envy of your algebra class. Try the site's great "roll-over outfits" feature: it pops up information on different pieces of clothing when you move your cursor over them.

Anthropologie www.anthropologie.com

Boho cool meets urban chic at Anthropologie, a store whose buyers troll flea markets and estate sales to bring you funky clothing and housewares. Pick up an embroidered sari curtain, a velvet wrap skirt, or a country French wooden table; the prices run high, so be sure to browse the sale links. The exceptionally courteous customer service policy assures they will take care of you.

StyleShop.com www.styleshop.com ©

When in Rome, shop as the Romans do: StyleShop.com's got city guides that tell you what's on sale in hundreds of cities across the country. Sample sales, store guides, and innumerable great deals await—just select the city, click the date, and find out what sales are on at Barney's, Armani, and Dolce & Gabbana, among others. The site even provides directions to your desired shopping destination!

Droog.com www.droog.com ⓓ

Droog.com isn't a site for mincing words (click Consume to shop), but when you're the bomb.com, you needn't be bashful. Aimed at teenage boys, the site offers high school fashion at its coolest, with pictures and sizing info that make it easy to buy online. The items are affordably priced to fit within the budget of the average after-school McJob, but if you're really strapped, enable the Save feature to view clothes with price cuts.

OshKosh B'Gosh www.oshkoshbgosh.com

The funniest name and the coolest overalls are at OshKosh B'Gosh. Shop here for denim basics for babies and kids, as well as stylish accessories like a little denim car seat headrest. Expectant moms will have to shop elsewhere for maternity overalls (no women's clothes here), but the large selection and frequent sales make this site worth a stop.

gapkids.com www.gapkids.com ⓢ

Where do Gap grown-ups come from? From Gap Kids, of course. The online version of the store is easy enough for a child to navigate but, luckily for parents, requires a grown-up's credit card for purchase. Find all the elementary school fashion basics, from backpacks and hats to small-sized versions of the Gap's classic khakis and vests. Sale items and maternity clothes are also available here.

Old Navy www.oldnavy.com

The Gap's hip younger cousin, Old Navy, has finally taken its surprisingly cheap and refreshingly stylish clothing online. Where else can you get a kicky, stretchy skirt for $9.99 or three cool, cotton T-shirts for 20 bucks? Faithful to the brick-and-mortar chain, the site has duds for men, women, boys, girls, and babies, with their notoriously wide range of sizes (women's jeans up to 20). Register, and the site will save your address for super-speedy checkout next time.

Payless.com www.payless.com ⑤

Don't let the name fool you: these shoes may be cheap but they hardly look it. Sure, some may give you a blister or two, but when you need a pair of glittery platform sandals that are priced to move, this is the place to go. In addition to dazzling dress shoes, Payless.com also has comfort and athletic footwear. Go to the Shoe Finder to search by size; if you have a particular shoe that you buy regularly, the Lot Finder link will take you straight to it.

Nike.com www.nike.com ⓓ ⑤

Nike deserves props for beefing up its site with stunning visuals, but with links labeled Duel, Force, and The Morning After, you may wonder whether you've stumbled on the site for *The Young and the Restless*. Don't panic, though; one click of the Store button will take you straight to the hundreds of styles of the revered athletic shoes. Or, if you prefer a custom look, visit the new NIKE iD section and put together the perfect combo of base, trim, and midsole colors.

Mondera www.mondera.com ©

There's truly something for everyone at Mondera.com, whether your style is elegant, casual, traditional, modern, or exotic. The site that claimed to have brokered the largest online diamond sale ever—a cool $96,000 for two loose stones—can hook you up with estate jewelry, an antique bracelet, or a wedding band. Also includes a jewelry users' guide of fashion tips and the top ten trends.

KennethCole.com www.kencole.com

Quintessential American cool straight from the New York stylemaker. The Kenneth Cole site is Flash-enhanced and sleeker than ever, with shoes, outerwear, accessories, and signature pieces for both men and women, easy to browse and slick to behold. Stick to the direct links to find what you want—the Shop By Look section is more like a magazine spread than a helpful tool.

eBags www.ebags.com ⑤

Ditch the pack mule look and get from point A to point B in style. eBags has a garment bag for your clothes, a messenger bag for your books, and a golf carrier for your clubs. For the packing-impaired, the bag recommendations and Ask the Road Warrior pages are filled with helpful advice. Free UPS shipping for registered shoppers.

Coach www.coach.com ⑤

The soft leather and distinctive stitching of a baseball glove were the inspiration that led to the Coach company. Now, more than half a century later, you can buy its renowned handbags, watches, and travel gear online. Treat yourself to a monogrammed satchel, or use the Corporate Gifts section to find a classy business gift. The prices are a study in inflation, but keep in mind that you're paying for a little history, a lot of quality, and impeccable customer service.

Shades.com www.shades.com

Protect your peepers and keep your wallet happy with stylish sunblockers from Shades.com. Aviators, wraparounds, clip-ons, sports shields, and cat-eyes from RayBan, Gucci, Swiss Army, Guess?, and others are always on sale. Browse through the brands or cut to the chase with the quick sunglasses finder, where you can search by brand, style, color, material, and activity.

Blue Nile www.bluenile.com ©

No idea where to begin shopping for that engagement ring? Start with Blue Nile's exhaustive Buyer's Guides, which explain terms like clarity, brilliance, and fire. Then browse through the 20,000 diamond rings and loose stones, all of which have been subjected to independent lab tests. Should you decide to buy, you'll have thirty days to evaluate your new rock and decide whether you'd like to return it for a refund.

consumer guides

BBBOnLine www.bbbonline.org

Separating the respectable from the disreputable. Before an online business can receive the Better Business Bureau's reliability seal, BBB representatives visit the company's physical location and verify its claims. Browse their site for an alphabetical list of companies that participate in the reliability program, or search for the name of the company you're thinking of patronizing. If you

feel you've been duped, you can file a complaint and get assistance in resolving your dispute.

ConsumerReview.com www.consumerreview.com ©

A simple and powerful idea: product reviews written by consumers. Read any one of more than 100,000 reviews in categories like sports and leisure, electronics, and baby gear, all written by people who actually bought the product. Or jump to one of ConsumerReview.com's 18 sister sites for reviews and information on skiing, PC games, audio equipment, and cars, to name a few. There are even top product picks in various categories with quotes from—you guessed it—consumers.

Gomez.com www.gomez.com © ⓓ

Gomez.com has taken those little comment cards you might find at your favorite restaurant, renamed them "Internet Scorecards," and applied them to the online world. Sites are rated by consumers and ranked in categories such as ease of use, customer confidence, and overall cost. Although the lists are a bit superstore-heavy (lots of Amazon.coms and Borderses), the content is enlightening.

jdpower.com www.jdpower.com

It may be tempting to jump into that online auction but, before you do, check with jdpower.com for invaluable information on the products and services floating around cyberspace and the real world. The self-billed "voice of the consumer" is one of the most respected independent product ranking organizations in the U.S. and has been empowering consumers with their purchasing choices for over 30 years.

Deja.com www.deja.com © d

To discuss Gucci boots with a rabid fan or digital cameras with others who bought them, dial up Deja.com. The site hosts discussion groups on just about any product you would ever want to buy (thousands of them) and rates the product according to user input. Though the user comments can be lukewarm individually, they provide valuable insight when taken together. This is also a fun place to browse, find out what's new and cool, and peek in on the online community.

Consumers Digest Online www.consumersdigest.com

The popular consumer magazine that's been arming buyers for years has an online component to further facilitate informed purchasing. Search for the Best Buy in your category or browse articles on products from gardening to home loans to airfare. The interface is intuitive and includes a compare function to view products side by side. Registered users may also save products and articles to a personal page.

Internet ScamBusters www.scambusters.org ⓞ

Credit card fraud, email viruses, urban legends—none can escape the watchful eye of this vigilant group. ScamBusters is an Internet fraud information station. And while it may not be the prettiest site, it does deliver serious, public service-oriented content, with trustworthy alternatives and recommendations for safe surfing. Check out the Scam Check Station to avoid being taken for a ride.

electronics

sharperimage.com www.sharperimage.com

For the person on your list who has everything—or just wants every-thing. Magic Q Balls, a pocket-sized wide-screen TV, and massagers for every occasion (and body part) are just some of the gizmos you'll find at sharperimage.com. Many of the prices might make you swallow hard, but there is a goodly amount of merchandise that won't break your bank account.

Point.com www.point.com © d Ⓢ

Don't have a cell phone yet? Point.com's comprehensive and content-rich site (which includes an 800-term glossary) should inspire even confirmed Luddites to join the 21st century, with comparison charts of more than 4,000 service plans, phone prices, and all kinds of tips and tricks—like how to screen calls and track battery strength on your new phone. And yes, you can buy a phone and sign up for service here.

etown.com www.etown.com © d Ⓢ

Now this is what an electronics Web site should look like! Make no mistake, though: etown.com is more than just a pretty face. Brimming with breaking news, expert reviews, and easy-to-follow tutorials, etown.com makes buying camcorders, cell phones, DTVs, and stereos almost pleasurable. Be sure to read the return policy for the specific etown.com dealer you're purchasing from: a higher price with a money-back guarantee may top a cheaper model with a restocking fee.

Crutchfield www.crutchfield.com

Low-cost shipping, tech-savvy customer service, the best brands in the consumer electronics industry. Simply put, Crutchfield is a terrific store. Why shop elsewhere when Crutchfield has car audio systems, home theater equipment, and all kinds of accessories backed up by a great tech-support team? The return policy covers returns for any reason for 30 days, no re-stocking fees or invasive questions.

LiquidPrice.com www.liquidprice.com

Just call it Priceline for tech gear. As one of the largest real-time buyer-driven marketplaces, LiquidPrice.com lets surfers pick a product—from camcorders to Palm Pilots—and kick back while retailers bid for their business. Search products by offbeat categories like Trendsetter and Technophile, throw in a bid, and hang out while Liquid does the rest.

Cellmania.com www.cellmania.com

Nokia may be the name you know, but this site's buyers guides can find you something on par for a better price. Scan their product index to see what's available (Motorola, Ericsson, etc.), then check the hundreds of product reviews to see how the phones actually stand up. Best of all, Cellmania's Quick Picks can suggest a cell phone and calling plan based on how you actually plan to use your phone.

Hifi.com www.hifi.com

Electronics shopping nirvana. Aside from sporting hundreds of high-end products, Hifi.com has gift-buying assistance, live consultants, and an installation support page. The seasoned audiophile can check out the I'm An Enthusiast section for expert technical opinions, while beginners can get click-by-click guidance. Ready to buy? Clever buttons and smooth navigation make puchasing a pleasure.

telstreet.com www.telstreet.com

Go from wired to wireless in one easy site. telstreet.com provides everything the comparison shopper needs to make a purchase on their mobile phone. Haven't tried it yet? The articles and FAQs here are brief and informative, with glossary links that spell out complicated jargon (anyone who thinks WAP is a cartoon sound effect should definitely log on). Check out the price lists for phone and service plans in your area, read the customer reviews, and cut the cord.

free stuff & coupons

coolsavings.com www.coolsavings.com

No more clipping coupons—coolsavings.com has thousands of printable money savers on its site. The coupons are all free and accepted at national chains like Kmart and Radio Shack as well as at Web retailers such as eToys and CDNOW. The site also offers freebies and email updates on new savings opportunities.

The Free Forum Network www.freeforum.com

Unlike most freebie sites, which offer little more than trial magazine subscriptions and coupons for product samples, The Free Forum Network has hundreds of links to useful products and services. Insurance information, travel discounts, long-distance calls, and more, sorted into categories like health and fitness, gardening, and sports.

beenz.com www.beenz.com

Fill out a survey: 100 beenz. Shop for insurance: 300 beenz. Once you've registered for a beenz account, this cool type of online currency accrues automatically as you interact with its partner sites. When your hill of beenz amounts to something, head to e-stores like Blockbuster, GiftCertificates.com, and Marshalls to spend it. Still not sold? Live customer service reps, called "betty beenz," can be contacted with one click.

FreeRide www.freeride.com

If you're shopping online already, you can beef up the bang per buck quotient by starting at FreeRide. Basically, the site links you through to top retailers like Amazon.com and Blockbuster, and awards FreeRide points while you shop that are redeemable for more merchandise. It takes a little effort since you need a minimum of 500 points—the equivalent of $5—to do anything, but if you're burning up the credit card anyway…

CyberRebate.com www.cyberrebate.com

If you can wait two weeks, you can get some hardcore bargains out of CyberRebate.com. That's how long it takes to cash in on the mail-in rebates that come with every product this site sells. Here's how it works: you buy an item (computer hardware, CDs, toys, books), print out and mail the rebate that the site posts online, track its progress, and cash the check. There is even a section for 100% cash back.

gifts & cards

RedEnvelope Gifts Online www.redenvelope.com   ⓓ ⓢ

According to Asian tradition, the most cherished presents come in a red envelope. No doubt anyone who receives an envelope containing one of this site's fine items will feel the same. Get gorgeous candles, sweets, tools, and other eclectic wares for the explorer, host, handyman, or epicure in your life. If you have a problem, log on and chat live with a service representative any time, day or night.

Flooz.com www.flooz.com

Cooler than paper gift certificates and classier than cash, Flooz are online "gift dollars" that can be redeemed at a long list of online stores. Participating sites include TowerRecords.com, Skechers, Art.com, and iGadget.com; the list is growing. A helpful customer service FAQ page and a toll-free number make this already convenient shopping experience even smoother. Hey, Whoopi Goldberg floozes; shouldn't you?

BlindGift.com www.blindgift.com   ⓞ

Generous stalkers and modest philanthropists alike can rely on BlindGift.com to send their tokens of affection. The site acts as a middleman between givers and recipients that keeps both parties' personal information private. To send a gift, you pick one from a BlindGift.com merchant's stock (bouquet, bottle of wine, etc.) and enter the other person's chat handle or email address. The site contacts him or her, requests a mailing address, and sends off the present.

Egreetings.com www.egreetings.com   ©

Paper cards look passé up against Egreetings.com's digital greeting cards. The site has a huge selection of moving, singing, blinking e-cards for traditional sentiments (Christmas, Halloween) as well as more modern ones (gay/lesbian, teen, etc.). Membership is free, and allows you to send cards, keep track of important addresses and dates, and keep a virtual photo album. For cards with character, this hits the cyber-spot.

Flowerbud.com www.flowerbud.com   ⓓ

Until other online florists pick up on the idea that there's a market for elegant, beautifully arranged floral bouquets, Flowerbud.com has got that market cornered. Stop here for arrangements that whisper, "I picked this just for you" instead of screaming, "This was the best they had for under $30." If you really want to bowl someone over, enroll them in the Year in Bloom, which will send your beloved fresh flowers once a week for an entire year.

Cut for you.

Flowerbud.com

Sparks.com www.sparks.com

When Sparks.com says they have cards for any occasion, they're not kidding—you can even use their art and quote library to make your own. These cool paper cards can be shipped to you or sent directly to anyone you want, complete with a personal message. You can also include a gift certificate from the nearly 80 companies featured here.

gifts.com www.gifts.com

Who'd have thought a collision of yuppie and hippie tastes would give birth to a Grateful Dead tie? gifts.com stocks that strange apparel progeny, as well as more general gifts for dad, daughter, boss, and other typecast recipients. Prices run high, but such is the cost of having so many options already sought and sorted. Orders over $50 often come with a free gift, like golf balls when you buy for Father's Day.

1-800-Flowers.com www.1800flowers.com

A pepper plant for a spicy surprise, a container of tulip bulbs for a delayed bouquet ... This site's motto, "flowers are just the beginning," isn't frivolous lip service. Check out the gift reminder service and the Giftology feature to search for presents according to astrological sign. The company promises that their flowers will live for at least a week; a complaint chat forum is ready 24/7 in case they don't.

Calyx & Corolla www.calyxandcorolla.com

Because a bunch of pink carnations and a small stuffed bear on a stick don't suit every occasion, Calyx & Corolla sells unfailingly classy arrangements—think calla lilies in a clear, cylindrical vase or six simple stems of orchids. Their Year Of options are equally unique, allowing you to send bouquets, bonsai trees, and other unusual flora on a bimonthly basis. To shop fast, browse their tasteful recommendations.

MuseumShop.com www.museumshop.com

The Louvre, the Brooklyn Museum of Art, and 38 other museums around the world have made their distinctive gift shop wares available here. Take the Flash tour for an overview, or just browse by museum. Art prints, greeting cards, jewelry, and designer furniture are some of the objects you can expect to find. While the selection is limited in some areas, a flat fee of $5.95 applies to domestic ground shipping and museum membership will often get you a discount.

GiftCertificates.com www.giftcertificates.com

Don't panic when you draw the computer guy in the next Secret Santa lottery; instead, head for GiftCertificates.com. Unlike similar services, this site helps you search vendors by category, occasion, recipient, or zip code. If you still can't decide what Mr. or Ms. Mysterian

would like, pick up a Super Certificate, redeemable at more than 100 merchants, including Banana Republic, iBeauty.com, or Dean & DeLuca.

Hallmark.com www.hallmark.com

From the company that invented gift wrap (no, really) comes a handy site for all the occasions you didn't even know existed. Send a free e-card to commemorate a new pet, observe Sweetest Day (October 21), or mark the start of a school year. Of course, Hallmark.com can also help you celebrate more traditional holidays with a variety of flowers, gifts, and ornaments.

CarePackages.com www.carepackages.com

Chances are, you know a bookworm who could use some snacks and a little Visine, or a camper with a craving for Chips Ahoy. This site takes the legwork out of sending treats by offering fantastic, pre-packaged boxes for students, sweethearts, or anyone else needing a boost. The site will also help you put together a personalized package, should the recipient have especially discerning tastes.

price comparisons

BottomDollar.com www.bottomdollar.com

Thirty discount listings for Tylenol alone should tell you BottomDollar.com's forte. Enter an item and BottomDollar.com searches online stores and returns a list of the cheapest prices. Available items fall into the full range of categories, with especially large sections for computers and home electronics. The more specific your request, the more successful—generic words like "wine" return less accurate results than "merlot."

mySimon www.mysimon.com

Meet your own personal shopper—even if he does have a maniacal expression on his face. mySimon is one of the best price comparison services around, searching over 2,000 merchants for the lowest prices on everything from a surfboard to a new hard drive. You'll also find daily shopping news, consumer resources, and detailed information on each merchant. Before you buy, be sure to check in with Simon first.

PriceSCAN www.pricescan.com

PriceSCAN will find you fabulous prices on the stuff you love by search-ing both e-tailers and merchants who don't have Web sites yet. Best of all, PriceSCAN doesn't accept money from vendors, so the search results are unbiased and amazingly thorough. The interface could be snazzier, but otherwise this a good source for bargain hunting.

DealTime www.dealtime.com

A Web site that calls you when it finds the price you want on a new digital camera? Believe it. Enter the price you want to pay for any item in their vast array and DealTime will notify you by email or pager when the product goes on sale. The site also provides links to product information and reviews. Not sure what you want to buy? Check out the New @ Deal-time link for the deal of the day.

BuyCentral.com www.buycentral.com

Though you can't actually buy anything at BuyCentral.com, you can use it to find a desired item online. It's a directory of e-commerce Web sites, as well as a price comparison tool that make it easy to see where goods are and how their prices vary. Each site is listed with a descrip-tion, a rating for security (or lack of), and a direct link to the store. Stores in France, Germany, and Italy are also included—check the Extras section for a currency converter.

Clickthebutton www.clickthebutton.com

Comparison shopping has never been easier. Download Clickthebutton's shopping software—which leaves a small bullseye in the corner of your computer screen—and surf your favorite e-commerce sites like normal. When you spy a product you love, hit the bullseye and Clickthebutton delivers a list of prices for that product as seen on other sites. Listed prices include taxes and shipping costs to boot.

sports   . . .. .

CBS SportsLine www.cbs.sportsline.com

SportsLine has the corner on comprehensive when it comes to sports Web sites, providing the same wealth of authoritative information that won your trust in the television channel. But you don't even have to visit the site to get the goods if you grab their free Sports Ticker. The program downloads in less than two minutes and constantly rattles off up-to-the-second details on the teams you tell it to track.

Outside Online www.outsidemag.com
Skateboard queen Cara-Beth Burnside and the members of the NYPD scuba unit don't appear to have a lot in common, except for the shared enthusiasm for outdoor activities that got them featured here. *Outside Magazine's* Web site is more than just a glorified archive of articles from the magazine, though you'll find plenty of past features distributed throughout. Each of the Web's different sections is hosted by a personality—Mr. Fit and Gear Guy are two—who dispenses expertise and answers reader questions.

ESPN.com www.espn.go.com
A-list sports news, fantasy games, athlete interviews ... ESPN.com is as comprehensive as one might imagine it would be, for mainstream American sports at least. The news coverage here will keep you coming back for more (as will the game schedules); be sure to check out indispenable columns by Peter Gammons and Dick Vitale and cool programs on ESPN radio.

Trails.com www.trails.com
The quickest way to find hiking and mountain biking destinations in your area, Trails.com sports a Trail Finder database with 10,000 unique listings, sortable by location, difficulty, length, and duration. When you find a trail that looks promising, print out a Topo Map of the path's topography, and use the Trip Planner to organize a group to go with you. Trails.com also offers an extensive e-commerce wing with 4,000 kinds of books, maps, and gear.

Total Sports www.totalsports.net
What makes Total Sports so cool? The awesome TotalCast coverage of in-progress games. Just select the game you'd like to watch (coverage ranges from NCAA basketball to major league baseball and soccer) and the site provides a companion window that summarizes the status and stats with play-by-play coverage, a real-time scoreboard, and photos. There's no video of the game here—but the TotalCasts are perfect when you want to track the game while you're at work.

GOLFonline www.golfonline.com

If spending hours on the greens isn't enough for you, then head to GOLFonline—the site is (perhaps too) crowded with news headlines on the major tours, information on courses and equipment, and tips to improve your game. The coolest part? GOLFonline's instructional videos, which let you watch mini-QuickTime movies of top golfers explaining their techniques.

CNNsi.com www.cnnsi.com

Bathing suits, sports, and … more bathing suits. CNNsi serves up all the features you love in *Sports Illustrated*, plus fancy multimedia tools you'll wonder how you did without. Check the daily news headlines, watch footage of game highlights, listen to interviews with players, or chat with other sports fans. And don't miss the swimsuit gallery, which contains years of archives, Web-exclusive pics, and even a zoom button.

Sports.com www.sports.com

With sports coverage for internationally-minded folk, Sports.com keeps track of it all: football, cricket, golf, tennis, rugby, Formula 1 car racing, sailing, boxing, and tips (for betting, not playing). The news is oriented toward European sports, providing links to the most popular pastimes in Germany, France, Spain, and Holland (clicking on the U.S. links will patch you through to CBS SportsLine). Hit the Fast Facts section to quickly find stats, or visit the topic-specific BBS to sound off about the latest *fútbol* game.

SkiReview.com www.skireview.com

Driven by consumer reviews, SkiReview.com aims to educate on the

best snowboards, bindings, and skis on the market this season. But while the product reviews are the site's focus, they are by no means the only offerings—slope and road conditions, a gear marketplace, and Ski Talk are some of the other options. See Skiing 101 for an exhaustive collection of instructions and tips for all styles and skill levels.

sportingnews.com www.sportingnews.com

Rare is the sports fan who needs complete and up-to-date information on all 700 pro and college teams, but if you can take it, sportingnews.com will dish it out weekly. The site's personalization feature lets users tailor the homepage to include news on some, none, or all of the teams it keeps track of. You can also choose which columnists' weekly rants you want to read, as well as whether you want to receive the updates via email.

MajorLeagueBaseball.com www.majorleaguebaseball.com

The only thing missing here is the smell of roasted peanuts, hot dogs and cheap beer. It's the official Web site of Major League Baseball—why go anywhere else for stats, schedules, and team info? You can tune in to live press conferences and game audio from local radio stations around the country. Take me out to the ball game? Nah, I'd rather catch it on the Web.

NFL.com www.nfl.com

NFL.com breaks down the professional football season week by week so you can relish each and every step of the climb to the Super Bowl. Fans can also buy tickets to upcoming games, brush up on stats, look over the career highlights of favorite players, and drop in on the Coaches Club page. There's even a kids page for pint-sized pigskin enthusiasts.

NBA.com www.nba.com

Affording a better (and cheaper) glimpse into pro basketball action than those $200 court-side seats, NBA.com has a minute-by-minute Live Scoreboard that keeps track of current games, and a news section that highlights yesterday's match-up. Don't miss the great Sight & Sound multimedia area—it has QuickTime video of the top plays of the week and a video archive of history-making shots.

NHL.com www.nhl.com

If your idea of 'slashing' has absolutely nothing to do with hockey sticks, you might want to skip the National Hockey League's official site—or visit their Hockey U link for some continuing education. But for those who know (and love) the sport that made Gretzky famous (or is it the other way around?), the site is a must-see, offering schedules, breaking news, interviews with coaches and players, video highlights of crucial games . . . even a separate NHL Kids page.

Boating.com www.boating.com

Who better for a beginning boater to talk to than a salty dog who has already mastered the tricks of smooth sailing? Boating.com packs its simple site with a myriad of discussion forums where week-end enthusiasts can swap advice and anecdotes on sailing, maintenance, fishing, and more. The homepage also offers news and nautical event listings, while the hefty Resources section has handy tools like tide predictors, surf cams, and weather reports.

Fogdog Sports www.fogdog.com

Don't be misled by the URL; you won't find any chew toys here, just tons and tons of sporting equipment. Get all the gear and apparel for your favorite athletic activity, from the majors (basketball, football, baseball, hockey) to the minors (lacrosse, gymnastics, wrestling). A wonderful alternative to chaotic sporting goods stores.

WWF.com www.wwf.com

The World Wrestling Federation is back with more force than a body slam by all three hundred pounds of Cactus Jack. The newly sleek WWF site serves as a companion to the televised action, providing bios of all the Superstars and Divas and results of recent face-offs. Though you can't watch matches online (unless you pay per view), the webcasts section archives past footage and Byte This interviews.

AthletesDirect www.athletesdirect.com

With direct access to the Web sites of over 200 living sports stars (hence the name), AthletesDirect's list includes Kobe Bryant, Ken Griffey Jr., Mia Hamm, and other news-making names. Link through to one of the extensive sub-sites to ask your sports hero a question, check on his stats, or read a story straight from his mouth. Feature articles on the homepage explore athletes' careers and, predictably, the latest sports news and commentary.

WNBA.com www.wnba.com

Yolanda Griffith, Rebecca Lobo, and other girls with game are featured on the official site of the Women's National Basketball Association. Each player gets a page with game highlights, stats, personal and injury details, and a complete game log; there is a printable version for those who keep track of such things. The site also has the stats, news, and Q & A (Ask Olympia with The Shock's Olympia Scott-Richardson!) you would expect to find on an official site, as well as a multimedia area with RealPlayer video of season highlights and nail-biting buzzer-beaters.

FitnessLink www.fitnesslink.com

Want to get fit but don't know where to start? FitnessLink is online to show you how to eat right, exercise right, and live longer. While the site is a little scant on content, a few notable features include the Virtual Gym (which shows you how to use the equipment in a real gym without straining your muscles), and the Home Gym (which guides you through your living room exercise routine.)

Explore.com www.explore.com

A cool primer on the adventure sports scene that covers rough-and-tumble activities like hiking, kayaking, and snowboarding. Explore.com lets you follow the trail of their "adventure van" with videos, journal entries, and photographs of the site's team of adventurers. There are also guides to sporting gear, adventurous travel spots, and various athletic competitions taking place around the world.

Tennis.com www.tennis.com

Whether you like to serve-and-volley, bash from the baseline, or just watch, this tennis info hub provides pro tennis news, gear shopping guidance, match listings, and an informative Instruction link for improving your game. The site is super-accessible and geared to fans (not fanatics) who like to play; the content is solid, if predictable, with a couple of pleasant surprises, like the Sport Science section.

Rocklist.com www.rocklist.com

Worth a site in and of itself, Rocklist.com's DataGuide is a growing database of the best scalable surfaces around the world. It's built on contributions from the climbing community—you too can add a listing, detailed text descriptions, photos, and maps. Rocklist.com also features a half-dozen new articles each month (with a complete archive), as well as a Learn the Ropes educational center that hands out climbing tips like how to block a knot and the best gear for women climbers.

Rivals.com www.rivals.com

Rivals.com, an online sports network, satisfies even the most rabid appetite with the scoop on over 500 sports teams and semi-independent sites on everything from professional hoops to competitive skateboarding. Expert commentary digs deep, and streaming videos of key plays and game rebroadcasts make Rivals.com an indispensable resource.

Olympics.com www.olympics.com

For anyone who wants to keep track of current trials and athletes or relive highlights of Games past, Olympics.com is the place to visit. The torch section is particularly fascinating, and details the 50 different modes of transportation used to carry the torch to the Sydney Olympics, including a train, a camel, a surf-lifesaving boat, and a scuba diver.

Quokka Sports www.quokka.com

Any sport site can give you the scoop from the sidelines, but Quokka Sports wants to get you inside the athlete's head. The site peddles what it calls Quokka Sports Immersion, using video, telemetry, biometrics, GPS data, timing, statistics, and email directly from the competitors to help you experience sports like the athletes do. You'll also find articles like "The Sherpa Series: Climbing Everest from the Guides' Perspective" and "Solo Travelers Keep Their Lifeline."

NCAA Online www.ncaa.org

Fans of college sports will find all the need-to-know info right here—for fencing, skiing, track, and wrestling, as well as baseball, basketball, and football. A searchable press release database, recruiting info, schedules, exhaustive coverage, and quality reporting make NCAA Online one of the hottest sports sites around.

World Wide Houseofboxing.com www.houseofboxing.com

Nifty to look at and easy to search, Houseofboxing.com gives fans everything they need to know about rankings, weigh-ins, fight schedules, and spotlight matches. It frequently adds interviews with the likes of De La Hoya and Jr. Jones to its list of videos, and covers who went down during the most recent major bout and who, exactly, bit off what. There's also a page dedicated to each of the major figures in international boxing.

Maxfootball.com www.maxfootball.com

With personalized audio and video programming at its core, the Max offers fans with broadband some of the latest in interactive sporting news. The site's field correspondents call in daily and provide a first person perspective, while the video section has team-by-team commentary from Jerry Glanville and Gary Horton. Of course, you can also drool over the latest news, scores and statistics, share your gripes with fellow fans or purchase team gear—all with a few clicks.

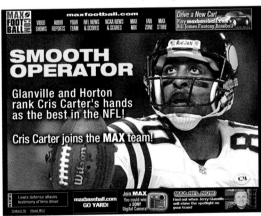

ZoomSoccer.com   www.zoomsoccer.com

ZoomSoccer.com is that rare place where soccer fans can congregate without risk of bloodshed. So if the fear of getting crushed by the crowds has kept you away from important games, listen to them live on this site via RealAudio. Also check out Zoom TV, which captures fans' memories of their favorite teams on video, and Picture Wire, a virtual album of classic plays captured on camera.

SportsUniversity.com   www.sportsuniversity.com

SportsUniversity.com gives you college sports from the campus perspective. Besides the standard coverage of recent games (including audio highlights), the site spotlights upcoming players and offers you a peek inside some of their journals. Air your thoughts and predictions for how they'll each perform this season in the forum, or link through to an individual team page for deeper content.

SchoolSports.com   www.schoolsports.com

Not much can be said for media coverage of high school sports—except on the local level. But fortunately, School-Sports.com has stepped up to the plate with this site for high school athletes, coaches, and fans. Catch the highlights from games around the country, see who'll be the hottest recruits for college teams, and get tips on boosting team spirit in the Coaches' Corner. Game schedules are updated daily.

REI.com   www.rei.com

The company that made it possible to look stylish while climbing a big hunk of granite has firmly established itself on the Net. After loading up on hiking, climbing, camping, cycling, and fishing gear at this massive store, be sure to pay a visit to the Learn and Share board, where you'll discover the best way to pack a backpack and the nicest places to hike around the world. There's even a gift registry here!

lifelounge.com   www.lifelounge.com   ⓓ

If you can surf through the jam-packed layout, lifelounge.com has the latest news and features on board, blade, and bike sports. For each category, there's a photo gallery, industry news, product reviews, and profiles of the biggest players. How-tos guide you through building ramps and finding a prime surfing location, while the sections on fashion, music, and videogames offer a slice of culture.

YogaDirectory.com   www.yogadirectory.com

Meditate on this: YogaDirectory.com has almost a thousand links to everything yoga. Though the site's strength doesn't lie in feature content (the only original material comes in the form of personals and discussion boards), it can direct you to other sites with details on different yoga traditions, the history of the practice, and instructional products for sale. A good place to know about in an arena that lacks a single comprehensive hub.

dsports.com www.dsports.com ©Ⓢ

An 18-year-old boy named Dick Stack, $300 from his nana's cookie jar, and a dream—these were the seeds from whence sprouted Dick's Sporting Goods. 50 years and 85 stores later, the company has developed dsports.com to sell its crazy range of products online. Everything from backpacks to hockey pucks comes with a buying guide to help you pick the right one, and a toll-free service number is available for further assistance.

MVP.com www.mvp.com ©ⓓ

Looking to buy a football but don't know your polyurethane from your polyvinyl chloride? Get the skinny on pigskin (and practically any other sporting equipment) directly from the pros who know: Elway, Jordan, and Gretzky. The powerhouse players have teamed up to bring you one of the most info-packed sporting goods sites online. Check out the buyer's guides here for expert advice on choosing equipment and protective gear; with advice from these guys, how could you possibly go wrong?

SportsRocket.com www.sportsrocket.com

Sports fans and gamers can combine their passions on SportsRocket.com. Play online games (some are Shockwave) of auto racing, baseball, golf, and soccer games, or try your luck at one of the many contests or trivia challenges. If you're the best in the field, you can win prizes like a free CD or $3,000. And if you've always wanted to get your hands on your favorite hockey player's old jersey, bring your winnings to the auction block where you can barter for sports cards, gear, and other memorabilia.

Sandbox.com www.sandbox.com

In fantasy sports, the winning and losing may be virtual but the gloating is very real. Sandbox.com is one of the more popular places to join a fantasy league—the site offers baseball, football, hockey, motor sports, and golf, and a Business league that follows the stock market. To keep you on top of your team's standing, there's tons of news and in-depth analysis; point your best friend towards the Casino arcade games to distract him from his stats.

AtomFilms www.atomfilms.com ©ⓓⓄ

Not for the weak-of-modem, AtomFilms begs surfers to "get into their shorts"—short movies, that is. With both live action and animated movies on offer here, you are just a 30-second download away from some of the best in abbreviated cinema. Stop by the Download Center on your way out to grab a few free flicks to share with your friends.

Yahoo! Broadcast www.broadcast.com

More than 400 radio stations, 60 TV and cable stations, 3,000 CDs, and 1,500 movie titles add up to a streaming media directory worthy of the Yahoo! name. Tune in for live sports play-by-play, preview a full CD, or attend a televised health seminar—helpful sidebars with show-times and descriptions of the day's main events make the otherwise overwhelming offerings somewhat manageable.

sputnik7 www.sputnik7.com

sputnik7 is a site offering a cutting-edge mix of streaming music, film, and anime programming. The scheduling here lends equal billing to both established acts and up-and-comers who don't ordinarily get widespread exposure. The upside? Viewers can rate the videos on offer and determine the direction of the programming. Downside? Technical difficulties (registration problems and slow-loading video) can be trying.

Pseudo.com www.pseudo.com

Pseudo.com is a trip into the world of interactive television. With 60 hours of original weekly programming, the sometimes educational, sometimes bizarre offerings here range from astronomy to underground hip hop, animated game shows to screeds on digital politics. If you can stand the wait, and you have the technology—Windows Media, RealPlayer—sit front row and watch for either the content or the thrill of seeing it unfold.

icast.com www.icast.com

Touting itself as a "new breed of entertainment site" and virtual community for those interested in the alternative film, music, and radio worlds, icast.com features news and tools for the observer and aspiring artist alike. Catch up on industry news, peruse member show-cases, or jump into chat rooms where users ask themselves penetrating questions like "Is electronic music the devil's work?"

Internet Radio List www.internetradiolist.com

Right now they're surrounding you, bouncing off your face, just waiting to be captured and enjoyed. So why not take advantage of those radio waves? Internet Radio List gives users a comprehensive guide to the airwaves (both AM/FM and Internet radio). One click allows search by genre (from sports to country and news), language, country, state, or keyword.

Live@ www.live-at.com

Condensing the wide world of online events into one byte-size Web site, Live@ makes it simple to search a comprehensive roster of upcoming goings-on. The site specializes in live video, audio, and chat events, presented by subtopic and day of the week. Try the super-handy sort function to narrow the selections down to blocks of time we'd call morning, noon, night, and shouldn't-you-be-sleeping.

eYada.com www.eyada.com

Move over, broadcast radio, there's a new kid in town. eYada.com has original talk programming on entertainment and sports that's just for the Internet (more categories to come). The shows' hosts are nervy and fun, and include some recognizable personalities like Johnny Rotten and Richard Johnson (the editor of the *New York Post's* Page Six). Tune in throughout the day—new shows air every couple of hours.

NPR Online www.npr.org

National Public Radio is a part of life for thousands of Americans, with unfaltering, quality news programs, interviews with figures of cultural interest, plus live jazz, classical, and new-music performances. A sure bet for news and entertainment—tune in right from the site, 24 hours a day.

SHOUTcast www.shoutcast.com

Mismatch your streaming audio and your connection speed and your music will sound like a drive-through speaker. SHOUTcast lets you sort radio stations by connection speed (from 28k to DSL), so you'll get continuous play rather than stutters and silence. Note: the site pushes Winamp, but RealPlayer works just as well.

NetRadio.com
www.netradio.com

With more channels than cable TV, NetRadio.com is one of the largest Internet broadcasting sites on the Web. Tune into one of 125 professionally-programmed

The Net Generation of Radio

stations to listen to music ranging from the Burundi Drummers in World Music to Weird Al Yankovic in Pop Hits. Click through for the option to buy the albums.

The Sync www.thesync.com

This brilliant site features interactive entertainment programs found nowhere else. Programs include *CyberLove* (20-somethings discuss love and sex), *Here and Now* (six college students live together in a house . . . wait—does that sound familiar?), *Snack Boy!* (a five-minute daily comedy show), and the classic weird *Jenni Show*. You'll also find short films here. Innovative and interesting.

Yack www.yack.com

Yack offers a streamlined way to find out about live webcasts, concerts, film festivals, or celebrity chats from a list of over 15,000 online events. Each listing includes the location, duration, and admission price (if there is one). Lest you worry about missing next week's Pamela Anderson chat, click the Add to My Calendar button to clip and save a listing in your Yack schedule, or request that the site email you a reminder the day before.

ShortTV www.shorttv.com

Digital camcorders are everywhere and editing software is readily available. Now it's time for some action. ShortTV appears to be one of the slickest and best-managed sites streaming independently produced short films like yours and mine. Flash-injected animation, a rock solid archive of flicks (like *Foggy Bottom*), and a cornucopia of comments by viewers are superfun for anyone with broadband.

Oddcast www.oddcast.com

Oddcast is one of the most innovative streaming media sites on the Web. Period. Exclamation point. Get ready for a refreshing dose of political activism and a whole-lotta Flash. The network's five heavy-weight channels include Witness for original documentaries and the Media Attack archive of sabotaged news talk shows. Stellar format and a commitment to "high concept" content make it worth watching.

Cammunity.com
www.cammunity.com

Let's 'fess up: we all like to watch. Cammunity.com is a well-designed gateway to the webcam world. The directory is super, organized by category and subcategory, with lists of the most popular cams in each. While the database is not as extensive as others on the Web, the search format makes up for it.

World Radio Network www.wrn.org

Catch up on news from your homeland, be it Australia, Austria, or South Africa. World Radio Network brings live and prerecorded radio broadcasts to your computer from 25 countries around the world. Tuning in is free, 24 hours a day—just choose English or another language, install the RealAudio Player or Windows Media Player, and get informed.

Scour www.scour.net

Scour is a colossal search portal for movies, music, and radio that catalogs Web entertainment alongside film and music previews. Check out the database of movie trailers here (both new releases and classics dating back to the 1950s), start your own online radio station, or snoop around for MP3s. The slick interface helps keep the pile of offerings manageable, while the site's toolbox provides all the software you might need—video and audio players, grabbers and rippers galore.

Channelseek.com www.channelseek.com

Streaming entertainment is one of the Web's best inventions, letting you watch videos and listen to music without downloading anything. Channelseek.com can help you find it all. This well-organized site lets you view its channel selector from any page. Click on Travel and take a virtual tour of the world. Click on Lifestyles and view actual surgery online. (We tried this, folks. It wasn't pretty.)

StreamSearch.com www.streamsearch.com
Take advantage of your high-speed broadband connection (or milk
your modem for all it's worth). StreamSearch.com provides an excellent
directory for the Web's ever-expanding selection of downloadable and
live multimedia programming. It covers all avenues of entertainment—
music videos, movie trailers, and hot shows like *New York Fashion
Weekly*—pointing out the best in the New Today sidebar.

teens

Bolt www.bolt.com
Providing a hip forum for discussing everything from after-school jobs
to your latest humiliation ("I bared my pit stubble to the whole class!"),
Bolt is a dynamic online community for people under 18. Personalizable
tools abound: register to start an online diary, receive comments in
your tagbook, and stash a list of friends who are also members. The site
has over 6,500 registered users (which could account for those pesky
Server Busy errors).

teenwire www.teenwire.com
A hearty round of applause goes to
Planned Parenthood for packaging its
reproductive health information in an

appealing and approachable Web site. The secret to the site's success is
hip design and content that goes beyond pregnancy and STD basics;
thought-provoking articles like "The Making of a Slut" and celebrity
interviews keep the facts engaging. Also an invaluable resource for
finding a clinic in your area.

Entertainment Asylum www.asylum.com
The Carson Daly of entertainment hubs, this pop culture dynamo sets
itself apart with interviews of a stellar list of celebrities ranging from
Neve Campbell to Forest Whitaker. You'll find 2,000 RealVideo interviews in the OnDemand section and behind-the-scenes clips from the
live online events hosted here. There are movie and TV listings as well,
but the emphasis is really on the celebrities.

TeenCentral.Net www.teencentral.net
An electronic help-line for teens, this site was developed by psychologists to provide a forum for young adults to discuss their issues: athletic
inability, weight, and peer pressure, to name a few. The site is pass-
word-protected and professionally monitored to ensure security and
appropriateness, and there are links to offline support in every state.

iCanBuy.com www.icanbuy.com
Surfing without a credit card can seem like driving without a license,
but iCanBuy.com enables teens to buy, bank, and even donate to
charity online, sans plastique. A parent sets up the account and gives
her teen a budget to squirrel away in a savings account or spend at cool
stores like CDNOW, Pacific Sunwear, Alloy, and Outpost. An airtight
privacy policy and a completely secure site (every page!) guarantee that
personal information won't leak into the wrong hands.

Link www.linkmag.com

The perpetual P.O. box fodder sent to college kids everywhere now has an online version. Read Link to unearth the dirt on schools across the nation—who went to class naked, what profs were recently busted, and other standard monthly fare. Feature articles also cover popular culture, from movie reviews to what coed just made her first million.com. There is even some coverage of deep topics like gay rights and affirmative action, though you'll have to dig to find it.

Sex, etc. www.sxetc.org

A Web site by teens and for teens, Sex, etc. is one of the few sites for young adults that discusses "the L word" (love) in addition to

male myths, bad breakups, and pregnancy panic. As its name implies, not everything here is about sex; there are also articles on drugs, divorce, self-image, and coping with stress, with a general push for abstinence underlying most features.

Getting Real www.gettingreal.com

This site provides an online community where teens can talk with peers from all different walks of life, all over the world. Channels cover the teen angle on careers, music, art, and culture, with a poetry and writing section of user-submitted works. Perhaps the strongest draw is the fantastic Clicks/Links section, which hones in on the best sites in each area—a cool way to keep up with the Web.

JVibe www.jvibe.com

JVibe addresses the same content as most teen community sites, but views it all from a Jewish perspective. Reviews of books and films about the Jewish experience, gossip about celebrities, even news on Jewish athletes can be had here. But the best parts are the original stories by the site's members and the descriptions of inspiring social activism that teens have taken on.

DoughNET.com www.doughnet.com   © Ⓞ

A finance site for teens that addresses the tricky parts of finance in decoded (rather than dumbed-down) terms. Teens can register here to try their hand at a fantasy stock portfolio and see how they'd do if they were really sinking money into it. The site also helps e-bankers under 18 open a joint account with parents, or an individual one if they already have a credit card.

travel

GORP www.gorp.com   ©

The nature site affectionately termed GORP is the information hub for outdoor enthusiasts and action-oriented travelers. Browse featured locations like Yellowstone or Aspen for ideas and inspiration, or scroll down to read useful and practical columns on health, safety, how-to, and what-to-see. Shop for gear, book a trip, find a trail; GORP does everything but tie your hiking boots for you.

travel

Concierge.com www.concierge.com
Like its namesake professional, Concierge.com is the site to hit for answers to the sundry issues that arise while on vacation. The online home for *Condé Nast Traveler* overflows with solid information for the average traveler (the budget and luxury extremes are less addressed)— destinations, hotels, airfares, books, and special sections on romantic getaways, beaches, and islands. For a little virtual sightseeing, don't miss the slideshows of lush places like Greece and Tuscany.

CitySearch www.citysearch.com
So many cities, so much to do! CitySearch gives you the hottest restaurants, arts, shopping, and entertainment listings for over 30 cities in the United States and abroad—each city has its own massive subsite. There's valuable info for locals as well as out-of-towners, loads of columns and interactive boards, and the kind of writing that's in-the-know without being snotty.

Visa-ATM Locator www.visa.com/atms
Putting another $20 at your fingertips at all times, Visa's ATM Locator knows where those elfin cash machines lie across the globe. Particularly useful for the traveler who isn't keen on carrying wads of cash around. Find out how close the ATM is to your hotel in Bangkok, the terminal at Narita, or your new office before you head out of the house.

ParkNet www.nps.gov
Aside from the massive listing of national and local parks in the United States, the NPS Web site is a rich educational resource for environmental and geological studies. Articles, photos, and fact sheets, as well as tour guides and contact information, supplement visits to the parks, while a fascinating historical section highlights the importance of conservation and open space.

TimeOut.com www.timeout.com
For more than 30 years, *Time Out* has been the champion of insider entertainment information, expanding its coverage to include major cities all across Europe and the U.S. (including London, New York, Las Vegas, Barcelona, Moscow, and Glasgow, to name six). Choose a city to view simple listings of where everyone will be eating and dancing this weekend. While the site doesn't leak any featured content from the magazine, the online interview archives do go back to 1998.

Biztravel.com www.biztravel.com
Pertinent travel information for the jet-setting CEO, convention-bound middle manager, or vacationing secretary. Biztravel.com's multitude of resources can be confusing at times (when looking for ticket prices, for example), but it multitasks better than bigger sites. The traveler toolkit gives the details on destination cities, maps, warnings about traveler safety, and currency conversions, while the flight info is continuously updated—departure times are accurate up to an hour before take-off.

MedicinePlanet www.medicineplanet.com

Without the proper precautions, exotic vacations can lead to exotic illnesses. MedicinePlanet is a personalized travel clinic where you can receive information on vaccinations, precautions, and travel hints according to your destination. Special sections for women, seniors, children, and adventure travelers go more in depth and in the instances where they recommend seeing an offline doctor, they'll also provide the name of the closest clinic.

Foreign Languages for Travelers
www.travlang.com/languages

The jackpot for language learning online, this amazingly useful and mind bogglingly immense site contains over 60 languages. Select your native tongue, the language you want to learn, and the kind of information you'd like your lesson to cover—basic words, numbers, shopping vocabulary, directions, or times and dates. Then, read the translations or click specific words to hear them pronounced in RealAudio.

Discovery.com Travel Channel www.travelchannel.com

Television's trusty travel pros have taken their documentary-style stories to the Web. From featured exhibits on equatorial wildlife (including 360-degree photo walking tours) to live video footage straight from the beaches in Maui, the Travel Channel is the first stop for practical education on hospitable destinations around the globe. News briefs, weather updates, currency converters, maps, and of course, travel planning and booking round out the offerings here.

Away.com www.away.com

Away.com is a site for those of us who need to get away from it all but don't know where to go. Designed with outdoorsy adventure-seekers in mind, it recommends outings like horseback riding, mountaineering, and ecotourism. Choose a place and the site presents activities; choose an activity and it lists the best places to do it. Want to party? Check the 1,001 festivals section for world-wide options. Drawing a complete blank? Check the idea generator.

Digital City www.digitalcity.com

Folks in big cities like New York and Los Angeles are used to consulting city guides like CitySearch for information on local happenings and services, but what about the rest of the country? Digital City is a nationwide source for information on tourism, shopping, entertainment, culture, sports, and local hangouts, plus a lot of practical advice on stuff like local garage sales and doctor- and lawyer-locators.

MapQuest.com www.mapquest.com

Get your motor running, head out on the highway . . . bust out a map? Even the born-to-be-wild need a little navigational nurturing sometimes. Enter your origin and destination and MapQuest.com delivers a zoomable map (available in multiple formats) and detailed directions. The site also offers a bit of leisure info (on national parks, scenic drives, etc.), plus live traffic reports and city guides.

Festivals.com www.festivals.com

Art festivals in Amsterdam, folk music in Seattle—Festivals.com event listings are truly global in scope. The database has 33,000 different goings-on in arts, kids, music, and sports, up to a year in advance. Each entry contains a description, phone number, and link to the event's site if it has one. Navigational note: the Backstage area is for the people who put on the festivals, not groupies hoping to score a pass.

CitySync www.citysync.com

Indiana Jones never had it this good. For $19.99 a pop, CitySync gives you the entire text of the *Lonely Planet* guidebook, straight to your Palm Pilot. Only 12 cities were downloadable to the Palm at press time, but look out for more guides in the coming months. After all, when you're climbing Mount Everest, the last thing you need is the extra weight of a book in your backpack.

Travel for Kids www.travelforkids.com

Think you can't visit Paris with the kids? Think again. The Travel Essentials section at Travel for Kids lets adventurous travelers know about tot-friendly restaurants on the Left Bank and local doctors (in case Junior chokes on the *escargot*). Europe and the Americas are covered extensively, with Asia and Africa getting fewer mentions.

Desteo www.desteo.com

A forest of 15,000 travel guides, maps, and pamphlets is free for the taking from brochure company and Web site Desteo. Would-be world travelers have only to select a destination or activity (dog sledding, dude ranch) to get a list of the brochures available. If you see a few that pique your interest, pop them into your virtual shopping cart and hit Place Order. The site will snail mail them to you at no cost.

Out & About Online www.outandabout.com

Out & About Online, a travel industry watchdog for the gay and lesbian community, has the skinny on gay-owned, -oriented, and -friendly locales and services. Before you book, the site can tell you which airlines honor same-sex partner frequent flyer miles, where to find a gay and lesbian film fest, or how the major airlines, car rentals, cruise lines, and hotels stack up in terms of anti-discrimination policies.

Geographia www.geographia.com

Did you know that the word "safari" is Swahili for "travel?" Geographia is a network of destination sites with encyclopedia-like information on countries in Africa, Europe, Asia, Latin America, and the Caribbean. Though by no means a comprehensive travel-planning site, the features are colorful and often have a soundtrack—try Pirates of the Bahamas or a virtual tour through Borneo's Mulu rainforest.

iExplore www.iexplore.com

iExplore is for the serious adventurer who wants to stray from the beaten path without trampling the local vegetation in the process. The articles describe average and extreme trips—like visiting Egyptian pyramids and rafting in the Rockies—with an eye to ecologically sound travel practices. Check out The Hot List for quick facts on ten popular destinations or pick the brains of a resident guru in the Experts section.

National Recreation Reservation Service
www.reserveusa.com

Now this is true innovation—reserving a camping space online! If you're an outdoorsy type who likes to plan ahead, The National Recreation Reservation Service provides directions, site amenities, availability, and rates for thousands of campgrounds across the U.S. For the less hardy, there are half a dozen states that offer federal cabins for rent.

travel guides

Lonely Planet Online www.lonelyplanet.com

The classic backpacker travel guide. *Lonely Planet* has practically peopled the earth with its scouts, writers, faithful followers, and travelers—now it's staked a claim on the Web. While the site lacks the play-by-play details on local restaurants and hostels that you find in the book, it does cover each country in the series with historical and cultural profiles, slide shows, getting there and away tips, and valuable information on visas, money, and climate, both political and meteorological.

Arthur Frommer's Budget Travel Online www.frommers.com

Despite the glaring "Budget Travel" logos, Frommer's Online is not just for the rugged traveler. Updated seven days a week, the articles and editorials here cover breaking news on special deals and hot vacation spots, plus insider advice on how to make traveling a little less taxing on the mind and the wallet. Peruse Arthur's Soap Box for thoughtful pieces on the impact we make on the places we visit.

The Rough Guide to Travel Online
www.travel.roughguides.com

Not every traveler wants a lazy vacation—for hands-on adventurers who really want to experience the culture, the Rough Guides travel series leads the way. Browse through their featured destinations or take a look at the city guides listed in their exhaustive database (Acapulco to Cairo to Zurich). With historical background and practical information on lodging, food, customs, and nightlife, the Rough Guide offers comforting introductions for those traveling less familiar terrain.

Fodors.com   www.fodors.com

An elegant, easily navigable Web site from one of the first names in travel. In addition to the usual resources on travel planning, Fodors.com lets you custom-tailor a "mini guide" for your trip. First choose your destination, then click through the checklist of options to select your budget, dining preferences, hotel, and nighttime activities. Print out the results and go to town—easy!

roadsideamerica.com   www.roadsideamerica.com

From the town atop a burning mine in Centralia, PA to the Fremont Troll of Seattle, roadsideAmerica.com ferrets out the obscure, bizarre, curious, and creepy to share with the rest of the world. There are more that 8,000 offbeat roadside attractions catalogued in the site's archive for curious road-trippers. Check out HyperTOURS for a picture gallery of crazy cross-crountry trips.

lodging

All-Hotels.com   www.all-hotels.com

All is a bit of a stretch, but the number of hotels, bed and breakfasts, and discount lodgings in this online directory is certainly impressive. Use All-Hotels.com to check out the options before you get to the taxi stand. You can even make reservations online for major hotels and chains planetwide—they guarantee that their price is the lowest.

CheapLodging.com   www.cheaplodging.com

CheapLodging.com can get you a night at the Sahara in Las Vegas (or any of 40,000 other hotels) for substantially less than other sites. Once you've chosen a city, the site will show you which hotels and rates are available—the same information travel agents use to find you a room. You can book the room online and get an instant confirmation, 24 hours a day. Car rentals, rail passes, and airline tickets are also accessible from the homepage.

Hostels.com www.hostels.com

For the budget, adventure, or just plain people-lovin' traveler, Hostels.com is the resource and community board of choice. What the hostel database lacks in comprehensivenes, the community-oriented features make up for, with some excellent articles on Hostelling 101 and advice and dispatches from travelers as far afield as Kathmandu.

BedandBreakfast.com www.bedandbreakfast.com

Modern sensibility meets old-fashioned charm at BedandBreakfast.com. Find B&Bs in major cities or the American heartland by searching a database of over 23,000 properties—even book online. If you're in need of inspiration, check out the site's themed guides for holiday getaways and relaxing retreats. The site also offers gift certificates for friends, and a B&B wedding planner.

petswelcome.com www.petswelcome.com

petswelcome.com

If you want to go on vacation and just can't bear to be parted from your little Snausage-eater, this is the site for you. Check the listings for hotels, camp-grounds, beaches, and ski resorts that will welcome (and/or pamper) your pooch. The Travel Info section is a helpful compendium of tips for traveling with animals. Airlines, for instance, require identification tags and a travel kennel, so fly prepared.

transportation

Expedia www.expedia.com © Ⓢ

What Microsoft's cyber travel agency lacks in cheap deals it makes up for in rock-solid consistency. The most reliable airline ticket purchase site on the Web includes hotels, cars, cruises and package vacations, and a feature called the Flight Price Matcher which is eerily reminiscent of Priceline. Specify your flight date, destination, and credit card number and the Price Matcher will automatically book your flight if it can match your price.

Travelocity www.travelocity.com

While the chances of actually purchasing any of the supercheap tickets at Travelocity are slimmer than you'd expect, the prices make persist-ence well worth it. More than any other airfare search site, Travelocity often turns up hard-to-find deals, making it a gem for the flexible traveler. Be sure to check out the Fare Watcher service, an email notification agent that reports fare hikes and dips for your specified destinations.

Bestfares.com www.bestfares.com

Money talks, and BestFares.com encourages you to listen up. This site finds the lowest prices on airlines, hotels, car rentals, cruises, even trains, and also teaches you how to make the most of frequent flier miles. Access to the best features costs $60 in membership fees—a paltry fee, considering the potential benefits for frequent travelers.

Priceline.com www.priceline.com

The site that made "name your price" a reality just keeps getting bigger—these days you can shop Priceline for airline tickets, hotel rooms, groceries, cars, and more. As always, you enter a bid, and Priceline.com notifies you within an hour if it's a go. While you may have to be flexible about brands, flight times, and the like, it's usually worth it for the money you can save.

TRIP.com www.trip.com

Some bargain flight sites just spit out a price, but TRIP.com actually tells you how to adjust your agenda to save more. After you use the Low Fare Finder, you can then book the flight, a rental car, and a hotel room right on the site. If you've got vacation time coming (but not yet scheduled), sign up for the impulseTRIP feature to get email notices of super-cheap tickets to the destinations you're considering.

Greyhound www.greyhound.com

Going Greyhound is a way of life in America. With such a corner on the market, you've gotta figure that Greyhound doesn't need to have perks like an easy-to-use Web site with schedules, fares, promotions, and specials, and yet it does. It's even available in Spanish. Students especially should check here for discounts and special passes.

Rail Connection www.railconnection.com

Backpacking across Europe has long been the boho adventure of choice, and how better to hostel-hop than Eurorail? This site is primarily a sales venue for the invaluable passes, with the added service of helping you choose the version that meets your travel needs. Free coupons, maps, and a guide to Europe accompany each online order.

tv

SoapCity.com www.soapcity.com

Don't you hate it when annoying things like work get in the way of enjoying your favorite soap operas? Now you can dial up SoapCity to get all the dish you missed. The site provides weekly updates on the major daytime serials, as well as behind-the-scenes stuff (like contract disputes) that makes it worth a visit even when you've seen the latest episode.

Comedy Central Online www.comedycentral.com

Whether you're just checking in with the tragically hip Jon Stewart or need to know who killed Kenny this week, Comedy Central Online can help. All the channel's politically incorrect shows are listed here (the *Daily Show,* the *Man Show, Ab Fab,* and *Strangers With Candy,* to name four), each with its own page and activities. But the main draw to this Web site may be the download section. It's packed with audio clips, streaming video, high-res images, and insane Shockwave games, "all designed to help you waste time in powerful new ways."

TV Guide Online www.tvguide.com © ⓓ

Addicted to both small screens? TV and Web fanatics will want to stop at TV Guide Online, which offers all the standard features of the print publication with one added perk: it's free. Find out the buzz on the actors, writers, and stars of television and film in the features sections; find weekly listings of what's on, or browse TV and film, past and present, in the searchable database.

FOX.com www.fox.com ⓓ

Once the laughing stock of the Big Three networks, Fox has emerged as a huge player in the ongoing television wars. Judging from its Web site, the little-network-that-could is living up to its wily mascot's reputation, offering a flashy showcase built around hit shows like *World's Wildest Police Videos, Greed,* and *King of the Hill.* The content here won't blow you away, but the presentation's admirable—each show gets a subpage with schedule, character info, and pictures of the actors.

Jump The Shark www.jumptheshark.com ⓞ

How do you know when a TV show has "jumped the shark"? The phrase is an oblique reference to an episode of *Happy Days* when Fonzie

actually jumped over a shark tank, and has come to mean the defining moment when a TV show starts to sour. Jump The Shark dedicates considerable disk space to determining that exact moment for a whole catalog of sitcoms by tallying the votes (and comments) of surfers. Uproarious and critical down to the minutest detail.

Court TV Online www.courttv.com

When hair-raising domestic disputes, international crimes, and generally gory goings-on get their day in court, they also get coverage on Court TV Online. While you won't get to see the television channel's extensive footage online, you can log on for news on recent arrests and current trials, and developments in the murder case of the moment. The video section offers RealPlayer snippets of last week's hearings, with a big bank of past clips in the archive.

NBC.com www.nbc.com

Perhaps the best organized of the major network Web sites, NBC.com is nevertheless a bit bland by even Hollywood standards. Still, it's a handy place to catch up on fave shows like *Friends, ER,* and *Saved By the Bell* (yep, it's still alive, thanks in large part to Dustin "Screech" Diamond). You'll also find clips of classic *Saturday Night Live* bits and coverage of the Olympic Games to liven things up.

BBC Online www.bbc.co.uk ©

The network Austin Powers worships through song. The British Broadcasting Corporation has created a fabulous site that encompasses both its radio and television programs. Dial it up to hear Scottish bagpipes, read up on the royal family, take in the latest rugby match, or drop in on *Dr. Who.* It's really impossible to describe the massive amount of content that's available here—click virtually anywhere and you'll find something fun.

CBS.com www.cbs.com

The Central Broadcasting System continues to spotlight its news programming as the driving force behind its network, even in cyberspace. However, if you're tired of hearing about the sorry state of the world, you can still opt for the harmless entertainment of shows like *Chicago Hope,* the *Bold and the Beautiful,* and the *People's Choice Awards*, all of which are covered in glowing detail here.

ABC.com www.abc.go.com

Like the television station, ABC.com asks for nothing but your undivided attention, and gives you the inside scoop on your favorite shows in return. Surf here for plot previews of the daytime and primetime lineups, video and audio clips, and a complete schedule of all of the station's shows, including news, sports, and cartoons. But bypass the site's store if you want something other than a mug—it must take a lot of coffee to keep those gals on *The View* awake.

AandE.com www.aande.com

Whether it's a good, old-fashioned mystery or a documentary on wildlife, A&E's Web site can direct you to quality programming like *Sherlock Holmes* and *Cry of the Wild*. Browse this bland but pleasing site only to find out what's airing when and leave the entertainment side of things to the network itself. An invaluable resource for programming your VCR.

Scifi.com www.scifi.com

This beautifully designed site is a sci-fi lover's dream, offering everything from chats with Stephen King to reviews of David Cronenberg movies. The fabulous news archive is organized by such categories as The Unexplained, Fandom, and Rumors, while the gift shop peddles everything from Clive Barker novels to *Mystery Science 3000* videos. If you're not a fan of the genre, this site could convert you.

Gist TV www.gist.com

Can't get enough of your favorite television show? Take your habit to the next level with Gist TV's celebrity photos, downloadable preview clips, and plenty of juicy gossip on perennially hot shows like *Ally, Sex in the City,* and *Survivor*. Or enter your zip code to view Gist's extensive TV listings by category (movies, soaps), date, or time. Almost as fun as flipping channels.

clickTV www.clicktv.com

Like *TV Guide* for the Net generation, clickTV tailors its show listings to your zip code, the current date, and hour. When you click on a show title, a window pops up with a description, duration, cast, and (if it's a movie) a link to buy a video of it from Reel.com. We especially like the genre search function—a search for cooking shows got us 60 different show times. The downside? The pop-up RealPlayer commercials reek of prime time.

PBS Online www.pbs.org

As a companion to its lush and informative programming, PBS has created a Web site that's both attractive and entertaining. The pages devoted to teachers, adult education, and independent films are particularly enticing, as are kids' pages that invite children to color, sing, and surf the Internet under guided supervision. Where else can you explore the cosmos and learn how to hang a door in one place?

Reel.com www.reel.com

A new partnership with Buy.com has left Reel.com free to pursue its dreams as an entertainment hub, which isn't that far afield when you consider how many thoughtful and entertaining articles it had before. Now there are simply more: a huge database of rental reviews, top ten lists of popular flicks, festival commentary from the front lines, and (still) links through to video and DVD shopping. Basically, the only difference is the name on the receipt.

TVTix www.tvtix.com

If you've ever wanted to see Bob Barker and his radiant tan in all their living glory, this site can get you tickets to a taping of the *Price is Right*. Likewise, TVTix has your free pass to *What's My Line, Rock and Roll Jeopardy*, and an ever-changing selection of mainstream programs. You peruse the schedule, choose the tickets, and print them right from your computer. Not surprisingly, all of the shows are in Los Angeles.

women

ChickClick www.chickclick.com

A women's portal with big attitude and bold design, ChickClick hosts a bunch of awesome, women-oriented sites (like Beat Box Betty and Maxi) that perk up the brain and get the estrogen flowing. Look here for hilarious e-postcards, smart articles, horoscopes, and free email and homepages. Just like the slogan says, these girl sites don't fake it.

Women.com www.women.com

Women.com's 18 channels each cover a different topic—health, home, and finance are three—making it a resource portal for every hat the modern woman wears. Some of the content is gleaned from partner publications like *Prevention, Redbook, Good Housekeeping,* and *Marie Claire,* but much of it is original. Because the site carries so much clout, it also gets actual celebs for its celebrity chats (recent ones included Senator Patty Murray and that helpful Heloise).

women

iVillage.com www.ivillage.com ©

You have fifteen errands to run on your lunch hour—where should you go first? iVillage.com. The network's 19 channels pack a whole host of e-tools around their feature content—buy stamps, plan your pregnancy, or learn keyboard yoga in a matter of minutes. You may even save enough time to take a break and read the excellent articles.

Cybergrrl www.cybergrrl.com

None of the trite, slumber party feel of your average women's site, Cybergrrl serves up sensible articles on solid subjects like reducing taxes, taking your workout outside, and the cool stuff that women are doing. We love the She's So Savvy section, which profiles women making it big in the Web economy. In addition, 25 different chat rooms prove the site's self-label, "the voice of women," isn't just lip service, and the links library offers some great sites for smart ladies.

Oxygen www.oxygen.com

Oxygen is a women's cable network and Web portal that's just a little more hip than its competitors. Articles on stuff like alternative medicine, feng-shui, and summer smoothie recipes show the site is smart but not snore-inducing. Branching out from the sharply-designed homepage are sites like We Sweat (with fitness and sports info), picky (a cool style and shopping resource), ka-Ching (with financial advice), and last but certainly not least, Oprah.

Jane Online www.janemag.com

Readers familiar with *Jane* won't be disappointed—its site mirrors the zany, neurotic vibe of the magazine, not to mention most of its departments: the It Happened to Me confessionals, Blind Date set ups, and Dish celebrity gossip. There's also some fresh Web-only material like sex Q & A with staffer Gigi Guerra. If you like Jane Online, you'll check in often. If you don't, well, rant on the site's boards.

UnderWire underwire.msn.com

A site that provides as much lift as the garment it's named after. Under-Wire addresses ponderous questions (Why do young girls obsess over the Backstreet Boys?) and daily frustrations (how-tos on controlling gas-guzzling cars and saving money), all in a low key, girlfriend-to-girlfriend style. The chat and bulletin boards are similar to those at all the other women's sites, but UnderWire does distinguish itself with a group-composed story that's built on user submissions .

womenConnect.com www.womenconnect.com

Not every article on this well-versed site is aimed at women—features on finance and career development are universally applicable. But along with the general run of topics, womenConnect.com addresses issues like the wage gap and equity, with an emphasis on the professional community of women. Members connect through active chat rooms and bulletin boards while recent grads can check out the Envision zine.

glossary

agent
A program that searches the Web on a continuous basis for information you have requested. Sometimes referred to as a bot. (*see also, bot*)

anonymizer
A service that works like a screen between you and the sites you browse, keeping personal information like IP address and email private from prying companies.

avatar
A Sanskrit word for "the form a god takes on earth" (so you know it was coined by a geek with an ego), your avatar is your character in a visual chat forum.

bandwidth
Refers to the size of the data pipeline. To have higher bandwidth is to have a faster Internet connection that carries more information.

banned
The chat world's version of exile, to be banned means you've obliterated all sense of human decency and can never log back onto that site.

beaming
Transferring songs (or CDs) to MP3s for storage in an online account.

bid increment
In an online auction, the amount by which bids are raised each round. This amount is set by the site, which will usually provide a table that explains how the bid increment is determined.

bot
The Web's version of personal shoppers. Tell a bot exactly what you're looking for and it scans sites for products that interest you and compares their prices. (*see also, agent*)

boolean operators
Words such as *and*, *not*, and *near* that help narrow down search results on search engines such as Yahoo! or AltaVista. You might search for "Elvis and peanut butter" to get info on the King's favorite recipe.

broadband
Refers to a high-speed Internet connection such as T-1 or DSL.

bulletin board system (BBS)
A message database where people can log in and leave broadcast messages for others, usually grouped into topics. These include biggies like Compuserve and thousands of little local bulletin boards run by amateurs out of their homes. (*see also, newsgroup*)

cache
Pronounced "cash," this refers to a temporary place to store files. Your browser's cache holds Web pages you've recently visited so it can load them again quickly if you return.

client
A client is a fancy word for a chat program, either a downloadable program or a simple Web interface.

cookie
A file put on your computer by a Web site so that it can "recognize" you at a later time. Though often used to target advertising, cookies also record things like passwords and shopping preferences that make surfing easier.

cyber
In chat rooms, to cyber is to type dirty.

cybercitizen
A citizen of the Internet, or a member of the cybercommunity. Also known as a netizen.

cybersquatting
Registering a dotcom and simply waiting for a company that would like to buy it. drugstore.com and furniture.com were both owned by cyber-squatters at one point.

egosurfing
Searching to see how many places on the Web your name appears. Try it! At AltaVista, simply enter your name surrounded by quotes in the search field like this: "Your Name".

encoder / decoder
Encoders are programs that allow you to trans-form a large WAV file (perhaps one you've uploaded from a CD) to a smaller, highly compressed MP3 file. A decoder is just the opposite: it transforms MP3 files into WAVs.

e-zine
The upstart Web counterpart of print magazines. Thousands of e-zines now dot the cyber landscape, offering a veritable feast of info on every topic from news to sex to snowboarding.

e-commerce
Electronic commerce is the buying and selling of goods on the Internet. Also called e-business or e-tailing (electronic retailing).

faq
A frequently asked question, or a list of questions posted on a newsgroup or Web site. Consult the faq page when you have questions about the newsgroup or site.

firewall
A computer system that functions like a security guard to make sure that certain types of information can't enter or leave a private network. Many large corporations have firewalls, which can make chatting and checking personal email at work difficult.

flaming
Posting an obnoxious message, or flamebait, on a public newsgroup, in a chat room, or in email. (*see netiquette*; flaming is a prime example of poor netiquette)

freeware
Refers to software that can be downloaded from the Internet at no cost.

geek
According to cyberlorist Eric Raymond: "One who fulfills all the dreariest negative stereo-types of hackers: an asocial, malodorous, pasty-faced monomaniac with all the personality of a cheese grater." But watch out—geeks, also called hackers, turbo nerds, and propeller heads—may yet inherit the earth.

geekosphere
The physical environment surrounding a hard-core geek's computer that's littered with sticky notes, stress balls, CDs, issues of *Wired*, wind-up toys, and half-empty coffee cups.

go private
To retreat into a quiet, two-person chat room, not necessarily to cyber.

handle
Your handle is your cyber identity—either your email username or the alias you use in chat rooms.

instant messenger (ICQ)
A small piece of software that allows you to chat and email with other friends on your "buddy list" who have the same software.

Internet Relay Chat (irc)
Any system, like chat, that allows you to communicate with others in text or audio in real time—that is, live.

jolt
Sometimes described as "the fuel on which the Internet is run," a typical can of Jolt cola contains about twice the amount of caffeine as Coke.

lurker
In a chat room, one who listens but doesn't say anything. Sometimes lurkers just want to listen; other times, they left the room and forgot to log out.

moof
To lose your your connection to a chat room or the Internet for no apparent reason.

mouse miles
Slang for time spent computing, as in "I covered a lot of mouse miles today," as well as an actual measure of the amount your mouse has been used.

MP3
A file format that makes music files small enough to download from the Internet.

netiquette
Etiquette on the Internet. Spamming or flaming your friends on the Web are examples of bad netiquette.

newbie
A Web freshman—new to the Internet and obviously so.

newsgroup
An Internet discussion group, or Usenet group, organized by subject, where you can post messages and see responses from others. Examples are alt.music.punk or rec.gardening.tulips.

nick
Also called a screen name or handle, a nick is the name you use while chatting.

opt-in, opt-out
A type of privacy policy where a user permits a company to use personal information (opt-in), or forbids a company to use it (opt-out).

personal digital assistant (PDA)
Those handheld organizers—like the Palm Pilot—that inspire in some users the other type of PDA (public display of affection).

plug-in
A tiny application that works in conjunction with your browser. Examples are RealAudio, which lets you listen to streaming music on the Internet, and Shockwave, which lets you view animations and games.

private message (pm)
A private note between two or more chatters that can't be seen by the rest of the group. Beware: you may think your pm is confidential, but the text can be cut and pasted for everyone else to see. Also called a whisper.

proxy bidding
In online auctions, placing a confidential maximum bid that the automatic bidding server will inch toward but not exceed to keep a bidder in the winning spot. The higher the maximum bid you enter, the better the chance you'll win.

glossary

remailer

An email program that strips a message of the identifying details of the sender before passing it along.

ripper

A program that allows you to copy a track from either a digital (CD) or analog (tape, LP) source and change it to a standard WAV sound file.

shilling

Caveat emptor: this is when the seller of an online auction item bids up his or her own item. Shilling is strictly prohibited but sometimes tough to detect.

simulcast

A text chat that is scheduled around a real world event. For example, fans of the *Simpsons* might log on to a simulcast during the show to exchange comments as they watch.

skins

Like wallpaper for your application windows, skins are fun patterns and pictures you can download and place on MP3 players, browsers, etc.

snail mail

Good old-fashioned mail that's delivered by the post office. You remember—the kind that needs stamps.

sniping

Placing a bid during a Web auction just seconds before an auction closes. Although sniping is technically legal, it's considered bad auction netiquette.

spam

Unsolicited junk email. Your email provider may offer spam-blocking, which filters out these annoying messages.

streaming

When data is transferred in a steady and continuous stream. Listen to an Internet radio station, for example, and you're listening to music that is being streamed to your computer.

thread

On bulletin boards or Usenet groups, a series of comments shown in the order they were posted. A dead thread is a discussion topic that has lost users' interest.

triplecast

Simultaneous broadcasts of a program over television, radio, and the Internet.

uploading

Transferring files from one computer to a larger computer or network.

WAP

(Wireless Application Protocol) A format that allows users to view wireless Internet sites on certain handheld devices like cell phones and Palm Pilots. Such devices are referred to as WAP-enabled.

WAV

The standard file format for storing sound on most computers, WAV files are larger than MP3 files.

webcam

A video camera, usually attached directly to a computer, that feeds footage to a Web site. A live cam is one that shows live streaming video.

webcast

A video program (often live) that is broadcast over the Web.

index

1-800-Flowers.com 160
4freequotes.com 83
6FigureJobs.com 38
24framespersecond 80
100hot 56
401Kafé 87

A
AAA Online 41
AandE.com 183
ABC.com 183
ABCNews.com 126
Activeworlds.com 45
Adagio Teas 91
addAshop.com 34
Adoption.com 131
Adrenaline Vault 92
Ain't It Cool News 78
AJR NewsLink 128
Alibris 30
alight 152
All About Jazz 122
AllBusiness.com 34
All-Hotels.com 179
All Movie Guide 77
All Music Guide 121
Allrecipes.com 89
AltaVista Live!: Translation 135
AltaVista: Shopping 146
Alternative Press Index 129
Alzheimer's Association, The 144
Amazon.com 145
American Anorexia
    Bulimia Organization, The 97
American Association of
    Retired Persons 144
American Bankruptcy Institute 84
American Civil Liberties Union 135
American Psychological Association 99
American School Directory 62
Ancestry.com 59
Anonymizer.com 57
Anthologia 116
Anthropologie 153
Antique Networking 26
AOL Instant Messenger 45
APBnews.com 127
AreYouGame.com 111
Argus Clearinghouse, The 135
ArtandCulture.com 22
ArtHire 37
Arthur Frommer's
    Budget Travel Online 178
Artistdirect 122
art & culture 22
Artstar.com 25
AsianAvenue.com 47
Ask Dr. Weil 96
Ask Jeeves for Kids 110
AskMe.com 138

Astounding B Monster, The 79
astrology.com 69
AstrologyGuide.Com 67
Athealth.com 98
AthletesDirect 165
Atlantic Unbound 73
AtomFilms 169
auctions & classifieds 150
AuctionWatch.com 150
AudioFind.com 122
Autoweb.com 42
Avatar Factory, The 46
Away.com 176
A Web of On-Line Dictionaries 135

B
BabyCenter.com 129
babystyle.com 130
Baby Zone 129
Bachrach 151
Backflip 57
Barbie.com 112
Barnes & Noble.com 29
Bartleby.com 138
BBBOnLine 155
BBC Online 182
beauty 27
Beauty.com 27
beautyscene 27
BedandBreakfast.com 180
beenz.com 158
Beliefnet 139
Best Book Buys 31
Bestfares.com 180
BET.com 47
Better Homes and Gardens Online 102
Bidder's Edge 150
Bigfoot.com 56
bigstar.com 79
Billboard Online 121
Biztravel.com 175
Bizzed.com 35
BlackVoices.com 48
Blaxploitation.com 81
BlindGift.com 159
Blipz 111
Bloomberg 82
Bluefly.com 151
BlueLight.com 147
Blue Nile 155
Boating.com 165
Body, The 100
Bolt 173
Bonus.com 109
BookBrowse 29
Bookreporter.com 30
books 29
BookSwap 31
Borders.com 29
Bottomdollar.com 161

Boulevards 74
BowieBanc 86
BrainPOP 110
BreezeNet's Guide to
    Airport Rental Cars 41
Brill's Content 75
Britannica.com 134
business 32
BusinessWeek Online 32
Butterfields 26
BuyCentral.com 162
Buyer's Index 146

C
Calyx & Corolla 160
Cammunity.com 172
Candy Direct 90
Car And Driver Online 40
careerjournal.com 38
CareerPath.com 37
careers 37
CarePackages.com 161
cars 40
Cars & Culture 42
CarsDirect.com 41
CartoonNetwork.com 66
Casino.com 93
CatalogCity.com 146
CBS.com 182
CBSHealthWatch 99
CBS MarketWatch 84
CBS Sportsline 162
CDNOW 123
Cellmania.com 157
CenterWatch 101
CEPA Gallery Online 24
Changeslive.com 27
Channelseek.com 172
Charles Schwab 84
chat 44
chatalyst 44
CheapLodging.com 179
Cherrybomb.com 118
Chess Cafe, The 92
ChickClick 184
Chumbo.com 50
CinemaNow 79
CitySearch.com 175
CitySync 177
ClassicCar.com 43
ClassicGaming.com 92
ClassMates.com 60
CleanSheets 115
clickthebutton 162
clickTV 183
CliffsNotes 64
clothing & accessories 151
CNET.com 49
CNET Gamecenter.com 93
CNET News.com 128
CNN.com 126
CNNfn 83
CNNSI.com 164
Coach 154
Coffee Review, The 91
Collectors Universe 68

College Board, The 64
CollegeClub.com 46
CollegeDates.com 114
Colors 73
Comedy Central Online 181
Comics.com 66
communities 46
Compaq 51
computers & internet 49
Concierge.com 175
Condom Sense 117
Connect for Kids 129
consumer guides 155
Consumers Digest Online 156
ConsumerReview.com 155
Cooking.com 88
Cooking Light Online 88
CoolSavings.com 158
coolshopping.com 145
Council on International
    Education Exchange 62
CountryCool.com 123
Court TV Online 183
craft.com 68
Crate and Barrel 103
Crayola.com 110
Crutchfield 157
C-SPAN.org 132
CultureFinder.com 25
CU-SeeMe World 45
Cybergrrl 185
Cyberkids 108
CyberRebate.com 158
Cyrano Server, The 117

D
DailyFashion.com 77
Dance Online 23
Darwin Awards 67
Dating911 116
dealnews.com 145
DealTime.com 162
Dean & DeLuca 89
Deja.com 156
dELiAs.cOm 152
Della Weddings 119
Dell.com 49
Delphi.com 44
Demandline.com 34
Desteo 177
DIAL 63
Dialpad.com 71
Digital City 176
Digital Theologian, The 139
directories & people finders 59
Discovery.com 141
Discovery.com Travel Channel 176
Disinformation 24
Disney.com 109
ditto.com 57
Divina Cucina 89
DLJdirect 83
DoDots 71
DoItYourself.com 105
Domania.com 107
Doonesbury Electronic Town Hall 132

index

DoubleTake Magazine 23
DoughNET.com 174
Dow Jones Business Directory 33
drkoop.com 95
Droog.com 153
drugstore.com 96
dsports.com 169

E
eArtGroup 26
eBags 154
eBay 149
E-Conflict World Encyclopedia 138
eCRUSH.com 114
EDGAR 35
eDiets.com 100
Edmunds.com 41
Edwina 116
education 60
eFax.com 72
eFridge 72
eGames 94
Egghead.com 51
Egreetings.com 159
eGroups 49
eHobbies.com 66
eHow 137
Electric Library 134
Electronic Arts 92
Electronic Frontier Foundation 133
electronics 157
ELLE.com 75
Embark.com 61
Encarta Learning Zone 136
English Server, The 135
Englishtown 64
EnSpot.com 65
Entertaindom 68
entertainment 64
Entertainment Asylum 173
Entertainment Sleuth 69
EntreNetwork.com 35
eNutrition 97
E! Online 65
ePALS 62
Epicurious Food 87
ePregnancy 130
e-services 70
ESPN.com 163
Esquire 119
etown.com 156
eToys 111
E*TRADE 85
Evite 70
EW.com 64
Excite Classifieds 150
Expedia 180
Expertcity.com 53
Exploratorium, The 141
Explore.com 166
explorezone.com 141
ExpressAutoParts.com 43
eYada.com 171
eyestorm 26
eZiba 104
e-zines 72

F
Fametracker 66
Family.com 129
familydoctor.org 131
familyeducation.com 61
FamilyStyle Movie Guide 81
FamilyWonder.com 112
Farmclub.com 124
farmersalmanac.com 138
fashion 75
FashionDig 152
FashionLive.com 76
Fashionmall.com 151
Fashiontrip.com 76
fashionuk 75
Fast Company 32
Fatbrain.com 30
FedEx 70
FEED 73
Festivals.com 177
FHM 120
FigLeaves 152
film 77
Film 100, The 79
Film.com 78
FinAid 62
finance & investing 81
FindLaw 113
FitnessLink 166
Flooz.com 159
Floss.com 98
Flowerbud.com 159
Fodors.com 179
Fogdog Sports 165
food & drink 87
Food.com 90
foodline.com 91
FoodTV.Com 88
Forbes.com 32
Foreign Languages for Travelers 176
Fortune 32
FortuneCity 47
foto8 22
FOX.com 182
FreeAgent.com 40
Free Forum Network, The 158
FreeRide 158
Freeskills.com 53
free stuff & coupons 158
FreetimeJobs.com 39
FSBON 107
FT.com 33
FunBrain.com 108
Funology.com 109
Furniture.com 103

G
Games Domain 92
games & gambling 91
GameSpy.Com 93
Gamestop 92
gapkids.com 153
Garage.com 36
Garden.com 102
Gateway 51
Gay.com 48

Gazoontite.com 97
Geographia 178
Geomancy.Net 102
getCustom.com 149
Getting Real 174
GiftCertificates.com 161
gifts & cards 159
gifts.com 160
GirlGeeks 53
Girls On 65
Gist TV 183
Global Mart 148
Global Music Network 125
Go Ask Alice! 96
GOLFonline 163
Gomez.com 155
GoodHome.com 104
Good Vibrations 115
GORP 174
Gospel Communications Network 140
govWorks.com's Jobs in
    Government 39
Grassroots.com 134
Greyhound 181
Gucci 76
Guru.com 39
Guyville.com 120
GYN 101 97

H

Hagglers.com 149
hair-news.com 28
Half.com 147
Hallmark.com 161
handheld computing 58
HandheldNews.com 58
Happy Puppy 94
harmony-central.com 122
Harrods Online 148
Headhunter.net 38
HealingPeople.com 98
health 95
HealthandAge.com 144
HealthGrades.com 100
healthwindows for kids 110
HerbVigor.com 101
Hifi.com 157
Hindu Universe, The 139
HistoryChannel.com 139
Holy See, The 140
HomeArts 101
homedepot.com 105
home & living 101
HomePortfolio 104
Homes.com 107
Homestead 55
Homestore.com 105
HomeworkCentral.com 110
Homeworkhelp.com 63
Hoover's Online 36
Hostels.com 180
HotJobs.com 38
Hotmail 57
How Stuff Works 136
H&R Block 84
Humor.com 67

Hungry Minds.com 60
HyperHistory Online 136

I

iBaby.com 130
iCanBuy.com 173
icast.com 170
iCastle 106
Iconfactory, The 53
ICQ.com 45
iDetour 75
i-drive 55
i-Escrow 150
iExplore 178
IFILM 78
iGive.com 147
IGN.com 93
iGrandparents 144
Images 80
iMotors.com 43
Inc.com 34
Individual.com 128
indulge.com 28
Infoplease.com 136
ingredients.com 29
Ink Blot 124
inshop.com 148
Institute for Global
    Communications 134
InsWeb 85
IntellectualCapital.com 134
IntelliChoice Car Center, The 42
Internal Revenue Service 86
InterNational Council on Infertility
    Information Dissemination, The 100
International Herald Tribune 128
internet 54
internet.com 54
Internet Legal Resource Guide 112
Internet Movie Database, The 77
Internet Public Library, The 135
Internet Radio List 170
Internet Sacred Text Archive 140
Internet ScamBusters 156
Intimategifts.com 116
iPrint.com 70
IslamiCity 140
iUniverse.com 31
iVillage Beauty 27
iVillage.com 185

J

Jalopy Journal, The 43
Jane Online 185
January Magazine 30
jcrew.com 151
jdpower.com 155
Jean Paul Gaultier 76
Jefferson Project, The 133
Jewish Community Online 141
JobMonkey.com 39
JobReviews.com 38
Jobtrak.com 37
Joe Cartoon 68
jokeswap.com 66
Journal E 73

index

Jumbo! 50
Jump The Shark 182
JVibe 174

K
Kaplan 61
KennethCole.com 154
kids 108
kidsDoctor 101
KingLove 118
Knot, The 118
Kozmo.com 147

L
Last Word, The 143
Launch.com 125
law 112
Law.com 113
Law School Admission Council 113
Lawyers.com 113
Learn2.com 62
Learn the Net 55
Library of Congress 136
lifelounge.com 168
Lightspan 63
Lightspan StudyWeb 61
Link 174
LiquidPrice.com 157
Liquor.com 90
Live@ 170
LiveDaily.com 124
living.com 103
lodging 179
Lonely Planet Online 178
Lotteries.com 95
lottery.com 94
love & sex 114
Lovingyou.com 115
Lucire 76
Lycos Gamesville 94

M
MacAddict.com 52
MacMall 51
macys.com 145
Mail.com 57
MajorLeagueBaseball.com 164
MaMaMedia.com 109
MapQuest.com 176
Maps.com 137
MarryingMan.com 119
marthastewart.com 102
Match.Com 115
Matchmaker.com 114
Maxfootball.com 167
MaximOnline.com 120
McAfee.com 52
mediabistro.com 38
Media Nugget 65
MedicalRecord.com 100
MedicineNet.com 96
MedicineOnline.com 99
MedicinePlanet 176
MemoWare 58
men 119
Men's Fitness 120

Mental Health InfoSource 99
Merriam-Webster OnLine 135
MetaMarkets.com 83
Metropolitan Museum of Art, The 25
Models.com 75
ModernBride.com 119
MoJo Wire 74
Moms Online 131
Mondera 154
Monster.com 37
Monterey Bay Aquarium
   E-Quarium 143
Morningstar.com 82
Mortgagebot.com 87
Motley Fool, The 82
Motor Trend Online 40
MotorcycleWorld.com 43
move.com 107
Moviefone.com 78
Movieline.com 79
moviesthatsuck.com 81
MP3.com 122
MP3Lit.com 29
MP3now.com 121
Mr. Showbiz 67
Mr. Smith E-mails Washington 133
MSNBC 126
MSN MoneyCentral 87
MTV Online 125
MUD Connector, The 93
Multex.com 82
Musee d'Orsay 24
Museum of Modern Art, The 23
MuseumShop.com 160
music 121
MusicMatch 122
MVP.com 169
MyEvents.com 72
MyFamily.com 47
MyHelpdesk.com 52
myhome.com 104
myjobsearch.com 40
myprimetime.com 48
Myria 130
mySimon 161
MyVirtuaLife.com 69

N
Namedroppers.com 56
NASA Human Spaceflight 142
Nation, The 127
National Charities
   Information Bureau 133
National Discount Brokers 83
National Foundation for
   Credit Counseling 84
nationalgeographic.com 141
National Institute on Drug Abuse 101
National Portrait Gallery, The 23
National Recreation
   Reservation Service 178
National Review Online 74
Natural History Museum, The 142
NBA.com 165
NBC.com 182
NCAA Online 167

Nearly-Wed Handbook, The 118
NearMyHome.com 107
NECX 50
Nerve 115
NetFlix 79
NetGrocer.com 89
NetLitigation 112
Netmarket.com 149
NetRadio.com 171
Netstock 86
Net-Temps 40
Newcity.com 127
news 126
Newsweek 127
NewWork News 35
New York Review of Books, The 30
New York Times on the Web, The 126
NextMonet.com 25
NFL.com 164
NHL.com 165
Nick.com 108
Nike.com 154
Nine West 152
Nolo.com 113
Noodle Kidoodle 112
Nordstrom.com 151
NPR Online 171
Ntouch 77

O
Oddcast 172
Office.com 33
OfficeDepot.com 36
office supplies 36
Ofoto 71
Old Navy 153
Olympics.com 167
Oncology.com 101
OneAcross 94
OnHealth 98
Onion, The 64
OnlineChoice.com 147
Onlinefood.com 90
Online Originals 31
Onna Maternity 131
Onvia.com 35
OrderZone.com 36
Oscar.com 78
OshKosh B'Gosh 153
OU.ORG 139
Out & About Online 177
Outpost.com 49
Outside Online 163
Overstock.com 148
Owners.com 107
Oxford English Dictionary 138
Oxygen 185

P
Palace, The 44
PalmGear H.Q. 58
ParenthoodWeb.com 130
parenting 129
Parents.com 131
Parent Soup 129
ParkNet 175

Park, The 46
Party411 105
Payless.com 154
PayMyBills.com 86
PBS Online 184
PBS.org: Arts 25
PBS Science & Technology 142
PC World.com 52
PDAStreet.com 58
Pets.com 106
PETsMART.com 106
petswelcome.com 180
Photography In New York 22
PhotoPoint.com 71
Phys.com 95
PickupTruck.com 41
Planet Alumni 60
PlanetOut 47
PlanetRx.com 96
PlanetVeggie.com 88
Planned Parenthood 97
Platform Network 125
Playbill Online 22
Playboy.com 114
Poets.org 137
Point.com 156
Politics.com 132
politics & issues 132
PollingReport.com 132
POP.com 80
PopSci.com 142
PowerStudents.com 64
Premiere Online 77
price comparisons 161
Priceline.com 181
PriceSCAN.com 162
Price Watch 50
Project Gutenberg 31
Pseudo.com 170
Purity Test, The 118
Puzz.com 95

Q
Quicken.com 81
Quokka Sports 167

R
RadioSpy.Com 125
Rail Connection 181
Real Beer Page, The 89
real estate 106
RedEnvelope 159
Redherring.com 85
Reel.com 184
Refdesk.com 137
reference 134
reflect.com 28
REI.com 168
religion 139
Rent.Net 106
Researchpaper.com 136
ResponsibilityInc.com 87
Rivals.com 166
Roadsideamerica.com 179
Rocklist.com 166
RollingStone.com 121

RoommateFind.com 105
Roughcut.com 78
Rough Guide to Travel Online, The 179
Rouze.com 119

S
Salon.com 72
Sandbox.com 169
SchoolSports.com 168
science & nature 141
Scientific American 142
Scifi.com 183
Scour.com 172
Sears.com 146
SecondSpin.com 123
Secular Web, The 140
SelfCare.com 96
SeniorNet 144
SeniorResource.com 143
seniors 143
Sephora.com 28
Service911.com 52
Sesame Workshop Online 110
Sex, etc. 174
Sexilicious.com 117
Sexual Health infoCenter 97
Shades.com 155
Shareware.com 52
Sharky Extreme 53
Sharper Image, The 156
Shockwave.com 65
shopping 145
ShoppingList.com 149
ShortTV 172
SHOUTcast 171
ShowBizwire 69
sixdegrees 48
Skinz.org 54
SkiReview.com 164
Slashdot 50
Slate 127
SmarterKids.com 111
SmartMoney.com 84
SmartOnline.com 32
SMARTpages.com 59
SmartPlanet 63
Smith & Hawken 103
Smithsonian Magazine 74
Smoking Gun, The 67
smug 73
SoapCity.com 181
SocialNet.com 116
SoftSeek 51
Songfile 123
Sothebys.com 25
Soul Strut Online 123
SoundDomain.com 42
SPACE.com 143
Spafinder.com 28
Sparks.com 160
Spin.com 124
Split-Up.com 118
Sporting News Online, The 164
sports 162
Sports.com 164
Sports Illustrated For Kids 109

SportsRocket.com 169
SportsUniversity.com 168
S&P Personal Wealth 86
sputnik7 170
Stamps.com 70
StampsOnline 70
Staples.com 36
StarChefs 88
State Hermitage Museum 24
Station@sony.com, The 91
streaming media 169
StreamSearch.com 173
Student Advantage 63
StudentU 63
StyleShop.com 153
Suck.com 72
SuperPages.com 60
Supreme Court Collection 112
Switchboard.com 59
Swoon.com 114
Sync, The 171

T
Talk City 44
Tantra.com 117
TapeHead 80
Target 145
Tavolo 90
Tech Museum of Innovation, The 142
TeenCentral.Net 173
teens 173
teenwire 173
teldir.com 60
telstreet.com 157
Tenants Resource Directory, The 108
Tennis.com 166
theglobe.com 46
TheMan.com 120
TheStandard.com 54
TheStreet.com 81
theweddinglist.com 119
ThirdAge.com 143
Ticketmaster.com 68
Tickets.com 69
TIME.com 128
Time for Kids 111
TimeOut.com 175
TimeTicker 138
Tire Rack, The 40
Topica 45
Total Sports 163
Tourdates.com 124
Town Hall 132
toys 111
Trader Online 42
Trails.com 163
transportation 180
travel 174
Travel for Kids 177
travel guides 178
Travelocity 180
Tribal Voice 46
Tricycle.com 140
TRIP.com 181
Tucows 51
tv 181

TV Guide Online 182
TVTix 184

U
U.S. Census Bureau 137
U.S. Department of Labor 33
U.S.News .edu 61
U.S. Patent & Trademark Office 33
U.S. Securities and
   Exchange Commission 83
Umbra 106
UnderGround Online 65
UnderWire 185
UPS 71
USAToday.com 126
uspublicinfo.com 59
Utne Reader Online 73

V
Value America 146
VarsityBooks.com 30
Vault.com 37
Vibe Online 121
Victoria's Secret 152
Vindigo 58
Virtual Jerusalem 48
VirtualKiss.com 116
Visa-ATM Locator 175
Vitamins.com 98
Vogue.com 76
Voice Chasers 69
Voice of Dance 24
Volumebuy 148
Voter.com 132
VZones 45

W
Walker Art Center 24
Wall Street Journal
   Interactive Edition, The 82
Wal-Mart Online 145
Washington Post Online, The 127
Webby Awards, The 56
Web of Culture, The 34
weddings 118
We Media 48
Weather by E-mail 126
Weather.com 128
WebMD 99
Webmonkey 55
Webopedia 55
Westerns.com 80
WetFeet.com 39
whatis 56
White House, The 133
Whitney Museum of American Art 22
Williams-Sonoma 105
Windowbox.com 103
Winebid 91
WineToday.com 90
WingspanBank.com 87
WinnerOnline.com 95
Wired 75
Wish-List.com 149
WNBA.com 166
women 184

Women.com 184
womenConnect.com 185
WON.net 94
WORD 74
World Book Online 137
worldlyinvestor.com 85
World Radio Network 172
World Wide Arts Resources 23
World Wide Houseofboxing.com 167
WWF.com 165

X
XseeksY.com 117

Y
Yack 171
Yahoo! Broadcast 170
Yahoo! Chat 44
Yahoo! Finance 85
Yahoo! GeoCities 56
Yahoo! Internet Life 54
Yahooligans! 108
Yahoo! People Search 59
YardMart.com 102
YogaDirectory.com 168
Yuckiest Site on the Internet, The 109

Z
Zagat.com 88
Zap2it.com 80
ZDNet 50
ZDNet FamilyPC 54
ZDNet GameSpot 93
ZoneZero 23
Zoological Society of San Diego 143
ZoomSoccer.com 168

index

credits

Editor-in-Chief Rula Razek
Senior Editor Tara Croft
Associate Editor Krista Prestek
Assistant Editor Sara Garlick
Designer John Manicke
Sales Associates Samantha Hill, Dave Hoffman
Graphics Coordinator Megan McEntire
Researchers Naomi Beckwith, David Mullett
Writers Colleen Bazdarich, Naomi Beckwith, Hanh Bui, Renee Canada, Maya Kremens, John Dyer, Sara Garlick, Walaika Haskins, Lisa Levy, Agnes Milewski, Steve Moramarco, David Mullett, James Porteous, Steven Raphael, Nicole Saunders, Michael Schiller, Lisa Schneider, Anna Sikora, Adam Swiderski, Minodora Tibrea, Charles Wolski, Phil Zabriskie, Marcy Zipke

First Edition
Distributed by
teNeues Publishing Company,
16 West 22nd Street
New York, NY 10010
Printed in Germany

 teNeues

internet cool guide

2001

A savvy guide to the hottest web sites

www.internetcoolguide.com